POWERFUL PRAISE FOR

WEIGHT TRAINING MADE EASY

"The safest, most effective, and, in the bargain, most time-efficient workout on the market. I will recommend this book to all of my patients—male and female alike. Not only will it reshape the body but it will build needed bone."

—Juce Barbera, M.D.,
assistant clinical professor of surgery,
Downstate Medical Center

"An example of why the American Chiropractic Association has made Joyce Vedral an honorary member. Here she provides a safe step-by-step way to a healthy, strong body—and a sure-fire method of achieving the sculpted, defined, toned look of an athlete—and all in minutes, not hours, a day."

—Jack Barnathan,
doctor of chiropractic, chairman,
Nassau County Council of Physical Fitness

"The answer for anyone who is willing to invest 20–30 minutes a day to reverse the aging process—not just in looks, but in health. This workout not only replaces atrophied muscles with reshaped, sexy 'tone,' but also reverses osteoporosis by zeroing in on each body part with exactly the right exercise. I would recommend it for the health benefits alone—but wow, what a body you get in the bargain!"

—Betty Weider,
cofounder of *Shape* magazine
and *Living Fit* magazine

A Featured Alternate of Doubleday Health Book Club™,
The Literary Guild®, and Doubleday Book Club®

WEIGHT TRAINING MADE EASY

TRANSFORM YOUR BODY IN FOUR SIMPLE STEPS

JOYCE L. VEDRAL, Ph.D.

WARNER BOOKS

A Time Warner Company

A NOTE FROM THE PUBLISHER
The information herein is not intended to replace the services of trained health care professionals. You are advised to consult with your health care professional with regard to matters relating to your health, and in particular regarding matters that may require diagnosis or medical attention.

Warner Books, Inc., 1271 Avenue of the Americas, New York, NY 10020

Visit our Web site at
http://warnerbooks.com

 A Time Warner Company

Printed in the United States of America
First Printing: November 1997
10 9 8 7 6 5 4 3 2 1

Library of Congress Cataloging-in-Publication Data
Vedral, Joyce L.
    Weight training made easy : transform your body in four simple steps / Joyce L. Vedral.
        p.   cm.
    Includes index.
    ISBN 0-446-67109-6
    1. Weight training.   I. Title.
GV546.V437   1997   97-13484
613.7'13—dc21   CIP

Bodywear provided by Dance France (1-800-421-1543)
Photography by Don Banks
Hair and makeup by Darianne
Bathing suits by Nicole's Perfect Fit
Gym shoes by Reebok International
Gym photographs taken at Ken's Fitness Center, Farmingdale, Long Island
Text design by Stanley S. Drate and Ellen Gleeson/Folio Graphics Co. Inc.

*To all the women
(and men too) who want
to get in shape in the most
uncomplicated and least
time-consuming way—
this one's for you!*

ACKNOWLEDGMENTS

To Joann Davis and Colleen Kaplein, for your continual support and enthusiasm.

To Mel Berger, my agent, for your cheerful wisdom.

To Jessica Papin for your indefatigable diligence.

To Diane Luger and Jacki Merri Meyer for your dedication to the cover art.

To Larry Kirshbaum, Mel Parker, Emi Battaglia, Debbie Stier, and Jimmy Franco for backing me up "to the hilt."

To Diane Mancher and Edna Farley for your relentless publicity efforts.

To Don Banks for your artistic photography.

To Darianne of New York, for your talented hair and makeup.

To Dance France for providing all of the workout clothing—cover and interior.

To Dawn Cohen, Danielle, Patricia Pless, Nanette De Falco, Stella Fiorentino, Antonetta Sivilli, and Robin Laimo of the Saks Fifth Avenue Club for the class and style you encourage.

To Ken's Fitness Center in Farmingdale, Long Island, for a wonderful gym where I shot the gym photographs, and to Frisco Panza, Lifestyle Consultant and Trainer, for your good-natured assistance with the machine photo shoot.

To the 24 Hour Fitness Center in Las Vegas, Nevada, and to Brad Marlow and Becky Most, managers, for providing an excellent workout environment.

To Mitch Beck, my most enthusiastic fan, who has now become a personal trainer!

To Kathy Harris, my back cover before-and-after model.

To Cynthia Malone, my anatomy shot before-and-after model, who is now getting all of Dallas, Texas, in shape as a personal trainer.

To Joe and Betty Weider—who started it all!

To you, the women and men who have written to me requesting such a book.

CONTENTS

WEIGHT TRAINING MADE EASY

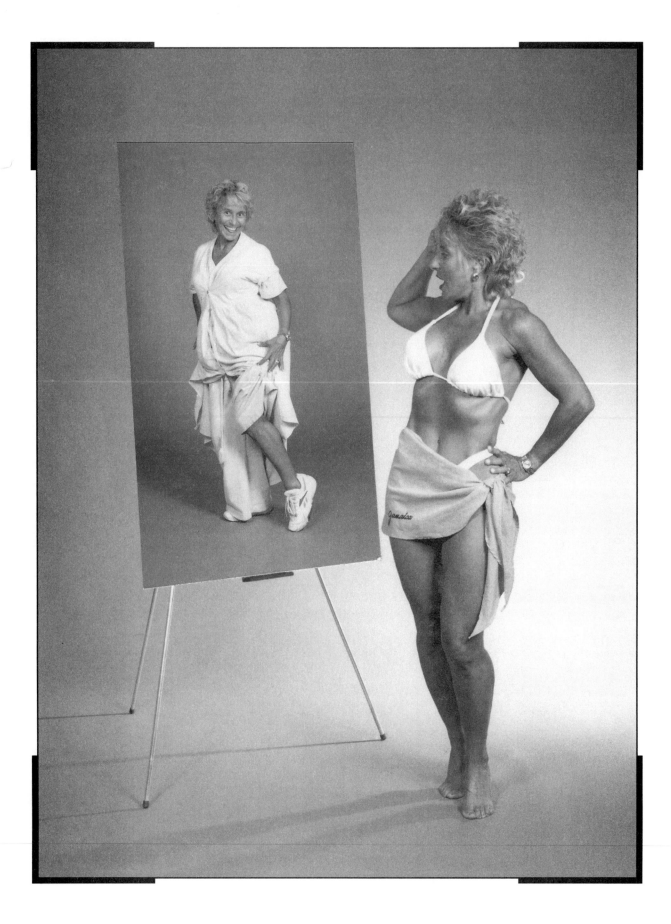

1

WHY YOU NEED THIS BOOK!

You want to get in shape—but you don't want to spend all day working out. You want to have a tight, toned, defined body, but you don't want to read an encyclopedia to figure out how. You want to look better and better as you go along, rather than being more and more apologetic about your body—and you'd like to have simple information in one book that will advance you from one level to the next without having to buy another book. If you feel this way, this book is for you.

There are four groups of people who can especially benefit from this book:

1. Anyone who has *never worked out* with weights before and would like a simple plan that moves along from one level to the next until the entire body is shaped, defined, tightened, and toned to her (or his) perfection.

2. Everyone who *has tried various weight-training programs (even one of mine)* and felt that it was "too much," too confusing, too demanding, too intimidating—too anything, and who wants to be taken in simple steps through the various levels of working out and would like to take advantage of the tear-out wall posters for each workout level.

3. *Experienced exercisers who are not confused about anything, but would like to challenge the body with some new routines and exercise combinations—* and would like to use this book as I do, as a "revolving workout" for guaranteed prevention of boredom.

4. Anyone who would like to know *how to substitute the dumbbells for barbells and machines*, or machines for dumbbells or barbells, if they are so inclined.

Why Did I Write This Book?

As you may know, this is not my first exercise book. I have written six others, and co-authored six more, for a total of *twelve* exercise books. Then why in the world would I write another exercise book?

This book is an answer to the cry I've received, time and again, from people who write to me. One letter seems to sum it all up:

Dear Joyce:

My best friend and I are thinking of working out, but we both feel overwhelmed before we even start. Barbells, dumbbells, reps, sets—we get a headache just thinking about it. Could you write a simple book that takes nothing for granted—that never assumes you know words common to people who work out—like set and repetition and so on.

I want a book that spells it all out and takes you from one step to the next until we have a beautiful body. I'm thinking almost in terms of those "dummy" and "idiot" books, you know, the ones they have for people who are trying to learn computers.

I love the idea of not having to leave the house—and working with the handheld inexpensive weights at home, but I would also like to solve the big mystery of how to use other equipment—you know, all those machines. I joined a fitness center, and although I'll probably work out at home most of the time, I do want to get my money's worth and use their equipment. Also, my husband bought one of those home-gym machines. I'd love to see him make progress by doing it the right way. Now the poor man just fools around—and I don't see anything happening in months. I know you could change all this.

I'm wondering if you could teach us in the book—in the simple way you always explain things—how in addition to using the handheld weights, we could use those machines and other strange equipment to do your workout. Let me not forget to ask you to also include those page-flip saving tear-out wall charts you included in Definition.

Oh, and by the way, in case you're wondering, I'm in my thirties and my best friend is in her forties—but let me tell you, Joyce (I feel as if I can call you Joyce because your books are so friendly), if you do write such a book, my aunt and her baby boomer friends told me that they will be first on line to get it too!
Sincerely, True Fan

When I read that letter I knew I had to write this book. Now, when working with dumbbells (and barbells and machines if you so choose), you will be able to fully understand what you are doing and why you are doing it, and you won't have to waste any time figuring things out.

So here it is. A book that assumes that you know nothing at all! A book that will lead you along step by step, and comfort you and, in a manner of speaking, hold your hand as you go along.

But what about those of you who do have experience working out? Don't worry, the book won't insult your intelligence. It will just read so easy that you will be able to progress more quickly than ever from one workout level to the next to achieve and perfect your body to your own specifications—and then to select a revolving never-be-bored maintenance plan for your particular body. (I'll tell you exactly how to do that in this book.)

I Wish I Had Such a Book When I Was Starting Out!

This book would have been my dream when I first started working out—and in fact for years after. I didn't know a dumbbell (handheld weights with a little ball-shape on each end) from a barbell (a long bar that holds disc-shaped plates—metal weights you place at the end of the barbell), and indeed, when I would confuse the two and get "the look" from some fitness trainer it would drive me to think of a bar and not a barbell!

I also wished that there were a simple book that didn't insult me with unchallenging exercises that would never reshape my body. In addition, I wanted to see a book that answered questions like "How many ways can you do the same exercise, and which way is best—and why?" (For example, the squat—you can do it with dumbbells, a barbell, a barbell and plates, at a squat station [a metal contraption that holds the barbell and allows you to crouch under it and lift it onto your shoulders without getting hurt], or on a machine.)

It bothered me to see that there were so many ways to do the same exercise—yet I had no idea how to take advantage of those other methods if I felt like doing so. I also wanted to know exactly what difference it would make to my body if I did use other methods besides the most convenient method that I used at home—dumbbells.

A Simple Plan

To make your workout life uncomplicated, in this book I will give you the four most effective (fundamental) body-shaping exercises for each of your nine body parts—and take these same exercises and use them again and again in different combinations—graduating you from workout level 1, the most elementary combination, to workout level 4, the most advanced combination. Each level will bring you one step closer to the body of your dreams.

The purpose of not changing the exercises as the workout levels advance is to prevent confusion. Instead of changing the exercises as you advance from one workout level to the next, I'm going to change the method—so you get more out of the exercises you are already doing! It's not only what exercises you are doing, but how you are doing those exercises that determines what happens to your body.

Yes. With this workout, as you advance from one level to the next, I'm going to ask you to first work very simply with one weight, then to add weights in a certain way, then group certain exercises together without resting, and finally to rearrange the entire exercise regimen. By the time you reach the final level you'll be a real pro, and your body will be the talk of the town!

Why These Particular Exercises?

But why did I choose the particular exercises I have chosen—rather than other exercises? The exercises contained in this book are the most productive. They get the most for your exercise time. They do more to reshape, sculpt, and define your body than any other exercises. That is not to say that other exercises are inferior. Many are equally good—but some are more difficult to perform, so I have left them out of this workout plan.

But as mentioned above, even though you will be using the same exercises in all four levels, each level will graduate you to a more advanced stage of body shaping. How so? You will be using these exercises in unique combinations, with varying repetitions (a repetition is one complete movement of an exercise, from start, to midpoint, to finish), with assorted weights and you will be working at different speeds.

All of this will become crystal clear as you read the book—and what's more, those of you who own some of my other books will better understand the difference between the various workouts in those books, and *will be able to use those books more efficiently*. But whether or not you have one of my other books, once and for all, you will be able to simplify the entire weight-training business, and know exactly what you are doing, why you are doing it—and the results you can expect from it.

Who Can Do the Workouts in This Book?

You can, that's who!

YOU CAN DO IT AT ANY AGE

First let's talk about age. You can do it at any age. I didn't even pick up a weight until I was almost forty! My Uncle Dave started in his fifties. My mother started in her late sixties, and I've gotten letters from women and men who started in their seventies, eighties, and older. We've all had the same great results.

Working out with weights adds lean muscle tissue to your body—and, in effect, reverses muscle atrophy that begins at thirty (we lose about half a pound of muscle every year after thirty). It is muscle that gives your body its shape and form. Without muscle your skin sags. Fat helps a little. It fills out the sagging skin with soft, mushy material. Not much comfort is it?

*So there's no choice. As you age, you need to *replace* the lost muscle to be tight and toned—and with this workout, you not only replace what you had, but you improve on it—because you shape and define your muscles. They end up looking better than they did when you were at your best.

INCREASED BONE DENSITY

Working out with weights also increases bone density. When I was going on fifty-two (I had already been into menopause for three years) I had my bone density tested (QCT-Bone Minerals TM Analysis) and discovered, to the amazement of the entire medical staff at the center, that my bone density is 219.3—a density of nearly double that of women my age—and indeed, the same density of a woman with great bones—in her twenties. Indeed medical research is beginning to proclaim that working out with weights increases bone density.

You can go as far as you want to go with this plan. The beauty of this book for you is, you can work at your own pace. You can begin with workout level 1 and remain there as long as you choose—only moving on when you feel ready to do so. And even if you remain at workout level 1 forever, you will achieve reversed muscle and bone atrophy by doing the workout exactly as prescribed.

But what about younger people—those in their teens, twenties, or early thirties? The workouts found in this book can give you the body you've always wanted. It can reshape your body into its ideal form—a shape you never had even at your best weight, because working with weights is the only way to sculpt and define muscle. More about this in Chapter 2.

MEN CAN DO IT TOO

What about men? Yes. If you're a man you can do the workouts in this book. See Wes (pp. 33–34) and Louie (pp. 35–36), who went from before to after. The workouts are exactly the same for you except for two things: 1) You don't have to do the hips/buttocks exercises (they are optional for you). 2) You may double the prescribed weight. It's that simple. Everything else is exactly the same. You can also use the books I have written that are specifically addressed to men: *Top Shape* and *Gut Busters.*

FROM SKINNY-FAT TO OVER 100 POUNDS OVERWEIGHT

Now let's talk about weight. Perhaps you are thirty pounds overweight. Perfect. This workout is for you. Suppose you are a hundred pounds overweight. Excellent. This workout is for you. What if you are a skinny-fat—not overweight, but not tight and toned. Wonderful. This workout is for you.

What? Am I crazy—telling *all* people that this workout is for them? No, I'm not mad—because yes, it is for everyone. How do I dare say so? Because for the first time in any of my books, this book starts at the easiest level. You can do it no matter how overweight, and/or out of shape you are, and very slowly, very gradually, advance to the next, and then the next, and then the next level—until your body has the look and feel that you desire.

I also tell you under what circumstances you can skip a certain workout level and go directly to the level that will give you the most immediate results. For more information on this, see Chapter 2, pp. 16–18, and the introductory section to each workout "Skipping Workout Level(s) _____ and Beginning Here." In other words, I won't hold you back or push you forward before you're ready. You'll move at your own pace!

How Long Will It Take to See Results?

No matter what shape you are in now—even if you're a hundred pounds overweight, and no matter which workout you choose to begin with—you will see and feel a change in your body in three weeks—twenty-one days. That's the magic number. Some parts of your body will be a little more firm to the touch, but you will feel stronger and have more energy. Some of you will even see certain muscles taking on a slightly different shape.

Then after that, as you continue to work out, in three months your entire body will begin to be reshaped, and will feel tighter and more solid. You'll have lots of definition (lines that separate your muscles and give you that sculpted, toned look) on your upper body, and the beginning of definition in your lower and middle body. Cellulite (bunched-up orange-peel-like fat) will begin to disappear.

In six months your entire body will have taken on a new shape. You'll think "But I need more work on _____" and you'll continue with "the plan" for your body (see pp. 16–18) working through to a year. At that point your friends will think you are perfect—but you'll know that you want to get even better in certain places. You'll read the section on pp. 19–20 "Extra Fine-Tuning Your Body." Finally, you'll be given a way to maintain your beautiful body for life—with a time investment of no more than thirty minutes four to six days a week!

How Much Time Is Involved?

Twenty to thirty minutes a day—four days a week. That's it. If you want to work out five or six days a week, you have that option. But a twenty- to thirty-minute investment four days a week is all you need to achieve your ideal body. Some of the workouts can be done in even less than twenty minutes. You'll find out which ones as you move through each level.

Ten Wonderful Changes: What You Can Expect from This Program

Turn the clock back. Project yourself back exactly one year. Now think of today. Look how fast the time went by. Zoom. There's one thing that no one can stop, and that's the passage of time.

Look at the calendar. What is today's date? Circle that date. Imagine another year going by. It will you know! And barring an act of God, you'll still be here. The question is, what shape will you be in? If you do what you've been doing, you'll get the same results you've been getting. Nothing! If, however, you follow the workout plan prescribed in this book, you will have a whole new body. Here's what you can expect in six months to a year.

(See Kathy, on back cover, after only twenty-five weeks.) But remember, as mentioned above, you will begin to see changes in your body almost immediately:

1. The loss of all excess body fat. (Between seventy-five and one hundred pounds of fat if you are that much overweight.)

2. The complete reshaping of your body with firm, beautifully sculpted, defined muscles.

3. Major reduction or total elimination of cellulite from thighs, hips, buttocks, and stomach—and anywhere else you may have it.

4. Healthful eating habits and lowered blood pressure.

5. The workout habit for life.

6. Raised metabolism that allows you to eat more without gaining weight due to increased muscle-to-fat body composition.

7. Improved bone density and posture.

8. Increased overall strength and energy.

9. A healthier heart and lung capacity.

10. A new outlook on life—added confidence and optimism.

Note: Make sure you read the introductions to each workout chapter to find out what each particular workout will do for you.

Exactly What You Will Find in This Book

Let's go through each chapter so you will know exactly what to expect in this book. Since you're reading Chapter 1, I'll start with Chapter 2.

CHAPTER 2: This chapter explains how and why weight training as prescribed in this book shapes your body, makes you tight and toned, reverses the aging process, allows you to eat more without getting fat, and demonstrates why aerobic activities (biking, treadmilling, swimming, etc.) are simply not enough. The chapter also zones in on *your particular body*, giving you a month-by-month game plan to achieve your ideal physique, and prescribes body perfection formulas for special body problems. The particular muscles you will be reshaping are described—and you are shown in detail how the "before" muscles all over your body will be reshaped. (Note: a woman who actually did the workout is the model for both "before and after muscles" and five other before-and-after women and men are shown and discussed.)

CHAPTER 3: This chapter explains the difference between dumbbells, barbells, and machines—and details how to make the most intelligent use of them all—giving advice on which pieces of exercise equipment are most valuable—and why. You are also given advice on workout schedules, clothing, equipment, where to work out, and so forth. Exercise names are cleared up and muscle soreness and injury are explained. You are taught how to "psych" yourself into a positive attitude about the workout. Finally, you are given an A–Z Quick-Start Dictionary that includes every word, term, or concept you will encounter in the various workouts. This dictionary will come in handy later if you encounter any word you don't understand. By referring back to it you'll get an instant answer to your question.

CHAPTER 4: "Learning the Moves." Here, workout level 1, the most simple of all the workouts, is introduced. You use only one set of three-pound dumbbells (handheld weights) and do the same number of repetitions (one complete movement of an exercise, from start, to midpoint, to finish) for each exercise. There's very little to remember. The goal of this chapter is for you to become familiar with the four exercises for each body part—exercises that will be used (although in different ways) in the following three chapters—workout levels 2, 3, and 4. You'll do this workout for three months (or less, depending upon your previous workout experience and/or goals and speed of progress) and then move on to the next workout level.

CHAPTER 5: Now you are taken to the next level—2, "Establishing a Muscle Base." Instead of using only three-pound dumbbells, you will use two additional sets of dumbbells—five- and ten-pounders—and you'll be taught to use the graduated weights by reducing the numbers of your repetitions (this is called the "pyramid system"). You'll learn how and why to raise your weights as you get stronger. In short, you'll find out how to use the weights in a way that makes for the best muscle development with the most efficient use of energy. You'll do this workout for three months (or less, depending upon your goal—this will be explained in that chapter) and then move on to the next workout level.

CHAPTER 6: Workout level 3, "Sculpting and Defining the Muscles," moves you to the next degree of muscular development. You'll learn how to burn extra body fat and at the same time define and shape your muscles into a more perfect form. You'll keep using graduated weights and the pyramid system introduced in Chapter 5, but there is an added element. You'll be taught how to combine the first two exercises for each body part (this is called the "superset within body parts"; it allows you to burn more fat, and get more definition, and in addition, complete your workout faster). You will do this workout for approximately three months or longer, depending upon your goal.

CHAPTER 7: Now you are advanced to the final workout level—4, "The Finishing Touch." This workout teaches you how to accomplish two muscle-enhancing goals at the same time: solidify your muscle mass (make your body harder and more shapely) and burn maximum fat and get more definition. You'll be shown how to combine the first two exercises of different body parts—(supersetting between body parts—twin sets) so that when one body part is resting, the other body part is working—and you don't actually have to rest at all. It's the most fat-burning of all the workouts, and requires the least amount of time. You will continue to use the pyramid system—and the graduated weights. You'll do this workout for approximately three months. Then you will use body-perfection techniques and maintenance, described in Chapter 10.

CHAPTER 8: In this chapter you will learn why you get fat—and the food facts that you will need to know to stop that process. You will find out how to eat a healthy, well-balanced diet that is in tune with the U.S. Department of Agriculture's food pyramid, but with lower fat, and you'll be given a food plan that tells you exactly how much of each food to eat in a given day. You'll learn how to deal with food emergencies (such as dining out) without breaking your diet. You'll be taught how to make your own meal plans, and learn the five basic rules of eating. Best of all, you'll find out how you can eat anything you want once a week—once you reach your fitness goal. Other food issues are also discussed. (Note: For a whole book on diet—and a month's worth of meal plans—get my book *Eat to Trim*.)

CHAPTER 9: This chapter tries to get one step ahead of you by nipping not-so-bright ideas in the bud. For example, it tells why it is not a bright idea to weigh yourself every day, leave out certain exercises, change the number of required repetitions, try thigh cream, and so on. This chapter also debunks common myths about working out, such as "muscle turns to fat if you stop" and "if you're fat, better wait till you lose the weight before you start working with weights." I also answer some general questions, such as "What about cosmetic surgery?" or "Can my five-year-old work out with me?" (I've used the many letters I've received from my readers as a basis for this chapter.)

CHAPTER 10: Here you will be given choices to select from—in order to stay in shape for the rest of your life—without being bored—and depending upon your particular goals. You are also advised about when and why to take time off—and how to cope with forced layoffs because of sickness or injury. This chapter also explains how to get back in shape quickly even if you've pigged out for two months and gained ten pounds—and tells why it is easier to get back in shape if you overeat for months at a time but do not stop working out, as opposed to both overeating and not working out. You are also advised about when and why to take a week off from working out.

By this point, you will be ready to write me with your questions, comments, and even beginning triumphs. You can do so—and I will answer, as long as you include a self-addressed, stamped envelope (see p. 245 for my P.O. Box).

APPENDIX (pp. 263–287): Here you will find the tear-out wall posters, so you can later do your workout without having to flip pages.

WEIGHTS—WHY AND HOW TO USE THEM TO RESHAPE YOUR BODY— FROM BEFORE TO AFTER

Is it necessary to work out with weights? Can working out with weights reshape your particular body—whether it is a skinny-fat, thirty pounds overweight—or even over a hundred pounds overweight? Is there a simple plan that will tell you exactly what you have to do to achieve the body of your dreams in a reasonable amount of time—and then keep that body for life?

Yes to all of it! *Yes*, you must work out with weights to reshape your body. *Yes*, working out with weights in a specific manner will reshape and de-fat (along with a low-fat eating plan) your body. *Yes*, there is a specific workout that you can follow to achieve your ideal body—and I will lead you gently along so that you can't miss it. You'll find out exactly what you have to do, and for how long you have to do it in order to achieve your ideal body.

Hello! Diet and Aerobics Alone Won't Do It

"I do aerobics—I run or ride an exercise bike—or swim—five times a week. I really keep my heart pumping. I feel healthier and I've lost a little weight, but my arms are still flabby—and my thighs are full of cellulite." "I've dieted myself down—I'm actually thin—but my body still feels fat." I've heard and read these words from frustrated women time and again. What's the problem?

YOU CAN'T RESHAPE YOUR BODY BY DOING AEROBIC ACTIVITIES BUT YOU *CAN* RESHAPE YOUR BODY BY WORKING OUT WITH WEIGHTS

You simply can't—not now, not ever—reshape and change the feel of your body by doing only aerobics. (Aerobics are physical fitness activities such as running, biking, or stair-stepping that are sustained by the body's continual supply of oxygen, and that cause your pulse to reach 60 to 80 percent of its capacity and to stay there for twenty minutes or longer. More about this below.)

But you *can* reshape and change the feel of your body by doing weight training alone. That's the truth. If you never did an aerobic activity in your life—you could completely reshape your body!

AEROBICS DOES NOT PREVENT OR REPLACE LOST MUSCLE TISSUE, BUT WORKING OUT WITH WEIGHTS DOES

One of the most important reasons to work out with weights is to prevent the loss of lean muscle tissue, and better, to replace what has already been lost. Medical doctors and the entire fitness community are now in agreement. Only working with weights is the right way to do it. In fact, we now know you can gain three pounds of muscle mass in eight weeks, while at the same time lose fat![1]

ADDING LEAN MUSCLE TISSUE TO YOUR BODY ALLOWS YOU TO EAT MORE WITHOUT GETTING FAT

For me, the best part of working out with weights (and mind you, I'm not talking about more than a total of seventy-five to eighty minutes *a week*) is, you raise your metabolism so that your body requires more calories to maintain itself. What does this mean? If, for example, you gain three pounds of muscle tissue, you raise your metabolism by about 7 percent and your body requires about 15 percent more calories to maintain itself. This means you can eat 15 percent more than you eat now to maintain your body. In short, you can eat more without getting fat.[2] (Also see "metabolism" in the A–Z Quick-Start Dictionary.)

People who are around me a lot and know how much I eat always wonder aloud: "I don't see how you could eat so much and not get fat. I look at food and gain weight." Well, I used to be this way too. If you look at me at twenty-six, in my before photo (see p. 36), I was eating less than I do now. But because I had little muscle tissue, my body required fewer calories to maintain itself than it does now.

THE VALUE OF AEROBICS

Then why do aerobics at all? Aerobics are great for burning additional overall body fat and increasing your heart and lung capacity. I do aerobics in addition to my weight-training workout because I love to eat and must burn that extra fat. Also, being in aerobic shape helps you to do everything easier—walk, work, run when you have to—everything physical—including the workouts in this book. You don't get out of breath as easy as you did before—and you don't have to stop to rest as often.

The ideal workout situation would be to do an aerobic activity in addition to your weight-training workout—for twenty to forty minutes, three to six days a week. But remember, *you can't reshape or tighten and tone your body, or add significant lean muscle mass with aerobics.* You must use weights—and in a very specific way. More about exactly how to use those weights later.

Where Does Diet Come In?

Now let's talk about diet. Diet alone will cause you to lose overall body fat. But what happens once you lose the fat? You could end up a skinny-fat, unless you have muscles on your body. After all, the body is made of skin, bone, water and other fluids, and—you guessed it—muscle. It is the muscle that gives your body its shape and form.

Without muscle, once the fat is gone, your body will feel soft and mushy, and even worse, your skin will just sag. And as you get older, and your natural muscle atrophies (the muscles you have from normal life—walking, carrying things, and so forth), your skin will droop more and more. In fact, as you get older, if you're not going to put some shapely muscle on your body, it's almost better to be a little fat. At least then your skin won't hang as much.

If you are overweight, you will have to follow the low-fat eating plan in Chapter 8, or use my new diet book *Eat to Trim* (see Bibliography), until your excess fat is gone, but don't worry, you won't have to starve to death. You get to eat a delicious, healthful combination of foods—high in complex carbohydrates and low in fat—and you eat often, and never go hungry. In addition, there are certain foods you can eat anytime, day or night. You'll get the details in Chapter 8.

How Do Weights Work to Reshape the Body?

Okay. So I've convinced you that in order to reshape your body you need muscle. But exactly how does working with weights form, and then sculpt and define, muscle on your body in exactly the places you need that muscle? Let's take the triceps as an example—the under part of the arm located between the elbow and the armpit—you know, the area that "waves like a flag" on older women if they don't work out with weights.

The triceps is the most neglected muscle on the female body. It isn't used very much in normal life. In fact, that's why it seems to be the first to go as we get older. There are four exercises in this workout that cause you to move your arm in a way that develops the triceps muscle from four different angles. In the end, you have a firm, defined triceps muscle and you'll never have to be ashamed of wearing sleeveless dresses or shirts.

Let's take a closer look at exactly how using weights does the job. In this workout, you will take a small handheld weight called a "dumbbell." I've mentioned this before—it has two ball-like shapes on either end, and you hold it in the middle—on the bar part. Imagine a three-pound dumbbell. Picture yourself taking it in your hand and holding it straight down at your side, your curled palm facing your body. (See p. 107 for a photograph of this.)

Now make believe you want to throw the dumbbell straight behind you—only when you extend your arm back as far as it can go, you don't let go of the dumbbell. Instead you bring it back to start position and repeat the movement twelve times. In addition, instead of using a throwing motion, you use a deliberate motion and squeeze your muscle (flex it) as you move the dumbbell back. What I've just described is one "set" (a group of "repetitions"—completed movements from start to finish and back to start again) of what is called a triceps "kickback." The only difference is, when you do the kickback, you bend over a little and bend at the elbow. (See p. 113. By the way, you don't have to memorize the names of the exercises—you just have to do them!)

But how does all of this relate to how weights reshape the body? In time, if you do a certain number of movements in a specific sequence for your triceps muscle, the muscle in that arm will respond to the "work" being demanded of it. The muscle will begin to be reshaped and will become stronger. It will say to itself, "Hey, I've got to develop, or I won't be able to cope with this work." And the muscle cells and fibers will become more concentrated and increase in number. And what does a stronger, more concentrated muscle feel like? It feels firm instead of mushy. It feels toned instead of loose. The reshaping part comes from the different angles you work. Each exercise hits the muscle from a different angle. I've figured out the best angles to get the best muscles. You don't want to go to a gym and just hope to get lucky. I've done the work for you. Look at my body—or the before-and-after people later in this chapter. If you like what you see, trust me.

The above example explains how only one muscle, the triceps, is reshaped by working with weights in a carefully designed way. In this book, you will be given exercises for all of your nine body parts: chest, shoulders, biceps, triceps (your biceps and triceps are your arms), back, thighs, hips/buttocks, abdominals (stomach), and calves. If you follow the workout plan in this book, in a matter of time your entire body will be tight, toned, defined, and beautifully shaped.

"But I'm athletic," you might argue. "I play tennis." "I ski." Sorry. It just won't do. Just like aerobics, sports and other physical fitness activities will help only the body part you are working. "Great forearm, tennis player Jane. You ought to enter a one-arm contest." "Nice legs, skier Lisa. What about your stomach?"

We can't get away from it. Aerobics, sports, or even the work we do in normal life, is not enough to reshape our bodies in the way that we want them reshaped. We need a system scientifically designed to get the job done. I've spent years working with the most knowledgeable experts in the field of body shaping—champion bodybuilders. It took them over fifty years to develop the science. They saved you and me the time. Now all we have to do is take advantage of that knowledge. I've applied that knowledge to myself and reshaped my body, and to over a million women and men who have used my workouts. Now I want to bring that knowledge to you.

I Don't Want to Look Like a Bodybuilder!

"But wait a minute. I don't want to look like one of those women on TV—the ones in those bodybuilding contests—who look like a man with a woman's face pasted on. Ugh." I know exactly what you're talking about.

Ironically, bodybuilders, the people to whom we owe our body-shaping knowledge, can turn people off and cause them to run the other way because of their bulky muscles. But don't worry. You couldn't look like a bodybuilder with this workout. Why?

Bodybuilders work out two to four hours a day. They lift very heavy weights. Instead of using three-, five-, ten-, or even twenty-pound weights they use hundreds of pounds. I know. I see them working out. I interviewed them for years for *Muscle and Fitness* magazine.

In addition, some bodybuilders take anabolic steroids, a male hormone called "testosterone," that exaggerates muscle growth. You will be working out only twenty to thirty minutes, four to six days a week. You'll be lifting three-, five-, and ten-pound dumbbells and going up to only about ten, fifteen, and twenty or slightly higher for your maximum weight. Bodybuilders go as high as 300 pounds—and more. And you will not ingest steroids.

So put your mind at ease. There's no way you will suddenly wake up one morning and look in the mirror in horror and see yourself all bulked up. It can't happen. In fact, bodybuilders wish it would happen that way. Then they wouldn't have to spend so much time working out!

What Will Working Out with Weights Do for Your Particular Body?

Traditionally, there are three body types. The first, and ideal one, is "mesomorphic" (a tendency toward muscle, ideal in shape and size). The next best is "ectomorphic" (a tendency toward being a little too lean). It is the last that most people dread and in fact think they are. It is "endomorphic" (a tendency toward fat).

But I have news for you. Anyone who makes it a goal to eat night and day—whether originally a mesomorph, ectomorph, or endomorph, will eventually *look like* a fatty endomorph. Now for the good news. Everyone and anyone, no matter what their original body type, can end up looking forever like a mesomorph (ideal in shape and size).

Forget "anyone." Let's talk about you. How can *you*, once and for all, no matter what your body type was to begin with, look great, now and forever? You must follow the workout levels in this book. Be calm, be patient, and go from level 1 to level 2 to level 3 to level 4—in the order prescribed for your particular body (see the following section). Then go on to the perfection techniques plan on pp. 19–20. Soon you will have the body of your dreams—no, better than your dreams, because frankly, I don't think you could imagine it. I know I couldn't before I started.

Let's talk about your specific situation. I'm listing the categories in order of the most common. Find yourself in one of the categories below and follow the workout plan designed for your situation. After you follow that plan, then go to the fine-tuning section to further perfect your body.

OVER SIXTY POUNDS OVERWEIGHT—EVEN A HUNDRED OR MORE— AND FLABBY

You're fat. You feel heavy and hopeless. Until now you may never even have dreamed of working out with weights. After all, doesn't working with weights bulk you up and make you look even fatter? No. Working with the kind of weights you will be using in this program will help you burn more fat—and the small muscles you will be forming will be there for you so once all the fat is gone, instead of feeling flabby and having skin hanging everywhere, you'll be firm to the touch.

Don't worry. You can do it. Just relax and enjoy the gentle lead-in program. I want you to do workout level 1 for three months and then advance. But what are you advancing to? Not workout level 2. I want you to *skip workout level 2 and go to workout level 3*. Yes. I want you to go out of order so that you can burn more fat before you build your solid muscle base.

Do workout level 3 for three months. Now you are ready to go to workout level 4. Do that for three months. Now I want you to go to workout level 2, "Establishing a Muscle Base," and do that for three months. Now look in the mirror. Your body will be reshaped and defined. Now read the section below to perfect your body still further.

Note: If you've worked with weights before and are familiar with weight training, and don't want to spend so much time on workout level 1, "Learning the Moves," just stay on that level for about three weeks—to get used to the exercises. (The same exercises are used in each of the four workout levels—in different combinations and with varying weights.) Then move right to level 3 and follow as written. (For more information on shortening or skipping workout level 1, see pp. 166–167.)

TWENTY TO SIXTY POUNDS OVERWEIGHT AND FLABBY

You don't know how you got here—but you did. You're fat, you're flabby, and you're out of shape. You've never worked with weights before.

You feel intimidated. What should you do and how long will it take you to get in shape?

I want you to begin with workout level 1, "Learning the Moves," and do it for three months, then advance to workout level 2, "Establishing a Muscle Base." Do that for three months, then advance to workout level 3, "Sculpting and Defining." After three months, go to level 4, "The Finishing Touch," and do that for three months. Now look in the mirror. You'll see a completely transformed body—but you may see troublesome areas that need more work. See "Fine-Tuning Your Body" below for instructions on what to do.

Note: If you've worked with weights before and are familiar with weight training, and don't want to spend two to three months on level 1, "Learning the Moves," just stay on that level for about three weeks—to get used to the exercises. (The same exercises are used in each of the four workout levels—in different combinations and with varying weights.) Then move right to level 2 and follow as written. (For more information on skipping workout level 1, see pp. 166–167.)

FIVE TO NINETEEN POUNDS OVERWEIGHT AND FLABBY

You're not really "fat-fat." In fact, some people say, "What are you talking about, you're not overweight." But you feel "pudgy," and in fact, you look, well, a little too "rounded" in the mirror. What should you do?

Do workout level 1, "Learning the Moves," for three months. Then go to workout level 2, "Establishing a Muscle Base," for three months. Then I want you to advance to workout level 3, "Sculpting and Defining the Muscles," for three months. Now I want you to go to workout level 4 for three months. Look in the mirror. Your entire body will be firm and reshaped.

Note: If you've worked with weights before and are familiar with weight training, and don't want to spend two to three months on workout level 1, "Learning the Moves," just stay on that level for about three weeks— to get used to the exercises. (The same exercises are used in each of the four workout levels—in different combinations and with varying weights.) Then move right to level 2 and follow as written. (For more information on skipping workout level 1, see pp. 166–167.)

A SKINNY-FAT—NOT OVERWEIGHT BUT FLABBY

You're not overweight yet you don't look great. It drives you crazy. You've even thought of going on a diet, but you know that is insane. If people hear you complaining about your body they give you a look of near hatred. "I wish I had your body," they say. But you don't like your body because although you look good in clothing, you're not happy with the way you look in the nude. In addition, your body doesn't feel as toned as you would like it to feel. It's too soft and mushy.

You need muscle! Plain and simple, your body is composed of too much fat and not enough muscle. I want you to begin with workout level 1, "Learning the Moves," and stay there for three months, just to get used to working out with weights. Then move to workout level 2, "Establishing a Muscle Base," and remain there for six months. Skip workout level 3. Finally, I want you to move to workout level 4 and remain there for three months. Now look in the mirror. Your body will be firm and defined.

Note: If you've worked with weights before and are familiar with weight training, and don't want to spend two to three months on level 1, "Learning the Moves," just stay on that level for about three weeks—to get used to the exercises. (The same exercises are used in each of the four workout levels—in different combinations and with varying weights.) Then move right to level 2 and follow as written. For more information on skipping workout level 1, see pp. 166–167.

All This Talk About Weight—Where's Your Height-Weight Chart, Joyce?

At the risk of seeming to contradict myself, after all that talk about X amount of pounds overweight, and Y amount of pounds overweight, I'm not going to give you a guideline as to what you "should" weigh. Why? Because there is no correct height-weight chart that takes into account muscle! I know I included them in previous books, but once a person starts working out, they are confusing. Why?

Height-weight charts assume that you do not work out with weights. Muscle weighs more than fat but takes up less space. For example, a five foot ten muscular male bodybuilder may weigh 270 pounds and be lean and gorgeous and have a thirty-two-inch waist—and a man who never touched a weight, of the same height and weight, may stand next to him and be as fat as a house and have a forty-two-inch waist. How can this be?

Simple. Muscle is like lead—it's heavy and condensed. Fat is like feathers—it's light and puffed out. I'll use myself as an example. I look thinner now and wear a smaller size at 120 pounds than I did when I was 110 pounds with no muscle. And look at Cynthia on p. 22 and 23. She looks as if she lost 30 pounds! I won't tell you now how much she really lost—how her makeover was due to muscle reshaping. I want you to look at her photo first and guess. Then find the answer on p. 21. So until they revise the height-weight charts to account for muscle, it's a foolish waste of time to force you to torture yourself with the charts.

Another point. I don't want you to become obsessed with that ——ed scale. I don't mean you can't weigh yourself ever. I just mean that once you have been working out for a while and follow the low-fat eating plan, if you're very fat—overweight (yes, overweight now, without muscle)—you will eventually lose pounds and pounds of feathers (fat) and gain a few pounds of lead (muscle). Your dress and/or pants size will go down. You will eventually not care a hoot about the scale. It's what you see in your mirror and your clothing that will count.

But how then can you tell if you're overweight right now? If you've never worked out with weights, ask your doctor, who will use a standard height-weight chart to tell you where you stand now. His answer will be relevant, because you have not yet worked out with weights. But once you get into the workout, you must give up the scale and charts and begin to look in the mirror. I'm not saying that you can never weigh yourself. You can. But realize that everything is different now that you're working out. The scale means something different as you lose fat and replace it with tight, condensed, sexy muscle. Eventually you'll become less and less addicted to the scale.

My motto is, just do it (the workout and the eating plan) and just look at it (in the mirror)—don't monitor it!

Extra Fine-Tuning Your Body

After you have followed your workout prescription above, and have finished the time frame, working your way through the various levels as prescribed for your particular body, I want you to take a hard look at yourself in the mirror. What do you see? Touch your body—what do you feel?

If you like what you see—if your body is as firm as you want it to be—see Chapter 10, "Preserving the National Treasure for Life," and follow the guidelines for your workout schedule.

If, however, you are still not quite happy with your body, here's what to do if:

SOME BODY PARTS ARE STILL SAGGING

For example, your triceps or thighs may still be too loose. You need to put more muscle in those body parts. Go to workout level 2 for those body parts for six months. For the sagging body parts, go as heavy as you can—gradually building up your weight so that you can form the muscle needed in that area. If the area is your thighs, you will need to use a squat rack, a barbell, and plates. (See pp. 54–55 for photographs and follow the machine alternatives in the exercise instructions.)

If you're still not satisfied, get a copy of Now or Never or Top Shape and do that for six months.

YOU STILL HAVE A LITTLE POUCH ON YOUR STOMACH AND IT IS NOT WELL DEFINED

First, you must be sure to keep to your low-fat eating plan. Any extra fat on your body will tend to linger around the midsection. Your stomach also needs extra work. I want you to get a copy of *Gut Busters* or the video *The Bottoms Up Workout: Middle Body*, and do that workout in place of your stomach workout—six days a week. After six months to a year—look out. You won't be able to believe your eyes.

YOUR BODY IS FIRM AND SHAPELY, BUT YOU WANT MORE DEFINITION

Go back to workout level 2 and do that for three to six months. If you're still not satisfied, get a copy of *Definition* and do the Dragon Lady routine for three months. Then get a copy of *The Fat-Burning Workout*, volume II, and do the insanity plan for three months.

YOUR BUTT IS STILL TOO BIG AND NOT QUITE SHAPED THE WAY YOU WISH

You need to "bomb away" at your hips/buttocks area. Get a copy of *Bottoms Up!*, or just get the *Bottoms Up* lower body video (see p. 245), and do that workout for the lower body for six months to a year. With that workout, you will hit your hips/buttocks area from every possible angle.

YOUR BUTT IS TOO FLAT AND LOW—YOU WANT IT ROUNDER AND HIGHER

You must do heavy squats using a squat rack, and heavy leg presses. Also increase the weight on your lunges. See pp. 48, 55 for photographs and follow the machine alternatives in the exercise instructions. Or, you can follow *Now or Never* for six months.

Note: See bibliography for all books and videos.

Focusing on the Human Anatomy: How Weight-Training Changes Your Entire Shape for the Better

Before I say another thing, I want you, as much as you hate to do it, to take an "anatomy" before photo—just as you see here of Cynthia. Why? I want you to later prove to yourself that this has worked for you! What good is it to look at lovely photographs of other people who have reshaped their body? For now you will use the photographs of Cynthia to understand how the specific exercises in this book will reshape each and every one of your body parts. (Note: I use Cynthia because she changed her body using these techniques.)

Later, I want you to take an after photo and put it next to your before.

Who knows, you may even use your own photos to encourage others to use the workout to change their bodies. You may even become a personal trainer. (I get letters from many women and men who do just that.)

Now let's take a hard look at the human body and study how working out with weights can actually reshape the body. Look at the anatomy photographs of Cynthia before and after. Notice the arrows pointing to specific muscles in both the before and after photos. Let's start with the top of her body and go down. In order to coincide this discussion with your workout, I'll talk about the body parts in the order that you will exercise them later—upper body on workout day one: chest, shoulders, biceps, triceps, and back. Then I'll talk about the lower body, which you will exercise on workout day two: thighs, hips/buttocks, abdominals, and calves.

Both men and women have the same muscles on their body. Women have fatty tissue over the chest muscles (breasts), but otherwise the muscles look exactly the same—except that women are naturally inclined to have smaller muscles than men (they have a smaller amount of the muscle-building hormone, testosterone).

Cynthia—From Before to After in One Year

Let's look at Cynthia, who is fifty-three years old—like me. She will be our before-and-after anatomy photo model—front and rear view. She weighed 136 pounds in her before photo. Now she weighs 132—a loss of only four pounds. But she looks as if she lost at least thirty pounds. How can this be? Cynthia is a perfect example of how muscle weighs more than fat but takes up less space. Cynthia has gone down three dress sizes—from an 11 to a 6! What happened? Cynthia lost thirty pounds of fat and replaced it with muscle that weighs more but takes up less space. The scale only went down four pounds—but her dress size went down three sizes. If Cynthia isn't proof positive that it's not the scale but the mirror that counts, I don't know what is.

Cynthia is the mother of two children, twenty-four and thirty-one. A former secretary, Cynthia now helps her husband run his business. Before this workout, Cynthia tried all kinds of diets. In fact, in her before photo, she had just lost thirty-five pounds and was quite disappointed to see that she still looked fat. So she went from one, as she puts it, "foolish tone-up program to another but I still looked like a sack of potatoes—no shape and no form. When I was sitting, my stomach still sat on my lap, and when I lay down at night, it lay down beside me."

Cynthia didn't look at her body until doing the workout for six weeks, and when she did she was shocked. "I saw muscles. From that day on, I started wearing tank tops," she says. "Now after a whole year people I meet can't believe it's me. I went to a high school reunion and all I got were raves all night long." Cynthia has now become a personal trainer.

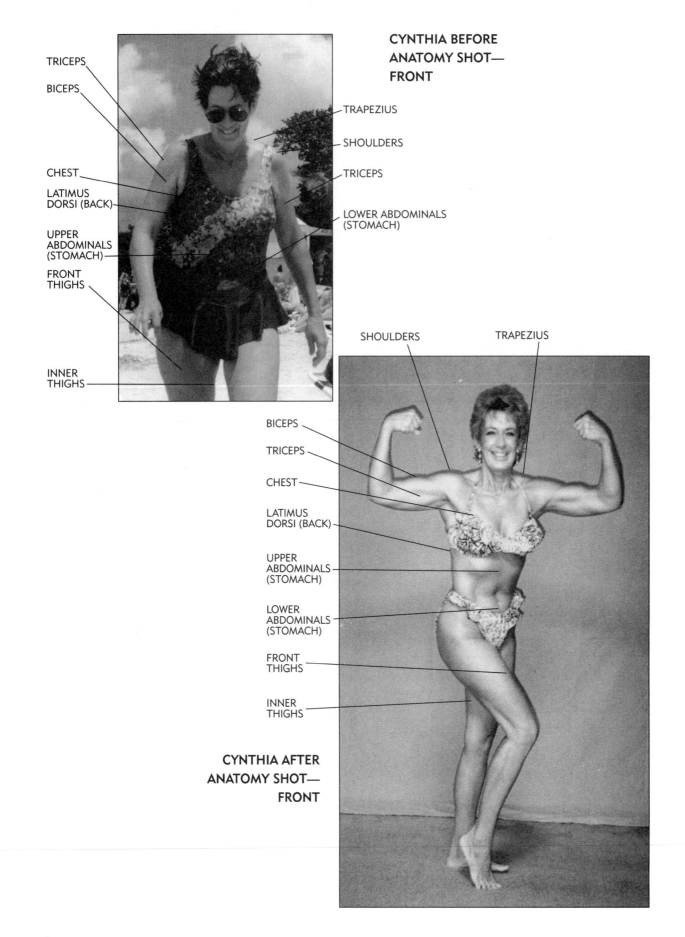

TRICEPS

BICEPS

CHEST

LATIMUS
DORSI (BACK)

UPPER
ABDOMINALS
(STOMACH)

FRONT
THIGHS

INNER
THIGHS

CYNTHIA BEFORE
ANATOMY SHOT—
FRONT

TRAPEZIUS

SHOULDERS

TRICEPS

LOWER ABDOMINALS
(STOMACH)

SHOULDERS

TRAPEZIUS

BICEPS

TRICEPS

CHEST

LATIMUS
DORSI (BACK)

UPPER
ABDOMINALS
(STOMACH)

LOWER
ABDOMINALS
(STOMACH)

FRONT
THIGHS

INNER
THIGHS

CYNTHIA AFTER
ANATOMY SHOT—
FRONT

CYNTHIA BEFORE ANATOMY SHOT— REAR

GLUTEUS MAXIMUS

BACK THIGHS

CALVES

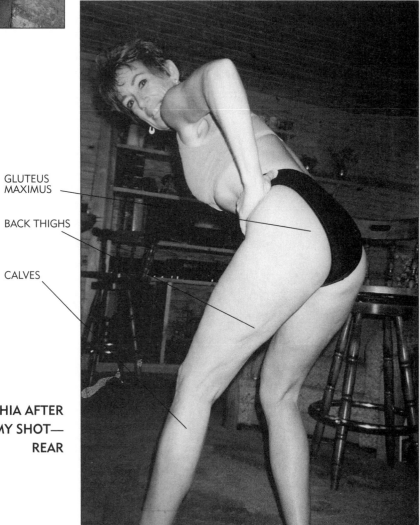

GLUTEUS MAXIMUS

BACK THIGHS

CALVES

CYNTHIA AFTER ANATOMY SHOT— REAR

Cynthia says her husband feels as if he's got a tiger by the tail. "I tell him, well, just don't let go. The workout really changes your self-image. You have so much self-esteem you can fly out the window. You don't walk anymore, you strut. Before this workout I used to feel like I was just waiting to be Grandma and go through the rest of my life cooking meals and then just die.

"I have one thing to say to all the women out there," says Cynthia. "Start this program. Go through all the stages, and no matter what you do, don't quit. Give yourself enough time because it does work. You'll never have to worry about your body again." Now let's take a closer look at Cynthia in her before-and-after anatomy photographs and analyze the specific changes the workout caused on her body—keeping in mind all the time that you will get the same results if you follow the workout.

The Chest, Breasts, Pectorals, Pectoralis Major or Pecs

The chest muscles are called the "pectoral" muscles, "pectoralis major," or "pecs." This muscle is shaped like a two-headed fan. The upper head (called the clavicular head) forms the upper pectoral area. The larger head (called the sternal head) forms the lower pectoral area. Look at Cynthia's before chest. There was no definition.

When you do the chest exercises in this workout, you shape and define your entire chest area. For example, your first chest exercise, the flat press, firms and defines the upper and lower pectoral area. The second and third chest exercises, the incline press and the incline flye, zone in on the upper chest area, giving definition, or to put it another way, the look of cleavage. The fourth exercise, the cross-bench pullover, covers the entire chest area— upper and lower—and helps to expand the rib cage. Look at Cynthia now. See how the specific four chest exercises, hitting her chest at different angles, have served to lift and reshape her chest.

What about breast size? Chest exercises can slightly increase the size of your breasts—but indirectly, by building the muscle under them. As you know, the breasts are made of fatty tissue. That's why most women who are extremely overweight have big breasts, but when they lose weight and come down to their healthy weight, they also lose a breast size or more. Actually, they are not losing a natural breast size. They are losing excess fat that was being stored in the breast area.

Some women are genetically gifted (or cursed, depending on how they feel about it) with large breasts. Even when they are very thin, their breasts are large. They were this way since puberty—when at a thin sixteen years old they had a breast size of, say, 34D or larger. If these women put on weight, their breasts would become so large that they would need a breast reduction operation—or it would be difficult to walk around.

So to summarize, your breast size is really a matter of genetics—but you can reshape and add a little size by working with weights—and you can add definition that increases the look of cleavage. Don't worry that you will reduce your breast size by working out. It won't happen. If you lose a breast size after working out and dieting (assuming you are overweight), realize that you've lost excess body fat—some of which was on your breasts. (Don't we all wish we could tell our bodies where to lose and where to retain the body fat?)

Shoulders, or Deltoids

The shoulder muscle is called a "deltoid" because it is shaped like an upside-down delta (the Greek letter delta). The three parts of this delta are front (anterior), side (medial), and rear (posterior). The deltoid muscle originates in the upper area of the shoulder blade and collarbone, and is attached on the bone of the upper arm.

Look at Cynthia's before shoulders. They were sloped down and basically had no shape or definition. Cynthia's shoulder muscles (deltoids) were developed by the four exercises presented in this book.

For example, your first shoulder exercise, the side lateral raise, zones in on your side (middle) shoulder area. The second shoulder exercise, the front lateral raise, focuses on your front shoulder area. Your third shoulder exercise, the alternate shoulder press, works on the entire shoulder area, and your fourth shoulder exercise, the bent lateral raise, zaps your rear shoulder area. By the time you finish your shoulder routine, you have hit your shoulder muscle from every possible angle—so that in time the end result is sexy shoulders. Look at Cynthia's before and after. Think of your own muscles being transformed.

Biceps

This muscle is intelligently named "biceps" because it is a two-headed muscle. The hump or rise of the biceps is caused by the coming together of the two heads of the muscle. The biceps originate at the shoulder blade and end at the forearm.

Look at Cynthia's biceps. They were weak and underdeveloped before. Notice now how firm and defined they are. The first and second biceps exercises, the alternate curl and the simultaneous curl, develop and shape the entire biceps muscle. The third and fourth biceps exercises, the alternate hammer curl and the concentration curl, zone in on the peak of the biceps muscle. In combination, the four biceps exercises reshape and strengthen this muscle, making it aesthetically appealing and firm to the touch.

Triceps

The triceps muscle has three heads ("tri" means three): inner, rear, and medial. The three heads originate at the shoulder blade and the upper arm, and insert at the elbow. Look at Cynthia's triceps muscle. It used to feel like jelly—and indeed it did wave like a flag. See how tight and toned it is now. In order to shape up the triceps, you must do exercises that attack each of the three heads of the muscle.

The first triceps exercise, the overhead press, focuses on the inner and rear heads of the muscle. The next exercise, the kickback, works on all three heads. The third exercise, the one-arm overhead extension, focuses on the medial head of the triceps, and the final exercise, the cross-face extension, zeroes in on the inner head of that muscle. In the end, the entire triceps muscle has been bombed in a way that will yield maximum tone and definition.

Back: Trapezius (Traps) and Latissimus Dorsi (Lats)

The trapezius muscle is shaped like a triangle. It looks as if it is only found between the neck and shoulder blade, but that's really just the tip of the iceberg. The trapezius originates along the spine and runs from the back of the neck all the way down to the middle of the back.

Look at Cynthia's back muscles in her rear-view before photograph. If you look closely, you can see the fat bulging below and above her bra line. I'm talking about the shot where someone candidly took a photo of her climbing into a cave. (She would never willingly stand for such a photo!)

Now look at her trapezius muscle—you can see it in her front-view before photo between her neck and shoulder area—or should I say not see it. She didn't have any muscle there—and it made her neck look scrawny in contrast with her fat body, making her body look even fatter. Now, notice that once she has developed her trapezius muscles, there is a smooth transitional line connecting her neck to her shoulders.

The first back exercise, the upright row, develops and shapes the trapezius muscle.

The other back muscle that will concern us is called the "latissimus dorsi," or abbreviated, "lats." The lats originate along the spinal column in the middle of the back and toward the shoulders and travel up to the front of the upper arm. They give the back a V appearance, and when developed, can make the waist look smaller.

Look at Cynthia's before photographs. You can see her absence of lats from her front-view before anatomy photo. Notice that she seemed to have a large waistline—not only because she had a lot of fat covering her middle, but because she had no V at all. Her back was straight, and it made her waist look larger. Once she developed her lats, her back took on a V shape, making her waist appear smaller.

The one-arm dumbbell row zones in on the lat muscles, and helps to develop those upper back muscles you can see on Cynthia (notice she didn't have them in her before photograph). The third back exercise, the double-arm reverse row, attacks both the trapezius muscle and the lats. The last back exercise, the seated back lateral, helps to put muscle and definition in the upper back—but it also works the trapezius muscles. In combination, the four back exercises work to develop the back of your dreams.

Front Thighs (Quadriceps, or Quads), Inner Thighs (Adductor), and Back Thighs (Hamstrings)

The front thigh, or quadriceps, is composed of four muscles ("quadri" means four). These muscles originate at the hip or thigh bones and meet at the knee. They give the front thigh its shape and form.

Look at Cynthia's front thighs in her before photo. They were not shaped well—and if you look closer, she had cellulite. Notice that in her after photograph, her front thighs are not only toned, but are beautifully formed and have definition.

She achieved this by doing the exercises in the thigh workout. The first and fourth thigh exercises, the squat and the lunge, zone in on the front thigh muscle.

The inner thigh (adductor) originates in the inner, lower pelvic area and rises to the inner thigh bone. It gives your inner thigh firmness.

Notice Cynthia's inner thigh in her before photo—it was loose and flabby. She was able to tighten up her inner thigh (adductor) muscles by doing the second thigh exercise, the side leg lift.

The back thigh (hamstrings) is composed of three muscle groups that originate at the bottom of the pelvis and end at the back knee joint. They give your back thigh its shape and form.

Look at all the cellulite on Cynthia's back thighs in her before rear-view anatomy photograph. Now look at her after rear-view anatomy photograph and note that not only is the cellulite gone from her back thigh, but major reshaping and defining have taken place. The leg curl is specifically effective in toning the back thigh (hamstrings).

Hips/Buttocks, or Gluteus Maximus

The gluteus maximus is the largest muscle in the human body. It originates at the crest of the thigh bone and runs down the tailbone. It gives your buttocks their firmness and form.

Look at Cynthia's hips/buttocks area in her before photograph. "Wide-load" would not be a faulty description. See the amazing transformation in her after anatomy photo. Her buttocks are higher, rounder, and are now beautifully shaped.

The first butt exercise, the standing butt squeeze, helped to lift, smooth, tighten, and tone that area. The second and fourth hips/buttocks exercises, the standing back-leg extension and the bent-knee kick-up, also helped to tighten and tone that area, but they zoned in on her outer butt or hip area, usually called "saddlebags." The third hips/buttocks exercise, the straight-leg kick-up, helped to tighten, tone, and lift her entire hips/buttocks area, but zeroed in on her upper-back-thigh area.

Abdominals, or Rectus Abdominis

The front abdominal area consists of a long powerful segmented muscle called the "rectus abdominis." This muscle runs above and below the waist.

Look at Cynthia's abdominal area in her before photograph. She looked pregnant! Notice how defined and shapely her waistline is in her after photograph.

The first and third abdominal exercises, the concentrated butt lift and the ceiling lift, helped Cynthia to tighten, reshape, and define her lower abdominal area—as you can see by the after photograph, although Cynthia feels that she wants it even flatter (it may take another six months for perfection). Now look at her before-and-after upper abdominal area, and notice how flat and defined she is now. The second and fourth abdominal exercises, the crunch and the knee-raised crunch, helped her to reshape and define her upper abdominal area.

Calves: Gastrocnemius and Soleus

The calf, which is called the "gastrocnemius" muscle, is a two-headed muscle. It also consists of the soleus muscle, which lies just under it. These muscles connect in the middle of the lower leg and tie in with the Achilles tendon. The calves help to balance out the leg. If you have well-developed thighs but tiny calves, your legs will look out of balance. Many women don't have to exercise their calves because they either run or wear high heels. Either one of these activities will automatically develop shapely calves.

Cynthia's before calves were just plain fat, as you can see in her rear-view before photo. She was able to shape and define her middle calf area by doing both the seated and standing straight-toe raise, and to sculpt her inner calf area by doing the seated angled-out-toe raise. She put the finishing touches on her calves—the outer edge—by doing the standing angled-in-toe raise.

Why Look at Cynthia's Before-and-After Photos and Think About How the Specific Exercises Reshaped Her Body?

It is crucial that you take the time to think, very carefully, about how each exercise discussed above was able to shape and define—to chisel each and every muscle on Cynthia's body and to create an after body from a before body. Why?

If Cynthia did it, you can do it too. She did the workouts in this book and ended up evolving from her before photo to her after photo.

Another reason to look at the before-and-after anatomy photographs is to help you to mentally focus on your working muscles as you work out. You can't do this unless you know what you're thinking about. Learn where the muscles are on your own body. Touch those muscles. Then, think to yourself as you work out, "This specific muscle is now being reshaped by this movement." Go a step further. Actually order the muscle to be reshaped. Tell it to become defined, tight, and toned. Visualize the muscle evolving into the shape you have in mind.

More Before-and-After Women—and Men Too!

You've met Cynthia. It took her twelve months to get into the shape you see her in. Here are some other women and men too who did the workout—most of them for less than a year.

KATHY, FORTY-THREE YEARS OLD—FROM SIZE 16 TO 6 IN
TWENTY-FIVE WEEKS

Kathy, also featured on the back cover, is a busy, happily married working mother of two children aged six and nine. "I remember how I was poured into my relaxed-fit size 16 jeans. They were so tight, they fit more like pantyhose than jeans. Now I wear a size 6 straight-cut jean—how do you beat it?"

Before trying this workout, Kathy tried aerobics, walking, swimming, cycling, and high-protein fad diets. "The diets, in the long run, made me gain more weight and none of the aerobics workouts reshaped my body. But once I tried this workout, my whole body began to become defined and sculpted, while at the same time any excess body fat began melting away. But the best part of it all was, I was now in total control of my body, and in a sense, my life. Instead of the center of control being 'out there,' now it was coming from within. I also followed the *Eat to Trim* diet.

"I'll tell you the truth," says Kathy, "at first it was hard. I was perspiring and I had thoughts like, 'Who am I kidding? Is this going to work?' But from reading the early manuscript of the book, it sounded so logical, and I

KATHY BEFORE

KATHY AFTER

decided to just have faith and keep going. Then in about three weeks I started seeing definition on my arms and I said, 'Oh, my God, it's muscles.'"

The best part of getting in shape for Kathy is a stronger sense of self and the added bonus of feeling sexy again. "Women tend to put everyone else first—so we shovel in cookies or ice cream or fast-food junk food to fill the gap. Now I take time out for myself first—to do the workout. Then I'm in a better mood all day and I can give the time to others. It's also nice to feel sensual. My husband is always after me now—it's really funny. I have to be careful not to let him see me walking around in underwear—especially on mornings when I'm in a hurry." Nice problem to have!

When I asked Kathy what was the best thing about this workout, she said: "If you're going to put energy into any kind of program, you're going to get the most return for your investment in this. Think of it—if you're going to take a half hour to walk or swim, you won't reshape your body. But if you invest the same time in this—you have a whole new body and a whole new life. And let me not forget the best part. You don't have to leave your house to do it. I prefer solitude—and especially when I was really fat. I didn't need anyone looking at my fat body—watching me sweat."

Note: Kathy did levels 3 and 4 from earlier versions of this workout—*The Fat-Burning Workout* and *Bottoms Up!*

STARLENE, THIRTY-TWO YEARS OLD, FROM SIZE 14 TO SIZE 8 IN SIXTEEN WEEKS

Starlene is a full-time single parent of two children aged six and eight. She is extremely busy because one of her children requires a lot of attention due to Down's syndrome. Starlene tried Jazzercize, health clubs, and starving, but she still had her "doughboy belly" and was getting scared because "my mom used to weigh 260 pounds and I was afraid I was going there." Starlene didn't have the money to spare or the time to invest in going to a gym. "That was one of the biggest appeals of this workout," she says. "I could do it for practically nothing—at home, between dealing with the children and the housework, and it looked easy."

Starlene says her friends can't believe the change in her body. But she admits that there were times, and there still are times, when she has to fight herself to put in those twenty to thirty minutes a day to work out. "But I always find a way to win the battle," she says. "I just reread the motivation section of the early manuscript of the book, and that gives me the energy to keep going. Also, I keep getting motivated by reading the issues of your *Joycercize* newsletter. I also use tricks by telling myself to start and only do one body part—five minutes. Then once I'm started I always finish the workout for the day."

When I asked Starlene what was the best thing about this workout, she

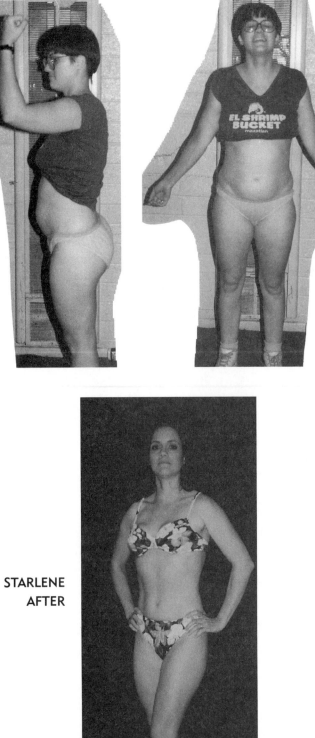

STARLENE BEFORE

STARLENE
AFTER

said, "I have so much more energy now—I mean, it used to be a big chore to clean the house. Now I'm going like a steam engine. Also, the workout is convenient. I don't have to do it on someone else's schedule—and I don't have to worry about getting a baby-sitter—and oh yes, as I passed thirty, instead of getting fatter and flabbier, I'm getting sexier and sexier—and I can eat more than I used to eat and still not get fat, because it is true—muscles do burn fat twenty-four hours a day!"

WES, FIFTY-TWO YEARS OLD, FROM SIZE 38 PANTS TO SIZE 32 IN A YEAR; HIS FIANCÉE, EMILY, TWENTY-NINE YEARS OLD, FROM SIZE 15 TO SIZE 9 IN SIX MONTHS

Take a look at Wes and Emily. Wes weighed 187 and wore size 38 pants. Now he's 164 pounds of lean muscle. Before Wes started working out, his blood pressure and cholesterol levels were sky-high. He was recently tested, and the doctor was amazed. "You couldn't get much better," she said to him. "This is astonishing. And your muscle tone's magnificent. What did you do?" He told her about the workout and the diet (Wes followed *Eat to Trim*).

When I asked Wes what's the best thing about this workout, he said, "You don't have to spend all day doing it. It's something you can go in, do it, get it done, and you're done with it for the day and you feel good! I put in a hard forty-hour workweek. I like to spend the rest of my time enjoying sports and other activities. I'm glad I only have to work out four times a week with the weights—and look at my body." Wes did an earlier verson of workout level 2 found in *Top Shape*.

Look at twenty-nine-year-old Emily before she met Wes, who told her about the workout. And look at her now—six months later. How did it happen? After going through workout level 1, Emily recalls, "I'm strong because of my greenhouse work. [Emily manages a greenhouse and regularly has to pick up heavy plants, dirt, and so forth.] I realized quickly that I didn't have to mess around too long with those three-pound weights." Emily quickly worked her way up to what she is now using: ten-, fifteen-, and twenty-pound dumbbells.

When I asked Emily what's the best thing about this workout, she said, "That it works! It will cause you to lose the weight and not only takes the weight off you but it shapes you. People are commenting—especially when I wear certain clothes. I'm really glad I met Wes—not only because he was very pleasing to the eye, but because he introduced me to this workout. Also we work out together. I like working out with someone because it motivates me and makes it fun. What I like too is, instead of relying on the scale, we measure ourselves and look in the mirror—and we see we're getting results. The scale may not always tell the tale."

WES BEFORE

EMILY BEFORE

WES & EMILY AFTER

LOUIE, FORTY-TWO YEARS OLD, FROM SIZE 36 PANTS TO 32 IN TWENTY-FIVE WEEKS

Louie spent many hours in the gym—and still looked the way he did in his before photo, even as he got older and older. I know this is true because that's where I met him—in the gym, working out and doing all the wrong things. In fact, I used to feel sorry for him. "Poor guy," I thought. "He spends more than double the time I do, and he seems to get nothing for his effort." I felt so sorry for Louie that I Xeroxed the pages of this workout and gave it to him. Since he had been working out awhile, I skipped him right to level 2—where he did the full workout from day one, without breaking in gently. What happened?

"After only three weeks of using this workout, people were already noticing my body. They kept asking me what I was doing different, telling me that I looked good. In a couple of months people started asking me to show them my workout. I wound up spending time teaching people—I was working for free. Now I've got everybody doing it—asking me what my secret is. You know, I'm thinking about becoming a personal trainer—but they can really just use the pictures and instructions the way I did."

LOUIE BEFORE

LOUIE AFTER

When I asked Louie what the best thing about his workout is, he said, "It's not only my body, but that I'm finished with the workout in no time—and those other guys take all day and don't improve at all. It's like you say in the book—it's the method, not the time—but even better, it's the fountain of youth. Look at me when I was twenty-six and look at me now at forty-two! I look better and younger and I feel a hundred percent healthier!"

Joyce Vedral—Before and After

Here's a photo of me at twenty-six years old. I was fat and getting fatter every year. Look at me now at more than double my age. I went from a size 11–13 to a 3–5! But what's more, my body is more toned and better shaped at fifty-three than it was at twenty-six! If I can do it, you can do it too.

Before

Joyce at 26

After

Joyce at 53

Before Front-View Anatomy Photo

After Front-View Anatomy Photo

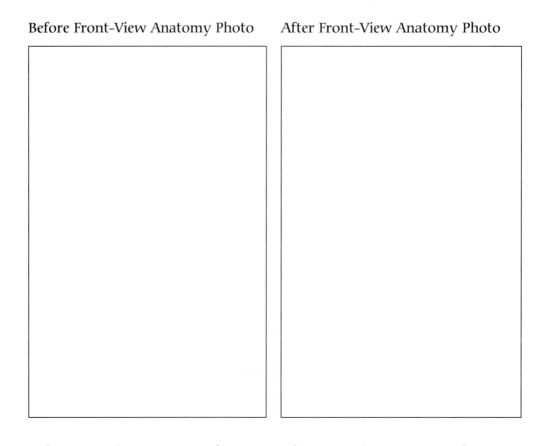

Before Rear-View Anatomy Photo

After Rear-View Anatomy Photo

Create Your Own Before-and-After-Anatomy Shots

If you haven't already done so, right now I want you to take a photograph in your bathing suit—front and rear view—and paste them into the spaces provided at left. Label your own before photographs. Find each of the muscles listed above: pectorals (chest), deltoids (shoulders), biceps, triceps, and so on. In the end, have a fully labeled front and rear view of yourself—before.

Now, in six months to a year from now, I want you to paste your new front- and rear-view photographs in the space and compare. You'll amaze yourself with your own progress. But don't just paste them in the book. You can be a star in my newsletter. Send them to me at the Joycercize Club! (See p. 246.)

NOTES

1. Wayne L. Wescott, Ph.D, "Strength Training Update," *Idea Today*, June 1995, p. 1. Studies cited in this article prove that working out eight to twelve weeks adds about three pounds of lean muscle and raises the metabolic rate by about 7 percent—and daily calorie requirement by 15 percent. "Adults who add muscle through sensible strength exercise use more calories all day long, so are less likely to accumulate fat," says Wescott.

2. Ibid.

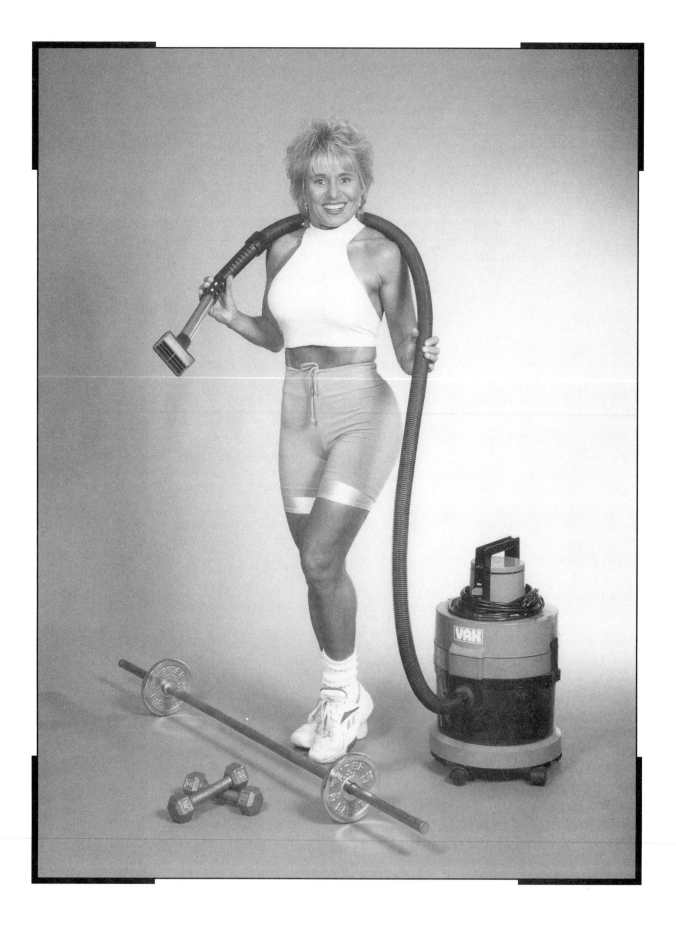

3

DUMBBELLS, BARBELLS, AND MACHINES

You know that in order to get into shape you must work out with weights—but what kind of weights are we talking about? There are two types of weights to choose from: free weights (weights that can be carried about) as opposed to machines that are nailed to the floor and/or are too heavy to be carried about.

Free weights divide into two different categories: dumbbells and barbells. As mentioned before, dumbbells are weights that you hold in each hand, while a barbell is a long bar that holds a disc-shaped plate on each end that must be held with both hands. I use dumbbells for all of the workout programs in this book because they are the least expensive, and can be used to do all the exercises. For those who want to keep their equipment down to a very inexpensive minimum, the best way to go is simply dumbbells.

But, and this is a big but—because it is a first ever for me—in this chapter, I'll show you *how to use barbells and machines* so that if you ever want variety, you'll have no problem making the substitutions.

I'll also talk about why, in general, free weights are considered superior to machines. I'll then explain why five certain machines are exceptions to the rule, and are great if you can gain access to them—and why the other machines are nice for a change, but not necessary. Finally, I'll finger the frivolous machines and tell you why most in-the-know weight trainers don't use them.

Next, we'll talk about the specific exercises found in this book and how to get started working out. We'll clear up any confusion you may have had about exercise names, talk about what to wear when you work out, where to work out, the time of day to work out, what days of the week to work out, setting up a workout schedule, making up a missed workout, muscle soreness, and getting psyched.

Finally, and most important, I'll give you a quick-start dictionary of terms and expressions that may come up as you work out, or that will help you better understand working out in general—so that if you ever have a question, you can come right back to this section and look it up.

Dumbbells Versus Machines

Machines come in many brands and styles, and can make you question your intelligence trying to figure them out. They get fancier and more expensive all the time. "Do I need this machine," you ask yourself, "or can I live without it?" By the time you finish reading this chapter you'll know the answer to that question.

Machines used to be simple mechanical devices that operated on pulleys and cams. Now many of them are so high-tech that they're operated by air pressure. You don't have to get off the machine to change the weight. All you do to increase or decrease the weight is press a button on either handle. Before you know it, they'll invent a machine that moves your working body part up and down—or in and out—whatever the case may be!

There exists a machine for every exercise you can do with dumbbells. But you need many machines to make up for a simple set of dumbbells, because *the most you can do on any one machine* is a few different exercises. In this workout, you will be given thirty-six different exercises, four exercises for each of your nine body parts—and you can do them *all* simply with dumbbells! (You remember—the handheld weights with a bell-like shape at the end.)

Dumbbells are more convenient than machines. You can keep them in your home or office—under a piece of furniture or in a closet—whereas machines may require a special workout room. You can also tailor dumbbells to your exact body size. For example, a machine is made to fit an "average" person. Even though machines have adjustments, you can never get a machine to be positioned perfectly for your body size. On the other hand, when you hold the dumbbells, you can move them up and down, in or out, over and under—in the exact range that your particular body structure demands.

Then why do people bother with machines at all? Machines do have some advantages. If you're working at a machine and you drop the weight, the machine will catch it. You won't hurt yourself. But this can be a disadvantage too—because many people use heavier weights than they should when working at machines. With free weights (dumbbells or barbells—you remember, a barbell is a long bar with a disclike plate at each end) you are more likely to use only the weights you can handle.

Let's think of the bench press as an example. Say you are using a bench press machine and boldly try to press eighty pounds. You push the weight bar halfway up and can't go any further. You drop it. The weight rack clangs down and the machine catches the weight. The gym manager gives you a look (dropping weights on machines eventually cracks the weight plates and does other damage), and you sheepishly continue your workout. Who cares! You're not paying for the ruined machine. But you did lose something after all. You got little out of the workout because you didn't do a full repetition—all the way up and all the way down—in a controlled manner.

Now picture yourself pressing dumbbells. You ignore everything I said about breaking in gently. In fact, you decide to start at workout level 2, and in addition, go right to the heavy weights. You take a set of twenty-pound dumbbells in your hands and lie on the bench, placing the dumbbells in start position. (See p. 87.) But the moment you try to press the dumbbells up, you realize that you've made a foolish mistake. There's no way you're going to lift these weights. Humbly, you put the weights down and opt for lighter five-pound dumbbells. Eventually, you become stronger and your body tells you to try a slightly higher weight. Someday you'll build yourself up to the point where twenty-pound dumbbells are not a problem—but you don't push yourself too fast. Free weights won't let you. You can see where working with free weights helps you to get into "fine tune" with your body.

Machines are important for those people who want to go extremely heavy, and need the guarantee that if they do drop the weight, the machine will catch the weight. This heavy-overload function of the machine is very valuable to power lifters and champion bodybuilders who use certain machines to do specific mass-building exercises.

Now let's talk about specific machines. There are some machines that are in fact very valuable—and a few that are better to use than free weights for particular exercises. I'll talk about these in a moment. Other machine exercises are equally valuable as free weights, and if available should be substituted, at least from time to time. Finally, there are some machine exercises that you could do without—although once in a while they can't hurt. First let's talk about the most useful machines.

The Five Best Machines and How to Use Them

The following five machines are used by all in-the-know weight-training experts. If they are available to you, I recommend that you use them. They can be purchased—and are not outrageous in price, and are available in virtually all fitness centers. The style and mechanism of the particular machine may differ, but if you ask the gym manager to show you to any of the five machines listed, he or she will be able to do so. (Note: By way of demonstration, photos show start and finish positions of each exercise.)

1. LAT-PULLDOWN MACHINE

You can perform a variety of exercises on this machine. Here are five on the pages that follow.

Although the free-weight exercises given with dumbbells in this workout do a great deal to build the lats (the back muscles that form the V look of the back and help your waist look smaller), the lat-pulldown machine is superior.

The advantage to doing *lat pulldowns to the front and/or rear* with the machine is the machine's ability to force you to position yourself safely, to move the weights at exactly the right angle, and to handle heavier weights (in order to widen the lats one often needs to lift heavier weights). Whenever I am in a gym, I will use this machine to substitute for the dumbbell exercises. If I were going to purchase only one machine, this would be the one.

As you read the exercise instructions, you'll see a section called "Machines, etc." In this section you will be told which machine exercise to do in place of a given exercise. For example, the second back exercise in all the workouts found in this book, the one-arm dumbbell row, can be substituted by the lat pulldown to the front. The third back exercise in all the workouts

START   FINISH

1. Back: lat pull-
down to the
front

2. Back: lat pull-
down to the
back or rear

START   FINISH

START FINISH

3. Triceps: triceps pushdown

START FINISH

4. Triceps: triceps overhead exten-sion

START FINISH

5. Biceps: biceps pulldown

START FINISH

found in this book, the double-arm reverse row, can be substituted by the lat pulldown to the back.

You can also do two triceps (the muscle located on the underside of your arm—between the elbow and the armpit—the one that waves like a flag if you're out of shape) exercises on this machine. They are excellent, and just as good as the free-weight exercises. From time to time, when I'm in the gym, I'll do the *triceps pushdown* and the *triceps overhead extension* in place of kickbacks and cross-face extensions (the second and fourth triceps exercises in the workouts found in this book). You'll be reminded where you can substitute what in each exercise instruction under "Machines, etc."

The *biceps pulldown* that can be done on this machine allows you to hit the biceps muscle from an angle not possible with any free-weight exercise. The closest free-weight exercise is the hammer curl. From time to time, when I am in the gym, I'll substitute the hammer curl for the biceps pulldown.

2. LEG EXTENSION MACHINE

You can perform only one exercise on this machine, the *leg extension*— but it is a very valuable machine for the front thigh. If everyone had a leg extension machine, I would make this a required exercise. If you have access to this machine, I suggest you add it to your four thigh exercises. If you don't want to do a fifth exercise, substitute it for the squat or lunge.

For those with bad knees, this machine is invaluable. It is often recommended by exercise physiologists for those people who are recovering from knee injuries, or who have back problems and cannot do bending exercises of any kind.

START   FINISH

If you have one of my other exercise books, you will notice that in most of them I give a free-weight leg extension exercise. I no longer include this exercise in my free-weight routine, because some of my readers have written saying that the exercise is uncomfortable and/or awkward, and they have trouble feeling the pressure in their front thigh muscle—where they should feel it. Instead, many of them say they feel it in their back. If you do it right with free weights you would feel it in your front thighs and not your back, but it is difficult to position your body and hold the dumbbell and move your legs—all at the same time along the right plane—to get the full benefit of the exercise. So, for this exercise, I must admit, the machine exercise is much more valuable than the free-weight exercise.

3. LEG CURL MACHINE

This is a back thigh machine. Using it will help you to do strict and/or heavy *leg curls*—more so than with dumbbells. If available, always substitute the leg curl machine for the dumbbell leg curl. (Note that sometimes the leg curl and leg extension machines are combined in one machine. If you are purchasing a home machine, make sure you get the combination.)

Whenever I am in a gym I will use the leg curl machine in place of the free-weight leg curl. It is a better bet because you don't have to worry about holding the dumbbell between your feet. You can concentrate all of your energy on the working muscle.

START   FINISH

4. LEG PRESS MACHINE

This is a thigh machine. It is used to do *leg presses* in addition to, or as a substitute for, the squat and sometimes the lunge. It allows you to use the kind of weight necessary for developing a significant front-thigh muscle. When doing this exercise, you either lie on your back or place your back against a flat surface—and press the weights. There is absolutely no pressure on your back.

People who cannot do squats or lunges because of bad knees rely heavily upon this machine. You can use it in place of the squat and/or lunge.

Note: You can also do lying calf raises, angled straight, in and out, on this machine—not demonstrated—but see seated dumbbell calf raise photos (pp. 151, 153) and you'll be able to figure it out.

START

FINISH

5. SEATED CALF MACHINE

The advantage to this machine over free weights is you can do *seated calf raises* with heavy enough weights to really make a difference on your calves. In fact, the only way to put on size on your calves, other than running or wearing high heels, is to use a calf machine with significant weight. (Note: The standing calf machine is just as good, and in fact is a welcome addition—if you are in a gym. I mention the seated calf machine here because it is not as expensive to buy as the standing machine, and also takes up less space.) This machine substitutes the seated straight-toe and angled-out-toe raise.

START

FINISH

Pulleys

What in the world are pulleys? They are small, fixed wheels with a grooved rim in which a steel rope runs—so as to raise a weight attached at one end by pulling the other end. Technically speaking, they are categorized as machines, but they are sometimes found attached to walls—and are not on machines at all. They are also attached to many and varied weight-training machines, and can be used for multiple purposes. (See p. 52 for photographs of a pulley exercise.) From time to time, in the exercise instructions, you'll be told the exercise can be done on a machine with a pulley device.

If you have access to pulleys, it is a good idea to take advantage of occasionally substituting your free-weight exercises with pulley exercises.

Those Thousand-Dollar-Plus Total-Body Home Machines

What about those total-body machines—you know, the kind you see advertised on TV all the time—Soloflex, Bowflex, Nautilus, Healthtrainer, and so on. Well, they're fine. They combine all of the above five machines in one—making for a gigantic many-faceted machine. But the problem is, you have to waste a lot of time rearranging bars and pins to convert the machine from one "machine" to the other (of the five above mentioned).

There's yet another catch. Even with all the things such multimachines do, you still can't do all the exercises you need to reshape your body on them. You will still need dumbbells in addition to the machine. This is very important—you'll see why as you read this book.

If you can afford such a machine and have the space for it, great. Use it to do the exercises described above—and even experiment with some of the exercises that come with the machine's manual. In fact, I use such a machine in my book *Top Shape*—the Healthtrainer. But in that book, I tell the readers which exercises are better done with dumbbells. So if you have a total-body machine, invest in some dumbbells and even go wild and buy a barbell and plates—and you'll really have a fully equipped gym.

What About Barbells?

As mentioned above, barbells are also considered free weights—but instead of two handheld weights, a barbell is one long bar to which you can add weights, called "plates." Plates begin as low as one and a quarter pounds and go as high as a hundred pounds each. You can purchase a barbell and plates in any gym supply store (look in your Yellow Pages under "Exercise Equipment" or "Sporting Goods").

Barbells have all of the same advantages over machines as dumbbells, only they are not quite as versatile, because you must work two arms at a time. However, for some purposes, barbells are more convenient than dumbbells. For example, it's more comfortable to do squats or lunges with a barbell if you are using relatively heavy weights, because a barbell is one long bar that you can rest on your shoulders. (See p. 54 for a photo of me doing a squat with a barbell and plates.) When you use dumbbells, you must hold one in each hand, and if the dumbbells are twenty pounds or more, your hands may get tired and give out. In the meantime, had you used a barbell, your shoulders could have easily supported the weight.

You can use a barbell in place of dumbbells even if you're not going heavy—just for the sake of variety. The lightest barbell is usually twenty pounds. If you are using a barbell to replace very light dumbbell work, that's a good place to start. As you get stronger, you can add plates to each side of the barbell.

Barbells are also an excellent addition to your dumbbell workout for upper body work. You can challenge your muscle from a slightly different angle than with dumbbells. For example, when exercising your biceps, you can do a barbell curl instead of the simultaneous curl with dumbbells. (I tell you this in the "Machines, etc." section of the exercise instructions. See p. 51 for a photo of me doing a biceps curl with a barbell.) You can also substitute barbells for chest work. For example, you can use a barbell to do the flat or incline press. (See p. 53 for a photo of me doing a bench press with a barbell and plates.)

Barbells are also good for doing shoulder exercises. For example, you can use a barbell to do your front lateral raise or your shoulder press. (Obviously, you can't do one arm at a time with a barbell, so if you are doing an "alternate" exercise, and the instructions say "you may use a barbell to do this exercise," you can assume that it is okay to work both arms at a time.)

You can use a barbell to substitute some triceps and back exercises as well. Whenever a barbell can be substituted, you will see it in the exercise instructions under "Machines, etc." If all of this is too much for you, you can ignore it and never use a barbell, or even look at the "Machines, etc." section. You will get in great shape either way, I promise.

Racks and Stations

What are racks and stations? They are setups where you can use heavier barbells and not injure yourself. For example, if you want to do heavier squats or lunges, sooner or later you'll have to switch to a barbell, because the dumbbells will be too heavy to hold. Then, sooner or later, as you add weight to the barbell, you'll need a squat rack so that you can get the heavy barbell on and off your shoulders without injuring your back (otherwise you would have to reach down to the floor and lift the heavy barbell to your back).

The squat rack holds the barbell in the perfect position for you to slide under it and get it on your shoulders, and then to get rid of when you are finished with your set. (See the photo on p. 54.) If you want to put a decent-sized muscle on your front thighs, or to raise and round out your buttocks, you'll eventually have to move on to a barbell with plates and a squat rack.

A station functions the same way as racks. They help you to position yourself so that you won't hurt yourself picking up and returning the weight when you start and finish a set. Bench press stations are attached to benches and are used when heavy chest work is done with barbells and plates. (See p. 53.) In my opinion, if you are a woman, you will never need to go so heavy for the chest as to need a bench press station. Men, who like bigger chests, may opt for them.

You Have a Choice: Dumbbells, Barbells, Stations, Racks, or Machines—How to Do the Same Exercise Four Different Ways

You don't have to use only dumbbells (the most simple and inexpensive method). You can add barbells, stations, racks, and/or machines. I'll make it easy for you. I'll tell you exactly how to do that—first in this chapter, and then at the end of each exercise instruction in "Machines, etc." By way of example, let me show you how to do an exercise for three body parts four different ways.

Look at the photographs of me doing the same biceps exercise four dif-

BICEPS / Simultaneous Curl

| 1. dumbbells, start | dumbbells, finish | 2. barbell, start | barbell, finish |

3. floor pulley, start

floor pulley, finish

4. machine, start

machine, finish

ferent ways. Notice that in each biceps exercise, the simultaneous curl, my arms are making the same curling movement. Whether I'm using the dumbbells, a barbell, a floor pulley, or the machine, my arms are curling up and returning to the arms-fully-extended start position each time. You can see where the saying holds true, "There's more than one way to skin a cat."

Whether you make the movement with dumbbells, a barbell, a floor pulley, or a machine, if you make that curling motion with weights, the muscle is challenged—and responds to the weight and becomes stronger, harder, and more defined—and eventually becomes more solid (firm) and strong. The fine points as to which device is superior to which have been discussed above.

Now look at the flat press. Notice that whether I'm using the dumbbells, a barbell, a barbell with plates at the bench press station, or a machine, my movements are basically the same. I am pressing (pushing) the weight away

CHEST / Flat Press

1. dumbbells, start

dumbbells, finish

2. barbell, start

barbell, finish

3. bench press station (with barbell and plates), start

bench press station (with barbell and plates), finish

4. machine, start

machine, finish

from my body and allowing it to descend back to my body each time. Again, no matter which method I use, eventually my chest muscles will respond to the demand of the weight as I press it up and let it return to start position. In time, my pectorals (chest muscles) will become stronger, more shapely, and more defined.

Ah ha! But notice the machine bench press has me in a sitting position. No matter. I'm still doing the pressing movement. Is the bench press more effective lying down? In my opinion, yes, because lying down you can rest on your back. You free up more energy for the press. But you can still get a lot out of it in the sitting position.

Next, look at the squat. Whether I'm using dumbbells, a barbell, a barbell and plates at a squat rack, or a machine, each time I am squatting down and allowing the force of weights to work on my front thigh muscles. I am then returning to the start, or standing position, where I can flex my thigh muscles for a full benefit of the exercise. No matter which of the four choices I have used, if I continue to make this up and down movement with

THIGHS / Squat

1. dumbbells, start

dumbbells, finish

2. barbell, start

barbell, finish

3. squat rack (with barbell and plates), start

squat rack (with barbell and plates), finish

4. machine, start   machine, finish

weights, eventually my thigh muscles will respond to the demand of the weights and become tighter, firmer, shapelier, and more defined.

What is the point of showing you the same exercise done four different ways, other than to confuse you? I want you to get the hang of it, so that whenever you see a familiar movement that you already know (and you will know many from this workout—using dumbbells) you will be able to translate in your mind and say, "Oh, that's similar to the _____ I do with dumbbells." And you will feel free to be adventurous and do the exercise with a barbell, a floor pulley, or a machine.

For example, you may notice someone using a shoulder press machine—where he or she is pressing a weight handle up, returning to start, and then pressing the other weight handle up and returning to start. Immediately you'll say to yourself, "Ah ha. That reminds me of the alternate shoulder press that I do with dumbbells" (see p. 97), and you will be right. This knowledge gives you many other choices to increase the variety of exercises available to you.

Using the same example, you may see someone lifting and lowering a barbell either to the front of their upper chest, or to the back of their neck. You will say to yourself, "Ah ha. This too reminds me of the alternate shoulder press, only the person is doing both shoulders at one time." And you will feel free to substitute a barbell for the dumbbells for your shoulder exercise. And so on. My goal for you is to be able to see any exercise done on any piece of equipment, and to figure out how it fits into what you are doing with the dumbbells. But as mentioned above, if this intimidates you, erase it from your mind. Even if you work out with only dumbbells till the day you die, you will get amazing results!

Other Valuable Machines, Some Totally Frivolous Machines—and Everything in Between

Now let's talk about machines not discussed above—machines that do not fall into the five-most-important category. Which are useful, and are okay for a change, and which machines are frivolous, and why. We'll go in the order that you will be exercising your body: chest, shoulders, biceps, triceps, back, thighs, hips/buttocks, abdominals, and calves.

CHEST MACHINES

In my opinion, if you have dumbbells and/or a barbell and plates and a bench press station, unless you have a shoulder injury (the shoulders are very much involved in chest exercises and the machine helps to balance the weight for you, taking some pressure off the shoulder) there is no reason, except for diversity, why you would ever need a bench press machine.

There is a chest machine that is quite valuable, and that is the pec-deck machine. It simulates the flye movement found in your chest routine. You can't get as much muscle development from the pec-deck machine, but you can get some added definition in the chest area. If a pec-deck machine is available, and you want a change of pace, use it from time to time.

There is one more chest device that is worthy of attention: the cable crossover. It is a way of doing the flye with cables that helps you to develop the center of your chest muscle (adds the look of cleavage). If you go to a fitness center that has a cable crossover machine (actually two pulleys spaced apart), it's a good idea to take advantage of it once in a while. Note: See the "Machines, etc." section of the exercise instructions for reminders as to when you can substitute for these devices.

SHOULDER MACHINES

If you have dumbbells and a barbell and plates, unless you have an injury, and need the machine to hold the weights for you, there's no reason, except for variety, that you would ever need a shoulder machine. It is true that champion bodybuilders sometimes take advantage of one shoulder machine, the shoulder press. But they use it because it enables them to allow the weight to come down lower than with a barbell and get more development in their front shoulder muscles. The kind of development we're talking about here is "contest" development, you know, the Arnold kind.

But what about all the shoulder machines you see in fitness centers? If free weights are not available, or if you feel like doing something different, use them. But as a general rule, you can't get away from the fact that dumbbells (and a barbell and plates if you have them) are superior to shoulder machines.

Pulleys, long metal ropes attached to a wheel-like device that pull weights—sometimes called "cables"—are good to use for a change of pace. You can do your side lateral raises one arm at a time with a single floor pulley device, and you can do your bent laterals on any double floor pulley device. These exercises allow for a little more resistance throughout the movement.

BICEPS MACHINES

For your purposes, biceps machine exercises are completely frivolous, and should only be used if there are no dumbbells or barbells available, or if you are bored and want to do something different. (Note: a biceps machine exercise is demonstrated on p. 45.) Champion bodybuilders use pulleys once in a while, and usually use biceps curl machines only occasionally, when they want to do a special exercise called "forced negatives," with heavy weights, where a weight-training partner will press down the machine weight while the weight-training person tries to lower the weight.

Pulley biceps exercises are good to do for the sake of diversity. As mentioned above, the most valuable biceps pulley exercise is the biceps pulldown (demonstrated on p. 45). It hits the biceps from a different angle than with any other exercise. If you have access to a pulley device, you either add this to your routine or, as stated in the exercise instructions, substitute it for the alternate hammer curl. Doing the alternate or simultaneous biceps curl with a floor pulley device is also good for a change, because it will help to add height to your biceps muscle.

TRICEPS MACHINES

Triceps machines are completely frivolous for anybody's purposes. Barbells, dumbbells, and/or pulley devices are always better. However, you may use a triceps machine if that's the only device available, or for a welcome change in your routine if you are bored with the usual fare.

Pulley devices are another matter entirely. As mentioned above, one of the most valuable triceps exercises is the triceps pushdown. It is performed on a high pulley device that is used by the lat-pulldown machine. (See p. 45 for a demonstration of this exercise.) It is usually done with a curved bar, but can also be performed by using a short, straight bar, or the middle part of the lat-pulldown bar. You may either add this to your triceps routine if you have the available pulley, or substitute it for the triceps kickback (as stated in the exercise instructions).

Another valuable triceps pulley exercise is the overhead triceps extension. It can be done using a high pulley (you can use the same pulley as is used in the lat pulldown—see p. 45 for a demonstration of this exercise). This exercise develops and shapes the entire triceps muscle. You can substitute this exercise for the cross-face triceps extension, as mentioned in the exercise instructions.

BACK MACHINES

There are some very useful back machines. As mentioned above, the lat-pulldown machine is the most valuable of all—and superior to dumbbells or barbells for developing the latissimus dorsi (lat) muscles—those muscles that create the V shape of the back and give the waistline a smaller appearance. If you have access to the lat-pulldown machine you can add it to your back routine, or substitute it for the one-arm dumbbell row and the reverse row, doing lat pulldowns to the front and the rear.

There are other worthwhile back machines. The seated pulley-rowing machine allows you to zone in on your lower lat muscles. For more versatile back development, you can use it from time to time, in place of any of the back exercises. The T-bar rowing machine allows you to develop your outer back muscles. For multifaceted back development, you can occasionally substitute this exercise for the seated back lateral, as mentioned in the exercise instructions.

Finally, there is a back machine called the "pullover," which is used by champion bodybuilders in order to work against circular resistance and hit the back muscles from a different range of motion. If you see this machine, and are in the mood for adventure, you may substitute it for any of your back exercises.

Pulleys are used for the back for one-arm cable rows. This exercise helps to develop the lower lats, and can be done on any floor pulley device. For a change of pace, you may substitute it for any of your back exercises.

THIGH MACHINES

The most valuable leg machines, as described above, are the leg extension and leg curl machines. If you have access to a leg extension machine, you should add it to your routine. If you don't want to do an extra exercise, you may substitute it for the squat or the lunge. For reasons stated above, if you have a leg curl machine, you should definitely use it in place of the dumbbell leg curl. (Note: The leg curl machines come in lying and standing versions. They are equally effective. Also, some machines allow you the choice of working one or both legs at a time. See which is more comfortable for you.)

There is another type of machine that you see in fitness centers—you know the ones I'm talking about—where you see people sitting opening their legs in the widest position—the one where women usually wait until no man is watching across the room! These are inner and outer (adductor and abductor) thigh machines. I advise you to go very light if you use them because they can build a muscle in your inner thigh (that will look like a piece of fat) and a muscle on your outer thigh—which is really your hips (that will look like a saddlebag).

What about squat machines? If you have dumbbells and a barbell and plates, as well as a squat station (see p. 54 for a demonstration of a squat done at a station), unless you have knee or back problems or, unless you want to go extra heavy, there is no reason to ever use the squat machine. (If you do have such problems, the machine helps take pressure off the knees and back—and may allow you to perform squats when otherwise it would be impossible. See p. 55 for a demonstration of the squat done on the squat machine.)

However, there is another squat-type machine called the "hack squat" machine that is quite valuable. You'll be able to recognize it right away because it has a large standing platform that is angled up from the ground. This machine allows you to develop your lower thigh area.

A very valuable leg machine is the leg press. (See p. 48 for a demonstration of this exercise.) It allows you to build muscle on your thighs without putting pressure on your back, and is in fact the only way people with back problems can achieve shape and definition in the thigh area. You can use this machine in addition to, or in place of, the squat and/or lunge.

HIPS/BUTTOCKS MACHINES

Hips/buttocks machines are a welcome change from the exercises performed in the hips/buttocks workout found in this book. If you have access to hips/buttocks machines, take advantage of them by substituting four different machines for each of the four hips/buttocks exercise presented here. If there are only one or two hips/buttocks machines available, then substitute only one or two of the exercises found in this workout. You may choose any one or two you wish.

ABDOMINAL MACHINES

Abdominal machines in general are completely frivolous. You can do a much better crunch without a machine than you can do with a machine. However, if you were looking to put thick muscles on your upper abdominal area, a crunch machine could be helpful, because it allows you to use heavy weights. (The heaviest weight you would be able to hold while doing a crunch would be about twenty-five pounds. The crunch machine lets you set the weight as high as 150 pounds—sometimes higher.)

Ironically, champion bodybuilders rarely—if ever—use abdominal machines. Instead, they hold a twenty-five-pound plate over their abdominal area while doing crunches or sit-ups, or a ten-pound dumbbell between their feet when doing knee-ins or leg raises.

But who wants to put thick muscles in the abdominal area anyway? Surely not I—and I daresay, not you. If you do want to put petite muscles and sculpt fine definition in that area, the routine described in this workout (or for extra work in *Gut Busters* or any of my other workout books) is quite sufficient without weights, or with a three- or five-pound dumbbell.

But what about all of those abdominal machines you see advertised on TV? I hate to say this, but I know a few of the gorgeous men who advertise them—and they are champion bodybuilders who I have personally seen doing all kinds of stomach exercises in the gym that have nothing to do with the machine they advertise. At most, those machines can be an addition to your stomach workout, but in my opinion can never, without additional work aside from the machine, give you the "ripped" stomach that you see on the models advertising them. They are, however, a godsend for those who have problem backs or necks, because they lend support and are sometimes the only way that certain people can work the stomach. The bottom line is, if you already have such a machine, fine, work it into your routine as one of the stomach exercises you do. For example, you can do three sets of 15–25 reps on the machine in place of one of the abdominal exercises in this book. If you have a problem back, then do your entire stomach workout on such a machine—using the variations provided with the machine manual (you will do 12 sets in all, four variations).

CALVES MACHINES

As mentioned above, calf machines are superior to dumbbells when it comes to working calves, because it is only with a machine that you can lift enough weight to significantly develop your calves.

Fortunately, for most women, calf machines are not absolutely necessary, because they wear (or have worn) high heels—and their calves are well developed. Other people, men and women alike, don't have to worry about developing their calves because they run, and runners usually have well-developed calves.

But what about the rest of you—those people who may have underdeveloped calves and want to build them up a little. Your best bet is to either buy a seated calf machine, or go to a fitness center where you can take advantage of the seated and standing calf machines (see p. 48 for an exercise done on the seated calf machine).

Time of Day to Work Out: Make a Plan

You can work out anytime—morning, noon, or night. Whenever it is convenient for you. If it's easier for you to get it out of the way in the morning, plan to get up thirty minutes earlier each day. Set your clock and just do it! I like to work out first thing in the morning because later I get busy or worse, lazy, and I find myself rationalizing as to why it's okay to skip a workout "just for today."

If lunchtime is your best time, write it into your calendar and follow through. If immediately after work is your only realistic time, then program yourself to go through the door and straight to your weights—after a quick drink of water.

Prepare for the unexpected. Make an alternate plan. For example, if you usually work out in the morning, scheme out another time during the day that you can work out, say, an hour after dinner. You won't like to work out at this time. You may resent it—but this will help you not to ignore that clock in the morning the next time you are tempted to do so.

But what should you do if you're tempted not to work out at your plan B time? Say to yourself, "All is not lost. Thank God I have an opportunity to make up the workout. If I do it, I'll be back on schedule and in control." And then do it.

You can govern what happens to you by making plans and using your mind to cooperate with those plans. Tell yourself ahead of time that you will not skip a workout. Help yourself with visualization and preconditioning techniques. (See entries for these topics in the A–Z Quick-Start Dictionary.)

The key is to set aside a definite time to work out—and allow yourself to get into a routine. Eventually, that routine will become a habit, and you'll rarely have to fight yourself to do it.

Days of the Week to Work Out—It's a Free Country!

You will work out four to six days a week. Four is the minimum, six is the maximum. Why is four the minimum? Since you are only allowed to exercise one half of your body on each workout day (the reason why will be explained below), and you must exercise your entire body at least twice a week in order to see muscle development, you will have to do a minimum of four sessions or days (two and two make four).

Why are six weight-training sessions per week the maximum? It's a good idea to take at least one day off a week or your body and mind will become fatigued and sooner or later you'll just refuse to do it.

What about five days a week? I tend to work out that amount. Some weeks I work four days, others five, and on ambitious weeks, six. You don't have to be consistent. You can work out four days one week, five the next, six the next, and back to four, or in any order you choose. Of course if you want to speed up your progress, you should work the maximum, six days a week.

You don't have to work out on the same days each week. You can work out Monday, Tuesday, Wednesday, and Thursday one week, and take the rest of the week off; and Monday, Wednesday, Friday, and Sunday the next week; and Tuesday, Thursday, Saturday, and Sunday the following week.

Although the real calendar begins on Sunday, most people think of Monday as the first day of their week, so I'll write the calendars you see below with Monday as the first day of the week. Your four-day workout schedule may look something like this:

MONDAY	TUESDAY	WEDNESDAY	THURSDAY	FRIDAY	SATURDAY	SUNDAY
Upper	Lower		Upper	Lower		

Or, it may look something like this:

MONDAY	TUESDAY	WEDNESDAY	THURSDAY	FRIDAY	SATURDAY	SUNDAY
Upper	Lower	Upper	Lower			

Or, it may look something like this:

MONDAY	TUESDAY	WEDNESDAY	THURSDAY	FRIDAY	SATURDAY	SUNDAY
	Upper		Lower		Upper	Lower

Here's a sample calendar for *five* days a week:

MONDAY	TUESDAY	WEDNESDAY	THURSDAY	FRIDAY	SATURDAY	SUNDAY
Upper	Lower	Upper	Lower		Upper	

Here's a sample calendar for *six* days a week:

MONDAY	TUESDAY	WEDNESDAY	THURSDAY	FRIDAY	SATURDAY	SUNDAY
Upper	Lower	Upper	Lower	Upper	Lower	

What You Work: Not a Free Country—Why You Can't Work the Same Body Parts Two Days in a Row

You may use any and every combination. But notice, and this is very key, you never exercise the same half of the body two days in a row. Whenever you get ready to start working out, you have to ask yourself, "What did I work last time?" Then don't work that *this* time.

But why can't you exercise the same body parts two days in a row? Simply put, except for abdominals, the muscles need forty-eight hours to recover from a workout. If you train them sooner, you are in danger of wearing them away rather than developing them. If you want more information or details about this, and the reason you can exercise abdominals nearly every day, look under "split routine" and "forty-eight-hour recovery principle" in the A–Z Quick-Start Dictionary below.

What About Aerobics?

You can choose any aerobic activity (see p. 68 in the Quick-Start Dictionary) and do it any day of the week—three to six days a week. It doesn't matter which body parts (if any) you work on the day you do aerobics. Ideally, do your aerobics before you work out, as a warm-up. But if it comes down to a choice—either aerobics or weight-training—choose the aerobics!

Upper Body and Lower Body: A Closer Look at the Workout

But exactly what will you be exercising on each workout day? Let's take another look at the entire workout. Turn to pp. 81. Notice that the workout is divided into "workout day one," which is the upper body, and "workout day two," which is the lower body. Notice that the upper body includes chest, shoulders, arms (biceps and triceps), and back, and workout day two, which is lower body, includes thighs, hips/buttocks, abdominals, and calves. In combination, the upper and lower body cover nine body parts—your entire body.

On workout day one, you do the upper body. On workout day two, you do the lower body. The next time you work out you do the upper body, and so on. All you have to do is remember what you worked last time, and next time you work out, don't work that half. Work the other half. You will notice that even though abdominals could be exercised six days a week, for the sake of simplicity I'm grouping them with lower body and you will do them every other workout. If you choose to do extra abdominal work, fine. Just add it in to your upper body workout, but don't forget to take one day off a week from abdominal work, or you'll feel burned out.

Write It Down

Sound simple? Well, the mind plays tricks. To make your life simple, I urge you to take the time to scribble on your calendar every time you worked out—the word "upper" or "lower." You may think, "Oh, I'll remember." But trust me, the day will come when for the life of you, you won't be able to remember what you worked the last time, and finally you'll choose upper (I know you will because the upper body is much easier to work than the lower body). But then all through your workout, you'll think you're getting flashbacks that you worked your upper body the last time, and it will drive you crazy.

Would it be the end of the world if you worked the same half of the body two days in a row? Of course not. But it's much better to alternate body parts, not only because muscles need forty-eight hours to recover from a workout, but it's the only way to ensure that your body gets a balanced look. (Abdominals—the stomach—always need extra work, so don't worry that you'll be out of balance if you choose to do that extra work for your stomach.)

Making Up a Workout—Can You Exercise Your Entire Body in One Day?

You can do it, but it's not a great idea with this workout because you may become fatigued and even discouraged. The more strenuous the workout, the more likely you are to become tired and not give your last few body parts the attention they deserve. (I do have a special workout designed to allow you to work your entire body on one day. It is found in *Definition: Shape Without Bulk in 15 Minutes a Day.*)

If you miss a workout and do decide to work your entire body in one day, remember that you will have to take the next day off. As mentioned above, you are not allowed to exercise your muscles (except for abdominals) two days in a row!

So unless you already know that you can't work out the next day (or don't want to) it's silly to work your entire body in one day to make up a workout. Just do the half of the body that is next, and the following day, do the other half—and you'll be back on schedule.

The Names of the Exercises—Why Do You Sometimes See the Same Exercises Elsewhere with Different Names?

For goodness' sake. One wonders why they don't create a central office for naming exercises! Why is it that sometimes you'll see "flat press," "bench press," "flat bench press," "flat dumbbell bench press," all naming *the same exercise?*

Here's the deal. It depends upon what part of the exercise the writer wants to emphasize and how complete the writer wants to be. The more complete, the longer the exercise name, and in my view, the more intimidating the exercise seems. My new trick is to keep the names of the exercises as short as possible. To do this, I only include the bare necessities of the name. For example, you will notice that the first exercise of your workout is for the chest, and it is entitled "flat press." Why didn't I call it "flat bench press"? Why should I? Who needs the word "bench" in there? Anyway, who knows, you may be doing it on a step. But why didn't I say "flat dumbbell press"? I've said it in other books after all. Well, I now see that the word "dumbbell" is not necessary. You know that you are working out with dumbbells. You can clearly see it in the photograph and throughout the instructions! And anyway, you do have the option of using a machine or a barbell to do the same exercise (as discussed on pp. 42–60 and the "Machines, etc." section of each exercise.

So getting back to that "flat press" title, what do we really need in the title? We do need "flat" (to distinguish it from "incline"—which you'll notice comes up next for another exercise). Why do we need the word "press"? It is the core of the description. You are "pressing" the weights up and down. Notice that the third exercise is "incline flye." Here you are "flying" the weights outward like a bird.

One more thing. The naming of exercises also depends upon the particular word the writer chooses to use. For example, one writer may like the word "lift" and another "raise" for a leg exercise. That's why you may see the same exact exercise entitled "side leg lift" in one book, and "side leg raise" in another—sometimes even by the same author!

Writers even rename their own exercises later on—when they discover a more descriptive way to name the exercise. Enough said. From now and forevermore, don't let the difference in exercise names bother you.

What Should You Wear?

Wear anything you want. Your survival instinct will not allow you to wear anything too tight or uncomfortable. Let your mood and circumstances determine what you wear. It is not unusual for a woman to admit to working out at home in her pajamas or underwear. I tend to keep an old T-shirt and shorts around. I think of it as a "uniform." It kind of symbolizes my "macho side." My power.

Set Up a Place

You'll feel much better, and be more likely to want to work out, if you can find a corner of a room where you keep your dumbbells and workout step or bench. Each day you could then approach that area, walking like a woman (or a man) with a mission.

Can This Workout Be Done in a Gym or Fitness Center?

Of course. You can use the dumbbells and a bench in any fitness center to do this workout. If you do go to such a place, you may even feel a wild streak pulling you toward the alternatives found in "Machines, etc.," and you may expand your borders by trying them out too.

Otherwise, you can take the dumbbells off into a corner and do your entire workout, like the hermit that you are. I go to a fitness center every so often just for a change of scene—and to take advantage of the five important machines discussed above. Kathy and Starlene never go to a fitness center, but Cynthia, Wes and Emily, and Louie do. I'd guess that less than one fourth of my readers do. They just don't have the time. It's up to you.

Muscle Soreness

Okay. Don't think it's a free ride. You're not going to work out and the next day feel as if nothing happened—even if you follow the "break-in gently" system. If your body is not used to the specific exercise given in this book, the day after you work out you should feel some soreness. How much? It depends upon how out of shape your muscles are when you start, and how hard you work the first time you work out. For example, some women ignore the break-in gently system and the next day they can hardly walk. But they love it, and tell me they are glad to see that their muscles are being awakened from the dead.

It's true. Muscle soreness can actually serve as a map indicating where you will see the most changes in your body. In fact, if you take a Magic Marker and circle every sore muscle, you will have a diagram of which muscles in your body are going to be the most tightened, toned, reshaped, and defined after a few months of working out. So instead of being upset when you experience muscle soreness, rejoice.

But what should you do the next day—when it comes time to work out—if you feel so sore that it's an effort to even move, much less think of working out? Work out anyway. Believe it or not, after about seven minutes, your muscles will feel a lot better—less stiff, almost as if they've been massaged. In fact, in a way, your muscles *will* have been massaged. You see, when you gently exercise a sore muscle, you cause the blood to circulate through that muscle, and as you move the muscle up and down, doing the exercise, the muscle is soothed and feels better.

The worst thing you could possibly do is to wait until the soreness goes away to start working out again. If you do this, every time you start working out again (say a week later) you'll experience the same soreness again, and you'll wait another week. In essence, you'll be taking one step forward and one step back.

Listen, I don't want to scare you with all this talk about soreness. The fact is, if you follow the break-in gently plans presented in each of the four workouts, your soreness will be quite bearable. And if you're really out of shape, and you've never worked with weights in your life, I suggest that you absolutely start at workout level 1. Otherwise you may get disgusted and be so sore that you won't care what I say about maps and massages— and curse me in your mind, and quit.

Before we leave the subject of muscle soreness, let's get a little scientific. Muscle soreness is the result of microscopic tears in the fibers of the ligaments and tendons connecting the muscles, and the slight internal swelling that accompanies these tears. The tears usually occur when you are doing the "elongating," or stretching part of the exercise, when the muscle fibers are lengthening, yet at the same time trying to contract in order to deal with the work being required of them.

These tears are normal and necessary in working out—and the soreness that comes from them is, as mentioned above, a good sign.

Injury

There's a world of difference between muscle soreness and an injury. An injury causes immediate pain—often sharp pain that sometimes makes it impossible to continue your workout. The most common injuries are tears to the covering of the muscle (fascia), stretching and tearing ligaments, and painful inflammation of a tendon (tendinitis). If you follow the break-in gently system, and if you follow the exercise photographs, keeping alert to the tips, you will avoid injury.

If you are at all suspicious that you have been injured, see your doctor immediately.

Getting Psyched for the Workout

Before you start the workout, make some mental preparations. Stand in front of the mirror and *visualize* your body evolving into the shape and form of your dreams. Tell your body to get to that form. Then set a *target date* and circle it on your calendar. Use your *unconscious mind* to help you achieve that goal. Your conscious mind tells your unconscious mind what to do—and like a well-programmed computer, it does it. (For more details, look up the italicized words in the A–Z Quick-Start Dictionary.)

In addition, take an *anatomy photograph*—front and rear view—and label that photograph the same way you see the photographs labeled on p. 38. Then six months to a year later, take another front- and rear-view photograph in the same poses, and again, label those photographs. You will see your wonderful progress.

Prepare for *sticking points*—times when there will seem to be no visible progress. Psych yourself ahead of time to not let that discourage you. Realize that growth and progress are not always immediately visible to the human eye. We can't see when children grow and we don't know the exact moment a seed is going to pop through the ground. Realize that sticking points are not really sticking points at all, but invisible growth and progress periods.

Finally, be patient with yourself. Realize that it took time to get fat and/or out of shape. For example, you probably didn't gain 104 pounds in a year—which would be only two pounds a week! Yet you want to lose five pounds a week, don't you? It's ridiculous. The human body doesn't work that way. It's a survival system. It works at its own pace. Cooperate with it. Be gentle and loving. Go with the flow. Easy does it.

And don't watch the scale anyway! Fat is light and feathery and takes up a lot of space—but muscle is dense and heavier—and takes up little space. Your clothing size may go down a lot faster than the scale weight—but who cares. It's what you see in the mirror that counts. Forget the scale if you dare. Just look in the mirror. That's the real measuring device, isn't it? What you see is what you get!

Now to the quick-start dictionary, and then to the workouts.

A–Z Quick-Start Dictionary
Terms and Expressions that Will Come Up as You Work Out

I'm going to ask you to do something strange here. I want you to read the dictionary! Yes. The following paragraphs, though, are a lot more than just a dictionary. Later they will serve as a reference dictionary, but for now they will give you an overview of what you need to know to work out. By reading, and for a moment thinking about what you read, and by doing this for the entire dictionary before you start your workout, you will put into your unconscious mind the vital information that will later help you achieve the body of your dreams. In addition, when you come across one of the terms later, you'll remember having read about it here—and when you look it up again for a refresher, this time it will really stay in your mind. It's one of the best ways to learn and retain information: preview, encounter, and review.

Aerobic: A physical fitness activity that involves the movement of the large muscles of your body, that is sustained by the body's continual supply of oxygen, and that causes your pulse to reach 60 to 80 percent of its capacity and to stay there for twenty minutes or longer. Aerobic activities are: running, walking very fast, riding a regular or exercise bike, using skiing, stair-stepping, rowing, and other machines. In addition, using weights in a certain way can be aerobic—for example, *circuit training* is an aerobic activity.

The two workouts in this book that come close to being aerobic are levels 3 and 4, because you take only occasional, brief rests, or no rests at all. I say "almost aerobic," because technically speaking, as mentioned above, to be aerobic you are not supposed to rest at all.

Anaerobic: A physical fitness activity that is too strenuous to be supported by the body's natural flow of oxygen, so that you have to take frequent rest periods to catch your breath. Heavy weight training is considered to be anaerobic. The workouts in this book are more aerobic than anaerobic.

Anatomy Photographs: Photographs (found in Chapter 2) of the front and back view of the body that are labeled so you can identify the nine body parts you will be exercising, locate those muscles on your own body, and then focus on each specific muscle as you exercise. You should take your own anatomy photographs before you start working out—label them, and then take another set in six months to a year and again label them and compare them to see your progress.

Barbell: A metal bar that is held in both hands and that holds various weights on each end. Barbells come in weights from twenty to forty pounds. You will only need a barbell if you choose to do the optional exercise variations found in "Machines, etc." in each exercise instruction.

Before-and-After Photos: Photographs of yourself now—both front and rear view—and photographs of yourself in six months to a year, front and rear view. These photographs can also double for *anatomy photographs*. As mentioned above, you should label them as you see the anatomy photographs labeled in Chapter 2.

Bench, Flat: A structure built specifically for the purpose of weight-training exercise. It is long, narrow, and padded, and parallel to the floor.

Bench, Incline: The same as a flat bench, only it can be raised at various degrees to a 45 degree angle, in order to do incline exercises, such as the incline flye found in the chest workout. You can purchase a flat bench that can be raised to an incline, or, you can put a stable block of eight to ten inches under the head of the bench to create an incline. (Two big telephone books taped together can also work.)

Bench Press Station: A device that is attached to an exercise bench consisting of bars that can hold a barbell. You will use a bench press station only if you choose to do the optional alternative barbell exercises listed under "Machines, etc.," in each exercise instruction and only if you intend to use a heavy barbell and plates.

Breathing Naturally: To inhale and exhale unconsciously—in an instinctive, as opposed to self-conscious, manner. You will notice that from time to time in the exercise instructions I remind you to not hold your breath and ask you to breathe naturally.

Some experts believe that you should breathe out (exhale) on the flex part of the exercise, and breathe in (inhale) on the stretch part of the exercise. This would be necessary if you were a power lifter and needed every bit of strength for the big thrust. For your purposes, though, it's much better not to think about your breathing at all. You have enough to worry about learning the movements and keeping up the pace of your workout.

Bounceback Action: The automatic impulse to come back and start punching. For example, if you get off track and stop working out and/or dieting, bounceback action forces you to start again. You program yourself to be just like those plastic blow-up toys with sand in the bottom that you punch and they get up. I used to have one as a child. It was called a "Joe Palooka Doll," a two-foot plastic blow-up of a boxer. When you punched hard, it toppled over, but two seconds later, it popped right up again, ready for the action.

Cellulite: Bumpy, craterlike fat that looks like an orange peel or multiple dimples. It is formed by enlarged fat cells joined together that attach themselves to connecting fibrous tissue just beneath the surface of the skin.

Cellulite appears on the thighs, stomach, and hips/buttocks area (also arms and other body parts) on women and some men.

Although some people are more inclined to develop cellulite due to genetic coding, everyone can get rid of it by low-fat eating *and* working out with weights. As you perform the specific muscle-shaping exercises in this book, and at the same time follow the low-fat eating plan, muscles develop in the formerly cellulite-ridden areas, and at the same time the fat in these areas burns up and disappears.

You can't get rid of cellulite by dieting or aerobic exercises alone. Diet and aerobics help to burn overall body fat. But in order to smooth out the formerly cellulite-ridden body part, you must place a firm, shapely muscle under the skin.

Circuit Training: (sometimes called "Nautilus," because the gym equipment Nautilus was the first to introduce circuit training): A method of exercising the entire body in one weight-training session. The exerciser performs one or two sets of an exercise for each body part by advancing from one weight-training machine (called "station") to the next, until the circuit is completed, at which time the person may opt to repeat the circuit. A circuit takes about twenty minutes.

It is impossible to reshape the body with circuit training, because in order to reshape the body, one must adhere to the principle of *muscle isolation*. In order to respond to the weights and become reshaped, toned, and defined, a muscle must be asked to do a minimum of nine sets (this workout goes the extra mile and asks you to do twelve sets) per body part before moving to the next body part. Circuit training is good for overall muscle stimulation and fat-burning (it is *aerobic* if you don't take rests), and is better than nothing—however, it is a waste of time if your goal is to reshape your body!

Collar: A device placed on the end of a barbell after heavy plates are added, and used to prevent the plates from slipping off the barbell. Many people who are using light plates learn to balance the barbell so that the plates don't slip off—eliminating the need for collars, and saving valuable workout time.

Concentration: To focus or direct toward a center. In working out, concentration involves mentally focusing on the specific muscle you are exercising by watching, touching, and/or thinking about that muscle as you perform your repetitions, and by picturing that muscle becoming firm, strong, shaped, and defined. Concentration also involves active telling of the muscle to grow and be reshaped. (This helps the *unconscious mind* go into action.)

Continual Pressure: Willfully squeezing (flexing) the muscle as hard as possible on the contraction part of the movement, and continuing to keep pressure on the muscle by willfully using as much dynamic tension on the muscle as possible on the stretch part of the movement. You can use continual pressure in workout level 1 after three weeks, since you will be using only three-pound dumbbells.

Definition: The clearly delineated lines that separate a muscle. Notice the definition in my shoulder muscles.

Density: The firmness or hardness of the muscle as a result of working out with weights. As you go from flab to firm, your muscles are becoming more dense.

Dynamic Tension: The willful force exerted on a muscle as it is being stretched or elongated. In a normal situation, when a muscle elongates, no pressure is exerted on the muscle. However, one can deliberately and consciously exert a pressure on the muscle, even as it elongates.

Let's take the biceps curl as an example. Pretend that your arm is in the curled position, and you are trying to uncurl your arm and bring it straight down. Someone is holding your arm in the curled position, but you, by force, are getting it to go down to the stretched position. You can create this force without anyone actually holding you back by imagining that someone is trying to do that.

You can use dynamic tension to increase the intensity of your level 1 workout since you will only be using three-pound dumbbells, but don't try it until at least three weeks (you've gotten used to the workout). Vacationers who don't want to carry even the three-pound dumbbells can do any of the four workouts found in this book using dynamic tension to replace the weights.

Exercise: A given movement for a specific muscle, designed to strengthen, reshape, and define that muscle. For example, the kickback exercise causes you to move your arm in a manner that will eventually strengthen, reshape, and define your triceps (the flag-waving arm) muscle.

Flex: To willfully contract (squeeze) the muscle, so that the muscle fibers are shortened. For example, if I ask you to "make a muscle" with your biceps, you would raise your arm, bend it at the elbow, and willfully squeeze your biceps muscle so that it bulges. As you read the exercise instructions, you will be asked, time and again, to flex your working muscle. If you have trouble doing this, just imagine that a doctor is coming at that body part with a long needle—ready to stick you. You will naturally flinch or squeeze your muscle, which if extended and held, is a flex.

Forty-eight Hour Recovery Principle: The allowing of forty-eight hours (or a day of rest) before rechallenging a muscle with a weight-training workout in order to allow the muscle optimum growth and to prevent overtraining and muscle attrition (wearing down). The only muscle that is an exception to this rule is the abdominals, which can be exercised consecutively because it is not exercised with weights, and because it consists of extremely small muscles.

Free Weights: Weights that can be carried about as opposed to machines that are nailed to the floor and/or are too heavy to be carried about.

Intensity: The degree of difficulty of the exercise program you are following. Intensity can be increased by raising the number of repetitions, adding to the load weight, flexing harder, using *dynamic tension*, or reducing the rest periods allowed between sets and between exercises.

Interset: A combined set of two exercises of complementary parts, also called a *superset*, between body parts, or a "twin set." For example, in workout level 4, you will be intersetting chest and triceps. Specifically, your first interset for your chest/triceps routine will consist of twelve repetitions of the flat press for the chest, and twelve repetitions of the overhead press for the triceps—without a rest between the two exercises. Intersets are also used in my *Bottoms Up!* book, only in that workout I ask you to interset different muscle groups—such as the chest and shoulders.

Machines: Exercise equipment designed to challenge one or more specific body parts operated by cams, pulleys, air pressure, etc. There are literally thousands of various exercise machines made by a multitude of companies.

Metabolism: The chemical and physical process continually going on in your body and in all living organisms, consisting of the process of changing food into fuel or energy, waste products, and living tissue. When referring to metabolism in this book, what is usually meant is "basal metabolism," which is the minimum quantity of energy used by an individual (or any resting organism) to sustain life.

When you develop muscles on your body, as you will if you follow the workouts in this book, your basal metabolism will rise, and you will use more energy (burn more excess fat, use up more calories) than you used to, doing the same activities. For example, if you used to burn sixty calories an hour sleeping, you will now burn about 20 percent more, say, seventy-two calories per hour. The more muscle you put on your body, the more you raise your basal metabolism, and the more fat you burn twenty-four hours a day. Champion bodybuilders burn at least twice as much or more fat twenty-four hours a day than average people—and in fact must eat twice as much in order to sustain their body. You can see why, if you love to eat, having muscles is a good idea!

Muscle Isolation: The method of exercising a body part completely and independently of other body parts. In order to ensure maximum shaping, defining, and strengthening of a given body part, it's necessary to provide that body part with uninterrupted work. In other words, it is not okay to do one *set* of exercises for the chest, and then skip to the shoulders, and then go to the back, and then to the biceps (as in circuit training for example). You must do a certain number of sets and exercises (usually a minimum of nine sets—three sets of at least three different exercises) in order to challenge the muscle to grow and change.

Muscle Mass: The actual size of a specific muscle.

Muscularity: The quantity of muscle as opposed to fat.

Negative Thinking and Verbalization vs. Positive Thinking and Verbalization: Nonpositive thoughts and expressions of those thoughts that hinder your progress. Learn to catch yourself the moment your mind or your mouth begins to express ideas such as "Nothing else worked, why should this work," or "I'm so fat I'll never get in shape," or "I'm a loser—I'll always be one."

Stop the music. In fact, learn to use those thoughts or verbalizations as signals to reverse the talk. Using the above examples, say "This time it will work. I'm determined. Nothing will stop me," or "I'm fat today, but every day, as I follow the low-fat eating plan and do the workout, the fat will slowly melt away and my muscles will shape and form and be defined. It took time to get fat. It will take time to get in shape. But it will happen. It must happen—it's scientific. Sooner or later my body must get in shape if I continue to do what I'm doing. It's like the law of gravity. It can't fail."

Plateau: The point where the exerciser decides that his or her muscles need no greater challenge in weights, because he or she is happy with the size of his or her muscles. For example, years ago, when I first started out, I used three-, five-, and ten-pound dumbbells. In under a year, I had in stages advanced to ten-, fifteen-, and twenty-pound dumbbells, and although I experimented with higher weights, I eventually returned to ten-, fifteen-, and twenty-pound dumbbells—and that's what I use to this day. I decided that I am satisfied with my muscles at this size and density.

Plates: Disc-shaped weights with a hole in the center that can be placed on the ends of a barbell, and ranging in weight from one and a quarter pounds to a hundred pounds.

Precondition: To mentally prepare for a future event so as to control that event. For example, if you want to prevent yourself from breaking your diet, you will use *visualization* to precondition yourself. You will picture yourself ahead of time being tempted to eat the wrong food, and then imagine yourself deciding not to put that food in your mouth. If you want to prevent yourself from skipping a workout, you can use visualization to precondition yourself to push aside the temptation and to forge ahead with the workout.

Progression: Occasional adding of weight to the specific exercises when the weight being used for those exercises is no longer enough of a challenge. In this book, the only workout that will not ask you to use progression (add weights to your exercises when they become too easy) is workout level 1—the most elementary workout level.

All other workout levels ask you to use the progression system—so that your muscles can continue to grow, be reshaped, and become tight and toned to your satisfaction. It is up to you to be honest with yourself and to admit when the weights you are using are too easy to lift. You'll know this when you find yourself being tempted to swing the dumbbells. If this happens, you must raise your weights or you won't continue to make progress (progression).

Pulley: A small, fixed wheel with a grooved rim in which a steel rope runs—so as to raise a weight attached at one end by pulling the other end. In this book pulleys are grouped in the machine category but they are found attached to walls—independent of an actual machine. Pulleys are also found in the mechanisms of many machines. You will note in the exercise instructions that certain exercises can be done on wall pulleys, or pulleys attached to certain machines used for multiple purposes.

Pumped: The state of a muscle when it is temporarily enlarged for about two hours after working out, due to the increased flow of blood caused by the stimulation of the exercise.

Pyramid System: (Actually, the modified pyramid system, but exercisers have come to just call it the pyramid system.) The adding of weight to each set with a simultaneous reduction of repetitions until a peak is achieved. You will be using this system in all workouts in this book except level 1. Here is a sample of how it looks:

Set 1: 12 repetitions, 3-pound dumbbells
Set 2: 10 repetitions, 5-pound dumbbells
Set 3: 8 repetitions, 10-pound dumbbells

(If it were a true pyramid, it would ask you to then go "down the pyramid" and perform two additional sets, a set 4 with ten repetitions, and a set 5 with twelve repetitions. This system is used in my book *Definition*. Forget about it for now.)

The pyramid system is reviewed in the workout chapters where it is used.

Repetition: Usually called a "rep." One complete movement of an exercise, from start, to midpoint, to finish (finish is actually back to start position). For example, one rep of the squat involves squatting down from the standing start position (now you are at midpoint) and raising yourself back up to standing position (back to start point). See p. 127 for photographs illustrating this exercise.

Rest: A pause between sets or exercises. The purpose of a rest is to allow the working muscle enough time to recover from the work it has just done, and efficiently perform the work of the next set. The rest time allowed in each of the four workout levels presented in this book varies according to the demand of that particular workout. See individual exercise instructions for length of rest.

Ripped: A muscle is said to be ripped when it has extreme definition—deeply marked, clearly delineated lines separating the muscle. Champion bodybuilders display ripped muscles.

Routine: The specific combination of exercises prescribed for a given body part. For example, your chest routine consists of the flat press, the incline press, the incline flye, and the cross-bench pullover.

Set: A specified number of repetitions (complete movements) of a particular exercise that are performed without a rest. In workout level 1, you will do ten repetitions for each set of exercises. The other workout levels will utilize the pyramid system and have descending repetitions for each set as the weights are increased.

Split Routine: The exercising of a given number of body parts on workout day one, and a given number of other body parts on workout day two, and so on. In all four workouts found in this book, the split routine consists of the upper body on workout day one and the lower body on workout day two.

The purpose and the necessity of the split routine is to allow the exercised muscle the required forty-eight hours recovery time before it is challenged again. Athletic experts agree that all muscles (except abdominals) need this amount of time to recuperate from a workout. If not allowed this amount of rest time, a muscle may become exhausted from overtraining, and development will be slowed down or even reversed.

The beauty of the split routine is you can work out with weights six days in a row if you choose to do so because you never work the same body parts on two consecutive days.

The reason you can exercise abdominals on consecutive days is due to the fact that abdominal muscles are very small in size, and are not in danger of being worn down by overtraining. In addition, little or no weight is used when exercising abdominal muscles. When little or no weight is used, overtraining is not as likely.

Starvation Dieting: The wrong way to lose weight. The body is a survival system. When you cut your calories below 1,000 a day, or go on a liquid diet, depriving your body of solid foods, or go on any fad diet that deprives your body of balanced eating (all pineapples, all eggs, or some such foolish thing), your body will lie in wait for the day when you are off guard and sabotage you—forcing you to eat until you have gained back every ounce of fat you lost—plus a hefty reserve for the threat of future famines! It's tempting to starvation-diet when you feel fat and want immediate results. But don't do it.

Step: A raised platform usually used for step aerobics, but that can be used in place of a bench, and is raised at least eight inches off the floor. Most steps come with removable parts, so that the step can be made higher or lower. If you are using your step as a bench, when you want to make the step go to an incline, remove only one end of the plastic and you will have an incline. (For a complete demonstration of how to use a step in place of a bench, see my book *Definition*.)

Sticking Point: A period of time when, although you are working out regularly, you seem to be making no visible progress. At such times, progress is being made under the surface. Think of it as a seed in the ground. You don't know that anything is happening until the green shoot pops through the earth. But in the meantime, a lot was happening under the surface—when you couldn't see a thing.

The body grows and changes in spurts. You can see this in children. No one ever sees a child grow. Yet from one year to the next, if the child is measured, there is progress. Your body will grow and change at its own pace. You may see something right away and then nothing for a month or two, then a great change, then nothing for four months. It is completely up to your body. But one thing is for sure. If you follow a combination of the workouts in this book (see p. 82 for your plan), in a year you will see amazing changes in your body.

Stretch: To lengthen the muscle fibers. Stretching is the opposite of flexing. Throughout the exercise instructions, I say "feel the stretch in your _____ muscle." I mean willfully stretch your muscle as it goes into the non-flexed position. Feel the muscle fibers elongate. Get into it!

Sublimation of Energy: Frustration and anger are really energy. When you were frustrated or angry, how many times have you kicked a door and maybe stubbed your toe—or even threw something across the room and broke something? Instead of using anger or frustration in a potentially destructive way, we can use it to benefit ourselves.

The next time you are angry or frustrated, channel that energy into the workout (sublimate your energy). Not only will you find yourself putting more into the workout, but in about ten minutes you'll feel calm and encouraged—and as a bonus, instead of having done damage to yourself or others, you will have done good!

Superset: The performance of two exercises without taking a rest. You can superset within body parts, as in workout level 2, where you do your first two and then your second two exercises for each body part without taking a rest, or you can superset between body parts, as in workout level 4, where you do one exercise for one body part, chest for example, and one exercise for another body part, triceps for example, before you take a rest.

To avoid confusion (or perhaps to add to it) I have given supersetting between different body parts a new name. I call it *intersetting*. (See also explanation in workout level 4.)

Symmetry: The aesthetic balance and proportion of muscles in relationship to other muscles on the body. The goal of the workouts in this book is to help you achieve your most perfect symmetry.

Target Date: The date you set for your visualized body to arrive. The date must be realistic. Give yourself plenty of time (look at the before and after photos on pp. 30–36 for a guideline). Set your target date, then mark the date on the calendar, and using your *unconscious mind*, tell your body to arrive at the condition you have visualized by that date.

Twin Set: This is another word for "interset." (See p. 72.)

Unconscious Mind: The subconscious. The part of your mind that goes on automatic, to deliver the goods when you tell (your conscious mind tells your unconscious mind) yourself to do a certain thing. For example, if you stand in the mirror and tell your body to become reshaped by a certain reasonable date, and you picture your body evolving into that shape, your unconscious mind will begin to cooperate and alert you when you are going off track, and remind you to do what is necessary to achieve that goal. The unconscious mind has been compared to a homing torpedo or a Scud missile that zigzags its way toward its target once you program it to do so.

Visualization: Picturing in your mind what you want to have happen. You will use visualization in three ways: 1) Stand in the mirror in the nude or in your underwear, and picture your body evolving into the shape and form you have in mind. Do this at least once a week. 2) As you are working out, see the body part you are working being reshaped into the form you have in mind. 3) Think ahead. You know when you will be tempted to miss a workout or eat the wrong foods. Imagine yourself in the situation, and then imagine yourself refusing to fall into the trap.

For example, ahead of time imagine yourself waking up in the morning and being tempted to push the snooze button instead of getting up thirty minutes earlier to work out. Then picture yourself getting angry at that impulse to give in to weakness, and imagine yourself jumping out of bed and going straight to the weights and doing that first step.

Picture yourself getting ready to stand at the refrigerator with a spoon in your hand and eat from your child's ice cream container. Then imagine yourself looking at the ice cream and getting a feeling of nausea, and see yourself closing the ice cream box, and picking some delicious vegetables or fruits from the refrigerator.

Weight: The heaviness or "resistance" of the weight used in a given exercise. For example, in workout level 1, you will be using three-pound weights. In workout level 2 you will be using three-, five-, and ten-pound weights—and later, you will increase those weights. The heavier the weight, the more resistance to your working muscles, the more your muscles grow and become reshaped and redefined.

Workout: All of the exercises performed on a given day. For example, your day one workout consists of all the exercises for your upper body: all chest, shoulder, biceps, triceps, and back exercises. Your day two workout consists of all the exercises for your lower body. All thigh, hips/buttocks, abdominal, and calf exercises.

The term "workout" can also be used to describe the overall exercise program. For example, you could say, "I'm doing the level 1 workout," or "I'm doing the level 2 workout," and it would refer to your entire workout, days one and days two.

And what better way to end this chapter than with the word "workout." In fact, that's just what you are ready to do right now. So go to the next chapter, Chapter 4, for your beginning workout—workout level 1.

4 LEARNING THE MOVES
WORKOUT LEVEL 1

This is the first of four workout combinations presented in this book. It is your most basic. It requires the lightest weights and the least to remember. You will be doing four basic exercises for each of nine body parts. Your entire body will be challenged!

In order to make your life simple—and to encourage you to go even further, the same four exercises will be used in workout levels 2 to 4—only there is a difference. I'll be asking you to perform the exercises *in a different manner* in each workout. This workout will ask you to do the exercise in the most elementary manner of all. You may be able to skip this beginner's stage. (See pp. 166-167.)

The Purpose of This Workout: Learning the Moves

The purpose of this uncomplicated workout is to make you familiar with the fundamental exercises of body shaping, to give you some muscle tone and the beginnings of definition—and to tease you into wanting to do more. It is also for those who never want to go further—who are happy with just stimulating the muscles and shaping them up a bit. It is also for those who are doing one of my other workouts, but are going on vacation and don't have weights or machines available—and don't want to lose their hard-earned muscles. If you are on vacation, and want to work without weights, do this workout with dynamic tension and continual pressure. (See A–Z Quick-Start Dictionary, and read below, "Getting More Out of the Workout by Increasing the Intensity.")

The Advantages of This Workout Over Other Workouts

This workout is easier to do than any other weight-training workout—and you still get results. It also requires less equipment than any other workout in this book. All you need is one set of three-pound dumbbells, and in fact, you can do the workout with no dumbbells at all! Finally, it is the least strenuous. It's the perfect workout to begin with if you're just starting out with weights, and is the ideal workout to return to when you're feeling burned out, but don't want to lose hard-earned muscle tone.

But it can also be your regular workout—forever. If you don't want to invest more time or energy, you can just stick to this workout and you'll get plenty out of it. In fact, I have a whole fan club who follow a workout similar to this (*The 12-Minute Total-Body Workout*) who would rather fight than switch to any other workout. This workout is different from that workout, however. In this workout you only have to work out four days a week, whereas in *The 12-Minute Total Body Workout* you have to work out nearly every day. In addition, the exercises and combinations are different in this workout.

How Much Time Is Involved?

Your time investment is twenty minutes, four to six days a week. Your actual workout time depends upon how fast or slow you move the dumbbells (eventually you will pick up speed). In the beginning stages, when you are learning the workout, it will probably take a little longer—maybe thirty to forty minutes. But don't worry. In about three weeks you'll be doing it in your sleep! (Don't laugh. To my horror, some nights I work out in my dreams. Then when I get up, I'm actually tired.)

The Split Routine

In this workout (and each of the following workouts as well) you will be using what is called "the split routine." Simply put, it is the exercising of a given number of body parts on one day, and a given number on another day. As mentioned in Chapter 3, the split routine used in this book divides the body into two halves, upper and lower. You exercise the upper body on your first workout day, and your lower body on your second workout day. The next time you work out, you go back to your upper body, and so on. In this way you make sure that you develop a balanced body. (We don't want to see you walking around with a flat stomach, sexy thighs, a tight butt, and flabby arms, a drooping chest, and with lumps of fat on your back!)

Why split the workout up in such a manner? The purpose of the split routine is to allow the exercised muscle the required forty-eight-hour recovery time before being challenged again in order to avoid fatigue or muscle attrition (wearing away of the muscle). The split routine is also a guarantee against overtraining. It allows you to work out with weights day after day, if you wish, without taking a day off—and yet you don't wear down the muscle.

The only muscle that is an exception to the split routine, and can be exercised day after day, is the rectus abdominis, or the abdominal muscles. For an explanation as to why, and further information on the split routine, see "split routine" and "forty-eight hour recovery principle" in the A–Z Quick Start Dictionary.

Workout Days and Exercises Used in This Workout

Here is the "division of labor." You will work certain body parts on workout day one, and other body parts on workout day two. As mentioned above, workout day one is the upper body, workout day two is the lower body. Could it be reversed? Yes. But there's no reason to reverse them, and I thought I'd give you the easier workout on day one, so as not to discourage you. (Take a look at what you are exercising on workout day two and you'll understand.)

▶ Workout Day 1	▶ Workout Day 2
UPPER BODY	LOWER BODY
Chest	Thighs
Shoulders	Hips/Buttocks
Biceps	Abdominals
Triceps	Calves
Back	

(At least you have one easy body part to exercise on workout day two—calves, and I put it at the end of the workout—something to look forward to.)

Now here's the breakdown on exactly which exercises you will do, and in what order—on each workout day. Don't worry about memorizing anything. You'll be led along gently, like a prize dog on a leash. Everything will be spelled out and crystal clear. I'm giving you this rundown because I want you to get a preview, a feel of where you'll be going.

DAY 1 WORKOUT

CHEST
- flat press
- incline press
- incline flye
- cross-bench pullover

SHOULDERS
- side lateral raise
- front lateral raise
- alternate shoulder press
- bent lateral raise

BICEPS
- alternate curl
- simultaneous curl
- alternate hammer curl
- concentration curl

TRICEPS
- overhead press
- kickback
- one-arm overhead extension
- cross-face extension

BACK
- upright row
- one-arm dumbbell row
- double-arm reverse row
- seated back lateral

DAY 2 WORKOUT

THIGHS
- squat
- side leg lift
- leg curl
- lunge

HIPS/ BUTTOCKS
- standing butt squeeze
- standing back-leg extension
- straight-leg kick-up
- bent-knee kick-up

ABDOMINALS
- concentrated butt lift
- crunch
- ceiling lift
- knee-raised crunch

CALVES
- seated straight-toe raise
- seated angled-out-toe raise
- standing straight-toe raise
- standing angled-in-toe raise

Equipment Needed

You will need one set of three-pound dumbbells. "What does she mean?" you immediately wonder: "a set of dumbbells weighing one and a half pounds each for a total of three pounds, or dumbbells weighing three pounds each?"

Okay. Let's clear this up now and forever. Whenever you hear "set" it means "each." For example, if I say a set of three-pound dumbbells I mean each dumbbell is three pounds. The fact that the total weight of the dumbbells is six pounds is completely irrelevant, and has, as my father used to say, nothing to do with the price of tea in China. So remember, set of three, set of five, set of ten—whatever—always means EACH DUMBBELL! End of story.

You will also need either a bench, preferably one that can be raised to an incline, or equally good, a step-type device, such as used by people who do step aerobics (one that is at least eight inches off the ground, preferably ten, and that has a removable piece so that you can put the step on an incline). As mentioned before, if you need a demonstration of using a step instead of a bench, glance through my book *Definition* (see Bibliography). But what if you have only a flat bench or step? Well, tape together two big telephone books and place them under the head of the bench or step.

Sets, Repetitions, Weights, and Rests

You will do three sets of ten repetitions for each exercise. It's that simple. As you already know, a repetition is one up and down (or in and out, or over and under, whatever the case may be) with the dumbbell, and a set is a *group* of the same. (See the A–Z Quick-Start Dictionary if you need a review of the definitions.)

> **SET 1:** 10 repetitions, 3-pound dumbbells. Rest 15 seconds.
> **SET 2:** 10 repetitions, 3-pound dumbbells. Rest 15 seconds.
> **SET 3:** 10 repetitions, 3-pound dumbbells. Rest 15 seconds.

You will, as a general rule, rest fifteen seconds after each set—but good news, you don't have to look at a stopwatch. Just try to feel it. You don't have to be very strict. With this workout, you won't lose any progress if you end up resting double the time (you'll just waste time). If you take shorter rests, even three-second rests, that's fine too—you'll save time. But in the beginning, while you're learning the moves, it's a good idea to take the full rest.

Getting More Out of the Workout by Increasing the Intensity

Later, when you really know the workout, and can do it without thinking, if you wish you can add dynamic tension and continual pressure to your regular workout, with the three-pound dumbbells. As mentioned above, you can also use this method without any weights at all—for example, if you're on vacation. The force you create by using dynamic tension and continual pressure make up for the lack of weight. (See the A–Z Quick Start Dictionary for review.) You can also later choose to shorten your rests to only a few seconds.

Changing the Order of the Exercises

The exercises in this workout have been placed in a certain order because, for physical and psychological reasons, they are easiest to do if grouped in this manner—for many people. However, after you have been working out for at least six weeks you may find that you have reason to change things around because your particular psychology and/or body prefers a different order. If so, here's what you can do.

You may change the order of the exercise within the body part. Let me explain, using the chest as an example. There are four exercises for the chest: the flat press, the incline press, the incline flye, and the cross-bench pullover, in that order. Instead of doing the flat press first, you can do the incline press first, or any other one in the group first. In fact, you can completely rearrange the exercises in this group in any manner you wish. But don't start mixing them with other body parts. You can only do that in a very special way—and I do it for you in workout level 4.

What about changing the order of the body parts you exercise in a given day? I'll use workout day one as an example. On that day you exercise chest, shoulders, biceps, triceps, and back, in that order. Suppose you want to exercise biceps first—or triceps first, or back? Suppose you want to scramble the body parts and make up your own order. Fine. You can do it.

What about mixing the body parts and completely rearranging what is done on the workout days—taking some body parts from workout day one and some body parts from workout day two—for example, doing chest, abdominals, biceps, and hips/buttocks on workout day one and the rest on workout day two. No. That's where I draw the line. I have changed the mix for you for very special reasons in workout level 4—and in some of my other books—again for very special reasons. After you have been working out at least a year, you may know enough to make the right kinds of changes in this area. For now, literally, "go by the book."

Stretching

Since you are using only three-pound dumbbells, you can think of the movements themselves as stretches. But if you want to feel as if you've officially stretched, you could do two or three repetitions of the exercises without weights just before you start your first set. Do I do it? Of course not!

Breaking In Gently

This is a very gentle workout to begin with. However, to be on the safe side, I suggest that you follow the break-in gently plan.

WEEK ONE: 1 set of each exercise for the body parts for that day.

WEEK TWO: 2 sets of each exercise for the body parts for that day.

WEEK THREE: 3 sets of each exercise for the body parts for that day. You're on the full program!

Do most people break in gently? From my letters, some do and some don't. Those who don't sometimes complain, "I didn't listen to you, and to my amazement, even though the weights are so light, I was in aches and pains the next day." But they survived and worked through the soreness. (See pp. 66–67. "Muscle Soreness."

Ready, Set, Go

Now you are ready to begin. At first you will want to read the exercise instructions carefully and follow the full-sized photographs. Later you will want to take advantage of the tear-out wall charts on p. 263–287, so you won't have to flip pages. You might also want to photocopy the sets, repetitions, and weights (p. 83) and paste it on the wall, though you probably will remember without having to do that.

Okay, enough talk. Let's begin the workout.

DAY 1

UPPER BODY WORKOUT

CHEST ROUTINE

1 | FLAT PRESS

This exercise develops, shapes, strengthens, and defines the entire chest (pectoral) area.

POSITION
Lie on a flat exercise bench with a dumbbell held in each hand, palms facing upward, and with the outer edge of the dumbbells touching your upper chest area. (Note—you may use a step instead of a bench.)

MOVEMENT
Flexing your chest muscles as you go, extend your arms upward until your elbows are nearly locked. The dumbbells should be in line with your upper chest in this fully extended position. Willfully flex your pectoral muscles and return to start position. Feel the stretch in your pectoral muscles and repeat the movement until you have completed your set.

Rest 15 seconds and perform your second set. Rest another 15 seconds and perform your third set. Rest 15 seconds and move to the next exercise— the incline press.

BEWARE
In order to get a full stretch in your chest, be sure to extend your elbows fully downward on the down movement. Keep your mind focused on your chest muscles throughout the exercise.

MACHINES, ETC.
You may use any bench press machine in place of this exercise. You may do this exercise with a 20-pound barbell. See p. 53.

SETS, REPETITIONS, WEIGHTS
Set 1: 10 repetitions, 3-pound dumbbells. Rest 15 seconds.
Set 2: 10 repetitions, 3-pound dumbbells. Rest 15 seconds.
Set 3: 10 repetitions, 3-pound dumbbells. Rest 15 seconds.

FINISH

2 | INCLINE PRESS

This exercise develops, shapes, strengthens, and defines the entire chest (pectoral) area, especially the upper pectoral area.

POSITION

Lie on an incline exercise bench with a dumbbell held in each hand, palms facing upward, and with the outer edge of the dumbbells touching your upper chest area. (Note—you may use a step positioned on an incline instead of a bench.)

MOVEMENT

Flexing your chest muscles as you go, extend your arms upward until your elbows are nearly locked. The dumbbells should be just over your forehead in this fully extended position. Willfully flex your pectoral muscles and return to start position. Feel the stretch in your pectoral muscles and repeat the movement until you have completed your set.

Rest 15 seconds and perform your second set. Rest another 15 seconds and perform your third set. Rest 15 seconds and move to the next exercise—the incline flye.

BEWARE

In order to get a full stretch in your chest, be sure to extend your elbows fully downward on the down movement. Keep your mind focused on your chest muscles throughout the exercise.

MACHINES, ETC.

You may use any incline bench press machine in place of this exercise. You may do this exercise with a 20-pound barbell.

SETS, REPETITIONS, WEIGHTS

Set 1: 10 repetitions, 3-pound dumbbells. Rest 15 seconds.
Set 2: 10 repetitions, 3-pound dumbbells. Rest 15 seconds.
Set 3: 10 repetitions, 3-pound dumbbells. Rest 15 seconds.

89

INCLINE FLYE

This exercise develops, shapes, strengthens, and defines the entire chest (pectoral) area, especially the upper pectoral area.

POSITION

Lie with your back flat against the bench, holding a dumbbell in each hand, with your palms facing each other. Extend your arms straight up so that the dumbbells are touching in the center of your chest.

MOVEMENT

With your elbows slightly bent, extend your arms outward and downward in a semicircle until you feel a complete stretch in your pectoral muscles. Flexing your pectoral muscles, return to start and repeat the movement until you have completed your set. Do not lock your elbows.

Rest 15 seconds and perform your second set. Rest another 15 seconds and perform your third set. Rest 15 seconds and move to the next exercise—the cross-bench pullover.

BEWARE

Don't hold your breath. Breathe naturally. Don't swing the dumbbells wildly. Maintain control. Keep your elbows slightly bent throughout the movement. Think of your arms as slightly curved steel bars that cannot be bent.

MACHINES, ETC.

You may use a pec-deck machine in place of this exercise. You may use a cable crossover device for this exercise.

SETS, REPETITIONS, WEIGHTS

Set 1: 10 repetitions, 3-pound dumbbells. Rest 15 seconds.
Set 2: 10 repetitions, 3-pound dumbbells. Rest 15 seconds.
Set 3: 10 repetitions, 3-pound dumbbells. Rest 15 seconds.

FINISH

CROSS-BENCH PULLOVER

Develops and shapes the entire chest area. Also helps expand the rib cage and develop the back muscles.

POSITION

Lie at the edge of a flat exercise bench with your head touching the edge of the bench. Hold a dumbbell in your hands, palms upward, between your crossed thumbs. Extend your arms straight up so that the dumbbell is held directly over your eye area.

MOVEMENT

Lower the dumbbell behind your head by lowering your arms and bending your elbows at the same time, until you cannot go any further. Feel a full stretch in your chest muscles. Flex your chest muscles as you return to start position, and give your muscles an extra hard flex as you reach start position. Repeat the movement until you have completed your set.

Rest 15 seconds and perform your second set. Rest another 15 seconds and perform your third set. Rest 15 seconds and move to the next exercise—and body part—the side lateral raise for the shoulders.

BEWARE

Do not let the weight nearly fall to the down position. Maintain control at all times. Try to keep your back flat against the bench as you work. Beware of the tendency to hold your breath. No one is trying to kill you. Open your mouth and breathe whenever you catch yourself holding your breath.

MACHINES, ETC.

You may perform this exercise with your feet on the ground and your shoulders resting at the edge of the bench. See my book *The Fat-Burning Workout* for this method.

SETS, REPETITIONS, WEIGHTS

Set 1: 10 repetitions, 3-pound dumbbells. Rest 15 seconds.
Set 2: 10 repetitions, 3-pound dumbbells. Rest 15 seconds.
Set 3: 10 repetitions, 3-pound dumbbells. Rest 15 seconds.

SIDE LATERAL RAISE

This exercise develops, shapes, strengthens, and defines the entire deltoid muscle, especially the medial area.

POSITION
Stand with your feet together. Hold a dumbbell in each hand with your palms facing each other, and extend your arms downward letting the dumbbells touch at the ends in the center of your body.

MOVEMENT
Flexing your shoulder muscles as you go, extend your arms upward and outward until the dumbbells are slightly higher than shoulder height. Willfully flex your shoulders and return to start position. Feel the stretch in your shoulder muscles and repeat the movement until you have completed your set.

Rest 15 seconds and perform your second set. Rest another 15 seconds and perform your third set. Rest 15 seconds and move to the next exercise—the front lateral raise.

BEWARE
Don't swing the dumbbells out and up. Use controlled movements, but do keep it moving. Don't hold your breath. Breathe naturally.

MACHINES, ETC.
You may perform this exercise on any shoulder side lateral machine, at 10 pounds. You may perform this exercise one arm at a time, on any floor pulley device. Set your weight at 10 pounds.

SETS, REPETITIONS, WEIGHTS
Set 1: 10 repetitions, 3-pound dumbbells. Rest 15 seconds.
Set 2: 10 repetitions, 3-pound dumbbells. Rest 15 seconds.
Set 3: 10 repetitions, 3-pound dumbbells. Rest 15 seconds.

START

FINISH

FRONT LATERAL RAISE

This exercise develops and shapes the front shoulder muscles.

POSITION
Stand with your feet a natural width apart. Hold a dumbbell in each hand, palms facing your body, and extend your arms straight down in front of you so that the dumbbells are in line with approximately the center of each thigh.

MOVEMENT
Flexing your shoulder muscles, nearly lock your elbows and extend one arm upward until it is parallel to the floor. Return to start position and raise the other arm to parallel to the floor position. Return to start and repeat the movement for the other arm. Continue this alternating movement until you have completed your set.

Rest 15 seconds and perform your second set. Rest another 15 seconds and perform your third set. Rest 15 seconds and move to the next exercise—the alternate shoulder press.

BEWARE
When raising the dumbbells, don't go higher than eye level. Don't swing the dumbbells up or nearly let them drop down to start position. Maintain control at all times.

MACHINES, ETC.
You may perform this exercise two arms at a time. You may use a 20-pound barbell instead of dumbbells (two arms at a time of course).

SETS, REPETITIONS, WEIGHTS
Set 1: 10 repetitions, 3-pound dumbbells. Rest 15 seconds.
Set 2: 10 repetitions, 3-pound dumbbells. Rest 15 seconds.
Set 3: 10 repetitions, 3-pound dumbbells. Rest 15 seconds.

START

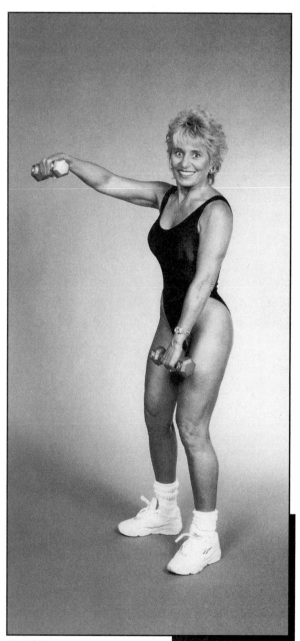

FINISH

3 | ALTERNATE SHOULDER PRESS

This exercise develops, shapes, strengthens, and defines the entire shoulder muscle, especially the front area of this muscle.

POSITION

Stand with your feet in a natural position, holding a dumbbell in each hand at shoulder height, with your palms facing away from your body.

MOVEMENT

Raise your right arm upward until it is fully extended. While returning your right arm to the start position, begin raising your left arm upward until it is fully extended, while at the same time lowering your right arm. Continue this alternate up-and-down movement until you have completed your set.

Rest 15 seconds and perform your second set. Rest another 15 seconds and perform your third set. Rest 15 seconds and move to the next exercise—the bent lateral raise.

BEWARE

Keep your upper body steady as you work. Remember to flex your shoulder muscle on each upward movement, and to feel the stretch on each down position.

MACHINES, ETC.

You may use any shoulder press machine in place of this exercise, one or two arms at a time, depending upon the machine. Set your weight at 10 pounds. You may use a 20-pound barbell for this exercise, placing the barbell on your chest (military press to the front) or placing the barbell on your shoulders (military press to the rear).

SETS, REPETITIONS, WEIGHTS

Set 1: 10 repetitions, 3-pound dumbbells. Rest 15 seconds.
Set 2: 10 repetitions, 3-pound dumbbells. Rest 15 seconds.
Set 3: 10 repetitions, 3-pound dumbbells. Rest 15 seconds.

START

FINISH

BENT LATERAL RAISE

This exercise develops, shapes, strengthens, and defines the rear and side shoulder (deltoid) muscles.

POSITION

Stand with your feet together, or a natural width apart, holding a dumbbell in each hand, with palms facing each other. Bend over until your upper body is parallel to the floor and extend your arms straight down in front of you in the center of your body. Let the ends of the dumbbells touch each other.

MOVEMENT

Keeping your wrists slightly bent, and flexing your side and rear shoulder muscles as you go, extend your arms outward until your arms are almost parallel to the floor. Willfully flex your shoulder muscles and return to start. Feel the stretch in your shoulder muscles and repeat the movement until you have completed your set.

Rest 15 seconds and perform your second set. Rest another 15 seconds and perform your third set. Rest 15 seconds and move to the next exercise—and body part—the alternate curl for the biceps.

BEWARE

Keep your upper body (torso) parallel to the floor throughout the movement.

MACHINES, ETC.

You may perform this exercise using any spaced-apart floor pulley machine. Set the weights at 10 pounds.

SETS, REPETITIONS, WEIGHTS

Set 1: 10 repetitions, 3-pound dumbbells. Rest 15 seconds.
Set 2: 10 repetitions, 3-pound dumbbells. Rest 15 seconds.
Set 3: 10 repetitions, 3-pound dumbbells. Rest 15 seconds.

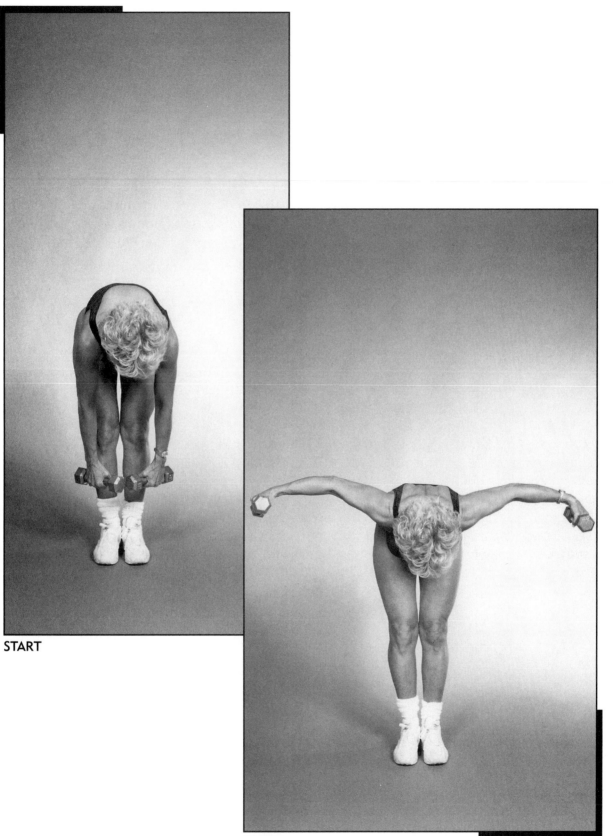

START

FINISH

101

ALTERNATE CURL

This exercise develops, shapes, strengthens, and defines the entire biceps muscle, and helps strengthen the forearm.

POSITION

Stand with your feet together or a natural width apart with a dumbbell in each hand. Place your arms at your sides and hold the dumbbells palms facing away from your body.

MOVEMENT

Flexing your biceps muscles as you go, and keeping your arms close to your body and your wrists slightly curled upward, curl one arm upward until you cannot curl it any further. Willfully flex your biceps muscles and return to start. As soon as your arm reaches start position, curl the other arm up and repeat the movement. Continue this alternating movement until you have completed your set.

Rest 15 seconds and perform your second set. Rest another 15 seconds and perform your third set. Rest 15 seconds and move to the next exercise—the simultaneous curl.

BEWARE

Don't rock back and forth as you work. Your body should remain stationary—only your arms are moving. Don't hold your breath. It won't be over faster that way.

MACHINES, ETC.

You may perform this exercise on any biceps curl machine (for photo, see p. 52) or on any close-set double floor pulley device. Set the weights at 20 pounds.

SETS, REPETITIONS, WEIGHTS

Set 1: 10 repetitions, 3-pound dumbbells. Rest 15 seconds.
Set 2: 10 repetitions, 3-pound dumbbells. Rest 15 seconds.
Set 3: 10 repetitions, 3-pound dumbbells. Rest 15 seconds.

START

FINISH

SIMULTANEOUS CURL

This exercise develops, shapes, strengthens, and defines the entire biceps muscle, and helps strengthen the forearm.

POSITION
Stand with your feet together or a natural width apart with a dumbbell in each hand. Place your arms at your sides and hold the dumbbells palms facing away from your body.

MOVEMENT
Flexing your biceps muscles as you go, and keeping your arms close to your body and your wrists slightly curled upward, curl your arms upward simultaneously until you cannot curl them any further. Willfully flex your biceps muscles and return to start position. Feel the stretch in your biceps muscles and repeat the movement until you have completed your set.

Rest 15 seconds and perform your second set. Rest another 15 seconds and perform your third set. Rest 15 seconds and move to the next exercise—the alternate hammer curl.

BEWARE
Don't rock back and forth as you work. Your body should remain stationary—only your arms are moving. Don't hold your breath. Breathe naturally.

MACHINES, ETC.
You may perform this exercise on any biceps curl machine, or on any floor pulley device (see p. 52 for photos). Set the weights at 10 pounds. You may perform this exercise with a 20-pound barbell.

SETS, REPETITIONS, WEIGHTS
Set 1: 10 repetitions, 3-pound dumbbells. Rest 15 seconds.
Set 2: 10 repetitions, 3-pound dumbbells. Rest 15 seconds.
Set 3: 10 repetitions, 3-pound dumbbells. Rest 15 seconds.

START

FINISH

ALTERNATE HAMMER CURL
Develops and shapes the entire biceps, and strengthens the forearm.

POSITION

Stand with your feet a natural width apart. Hold a dumbbell in each hand, palms facing your body. Let your arms hang down at the sides of your body.

MOVEMENT

With palms facing your body and the dumbbells in the "hammer" position (see photograph), curl one arm up to your shoulder as far as you can go. Flex your biceps muscle and return to start position. Feel the stretch in your biceps. Without pausing, immediately repeat the movement for the other arm. Continue this alternating curling movement until you have completed your set.

Rest 15 seconds and perform your second set. Rest another 15 seconds and perform your third set. Rest 15 seconds and move to the next exercise—the concentration curl.

BEWARE

Remember to flex your biceps on the upward movement and feel the stretch on the downward movement. Don't rock your body. You're not on a skiing expedition and you don't need momentum to propel your body. Be still and let your biceps do the work.

MACHINES, ETC.

You may perform this exercise two arms at a time, standing, seated, or lying on a flat or incline bench. You may substitute this exercise for the machine biceps pulldown, as demonstrated on p. 45. Set the weight at 20 pounds.

SETS, REPETITIONS, WEIGHTS

Set 1: 10 repetitions, 3-pound dumbbells. Rest 15 seconds.
Set 2: 10 repetitions, 3-pound dumbbells. Rest 15 seconds.
Set 3: 10 repetitions, 3-pound dumbbells. Rest 15 seconds.

START

FINISH

CONCENTRATION CURL

This exercise develops, shapes, and defines the peak of the biceps, and strengthens the forearm.

POSITION

Sit at the edge of a flat exercise bench and lean forward, placing your elbow against your inner knee. Hold a dumbbell in your working hand, palm away from your body. Extend your working arm straight down. Keep your upper body down throughout the exercise.

MOVEMENT

Flexing your biceps as hard as possible, curl your working arm upward until the dumbbell reaches approximate chin height. Without looking up, return to start position. Feel the stretch in your biceps muscle. Repeat the movement for the other arm.

Rest 15 seconds and perform your second set. Rest another 15 seconds and perform your third set. Rest 15 seconds and move to the next exercise—and body part—the overhead press for the triceps.

BEWARE

Keep your elbows against your inner knee at all times. Do not fall into the trap of swinging the dumbbell to the up position and letting it drop to the down position. Grip the dumbbell as if it were a treasure, not something you can't wait to get rid of.

MACHINES, ETC.

You may perform this exercise in a standing, bent position. See *The Fat-Burning Workout* for this stance.

SETS, REPETITIONS, WEIGHTS

Set 1: 10 repetitions, 3-pound dumbbells. Rest 15 seconds.
Set 2: 10 repetitions, 3-pound dumbbells. Rest 15 seconds.
Set 3: 10 repetitions, 3-pound dumbbells. Rest 15 seconds.

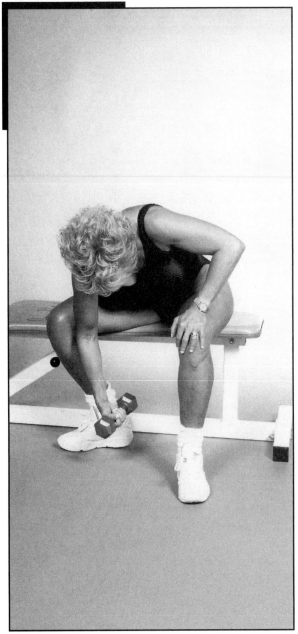

START

FINISH

1 | OVERHEAD PRESS

This exercise develops, shapes, strengthens, and defines the entire triceps, especially the inside and rear heads of this muscle.

POSITION

Grasp a dumbbell with an overhead grip, holding it on either side of the ball shape. Stand, or sit on a flat bench or chair, and raise the dumbbell straight up, locking your elbows and keeping your biceps close to your head.

MOVEMENT

Keeping your biceps close to your head, and your elbows stationary, lower the dumbbell in an arclike movement by letting your arms descend behind you. Feel a full stretch in your triceps muscle, and without resting, and flexing your triceps muscles as you go, return to start position. Willfully flex your triceps muscle and repeat the movement until you have completed your set.

Rest 15 seconds and perform your second set. Rest another 15 seconds and perform your third set. Rest 15 seconds and move to the next exercise—the kickback.

BEWARE

Your upper arms must remain close to your head throughout the movement. Don't hold your breath. Don't think "Wake me when it's over." Breathe and enjoy the exercise.

MACHINES, ETC.

You may use either a 20-pound barbell or an "EZ Curl bar" with 10-pound plates on each end to perform this exercise.

SETS, REPETITIONS, WEIGHTS

Set 1: 10 repetitions, 3-pound dumbbells. Rest 15 seconds.
Set 2: 10 repetitions, 3-pound dumbbells. Rest 15 seconds.
Set 3: 10 repetitions, 3-pound dumbbells. Rest 15 seconds.

START

FINISH

KICKBACK

This exercise develops, shapes, strengthens, and defines the entire triceps.

POSITION

Stand with your feet in a natural position, bending at the waist and at the knees, and hold a dumbbell in your working hand, palm facing your body. Place your nonworking hand on your corresponding knee. Bend your waiting arm at the elbow so that your forearm is parallel to the floor and your elbow is touching your waist.

MOVEMENT

Keeping your working upper arm close to your body, and flexing your triceps as you go, extend your working arm back as far as possible, and flex your triceps muscles. Without resting, return to start position and feel the stretch in your triceps muscle. Repeat the movement for the other arm.

Rest 15 seconds and perform your second set. Rest another 15 seconds and perform your third set. Rest 15 seconds and move to the next exercise—the one-arm overhead extension.

BEWARE

Keep your working upper arm close to your body throughout the exercise. Don't jerk the dumbbell back as if you were going to hurl it behind you. Maintain control at all times.

MACHINES, ETC.

You may substitute this exercise for the triceps pushdown (see p. 45 for photos) on any high pulley device, or on the lat-pulldown machine, using a narrow curved or straight bar, or using the center part of the lat machine bar (as seen in *Top Shape*). Set the weight at 20 pounds.

SETS, REPETITIONS, WEIGHTS

Set 1: 10 repetitions, 3-pound dumbbells. Rest 15 seconds.
Set 2: 10 repetitions, 3-pound dumbbells. Rest 15 seconds.
Set 3: 10 repetitions, 3-pound dumbbells. Rest 15 seconds.

START

FINISH

ONE-ARM OVERHEAD EXTENSION

This exercise develops, shapes, and defines the entire triceps, especially the inner and medial heads of that muscle.

POSITION   Stand with your feet together or a natural width apart. Hold a dumbbell in your working hand, palm facing in toward your body, arm extended straight up, with your upper arm touching your ear.

MOVEMENT   Lower the dumbbell behind your head until it grazes your neck and upper back. Flexing your triceps as hard as possible, return to start position, and repeat the movement until you have completed your set. Repeat the set for your other arm.

Rest 15 seconds and perform your second set. Rest another 15 seconds and perform your third set. Rest 15 seconds and move to the next exercise—the cross-face extension.

BEWARE   Keep your upper arm close to your head at all times. Make believe you are trying to block your ear from hearing odious music. It's fun to let your fingertips gently touch your working triceps muscle as it flexes and stretches—this way you really know you're working.

MACHINES, ETC.   You may perform this exercise using two arms at a time, with twice the weight.

SETS, REPETITIONS, WEIGHTS   Set 1: 10 repetitions, 3-pound dumbbells. Rest 15 seconds.
Set 2: 10 repetitions, 3-pound dumbbells. Rest 15 seconds.
Set 3: 10 repetitions, 3-pound dumbbells. Rest 15 seconds.

FINISH

CROSS-FACE EXTENSION

This exercise develops, shapes, and defines the inner head of the triceps muscle.

POSITION Lie on a flat exercise bench, or the floor, with a dumbbell held up in your fully extended working arm, with your palm facing your legs. Turn your face so that your nose (depending upon its size) and mouth are touching your upper arm area. The goal is to avoid smashing yourself in the face when you bring the dumbbell down!

MOVEMENT Bending your working arm at the elbow, lower your arm until the dumbbell touches your nonworking neck-shoulder area. Feel the stretch in your triceps muscle. Return to start position and flex your triceps muscle as hard as possible. Repeat the movement until you have completed your set. Perform the set for the other arm.

Rest 15 seconds and perform your second set. Rest another 15 seconds and perform your third set. Rest 15 seconds and move to the next exercise—and body part—the upright row for the back.

BEWARE Keep your working triceps close to your face at all times.

MACHINES, ETC. You may substitute this exercise for the triceps overhead extension, which can be performed on any lat-pulldown machine or any high pulley device, using a short curved bar, (see p. 45 for photo), or the center part of the lat machine bar, as seen in *Top Shape*. Set the weight at 20 pounds.

SETS, REPETITIONS, WEIGHTS
Set 1: 10 repetitions, 3-pound dumbbells. Rest 15 seconds.
Set 2: 10 repetitions, 3-pound dumbbells. Rest 15 seconds.
Set 3: 10 repetitions, 3-pound dumbbells. Rest 15 seconds.

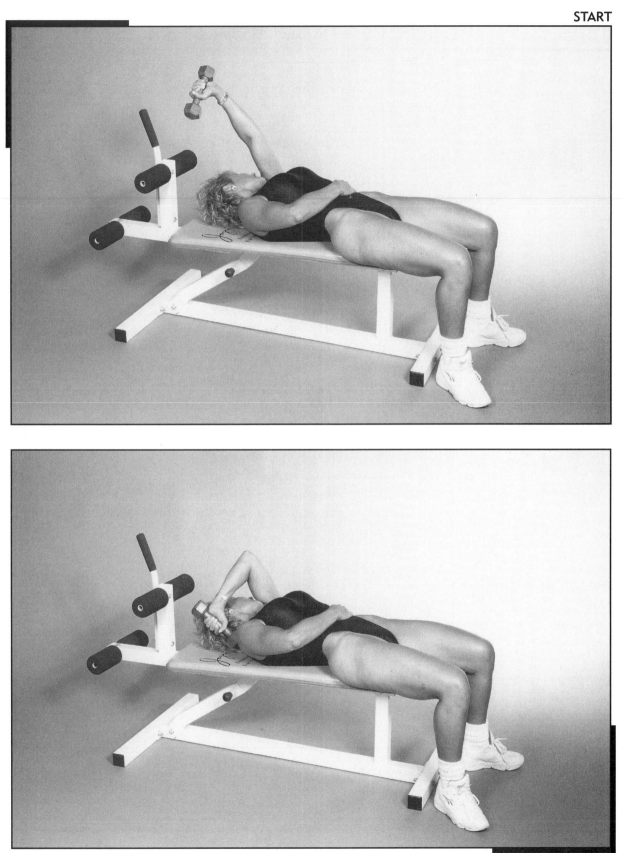

FINISH

1

UPRIGHT ROW

This exercise develops, shapes, strengthens, and defines the entire trapezius muscle, and also strengthens and defines the front shoulder muscle.

POSITION

Stand with your feet a natural width apart, and hold a dumbbell with both hands in the center of the dumbbell, palms facing your body. Extend your arms fully downward and keep the dumbbell centered and close to your body.

MOVEMENT

Flexing your trapezius muscle as you go, extending your elbows outward, and keeping the dumbbell close to your body, raise the dumbbell until it reaches chin height. Willfully flex your trapezius muscle and return to start position. Feel the stretch in your trapezius muscle and repeat the movement until you have completed your set.

Rest 15 seconds and perform your second set. Rest another 15 seconds and perform your third set. Rest 15 seconds and move to the next exercise—the one-arm dumbbell row.

BEWARE

Don't let the dumbbell wander away from your body. Don't shorten the movement—go all the way up to your chin and let your arms extend fully down.

MACHINES, ETC.

You may perform this exercise with a 20-pound barbell, or by attaching a bar to any floor pulley machine, as seen in *Top Shape*. Set the weight at 20 pounds. You may use any floor pulley to perform this movement. Set the weight at 10 pounds.

SETS, REPETITIONS, WEIGHTS

Set 1: 10 repetitions, 3-pound dumbbells. Rest 15 seconds.
Set 2: 10 repetitions, 3-pound dumbbells. Rest 15 seconds.
Set 3: 10 repetitions, 3-pound dumbbells. Rest 15 seconds.

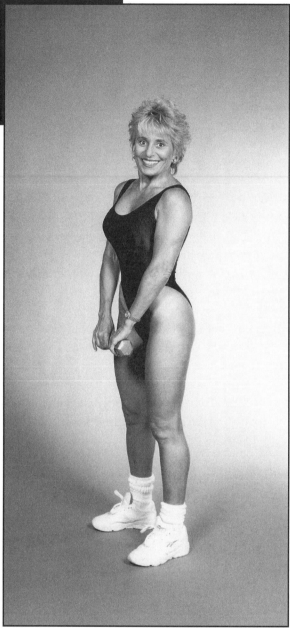

START

FINISH

ONE-ARM DUMBBELL ROW

This exercise develops, strengthens, shapes, and defines the latissimus dorsi and upper back muscles, and as a sideline, helps to develop the biceps.

POSITION

Bend at the waist, with a dumbbell held in your working hand, palm facing your body. Extend your nonworking leg out, and bend at the knee. Place your nonworking hand (to keep it out of trouble) on your nonworking knee. Extend your working arm out until you feel a stretch in your latissimus dorsi muscle.

MOVEMENT

Raise your working arm toward waist level, while at the same time flexing your back muscles to the fullest extent. Continue to raise the dumbbell until your elbow is extended as high as it can go (the dumbbell should reach approximate waist height at this point). Without resting, and vigilantly keeping your working arm close to your body, return to start position and feel the stretch in your back muscles. Repeat the movement until you have completed your set. Repeat the set for the other side of your body.

Rest 15 seconds and perform your second set. Rest another 15 seconds and perform your third set. Rest 15 seconds and move to the next exercise—the double-arm reverse row.

BEWARE

This is one of the more relaxing exercises. Enjoy it—but don't take it for granted. Work hard. Concentrate on your working muscle throughout the movements.

MACHINES, ETC.

You may substitute this exercise for the lat pulldown to the front, by using any lat-pulldown machine, as seen on p. 44. Set the weight at 20 pounds.

SETS, REPETITIONS, WEIGHTS

Set 1: 10 repetitions, 3-pound dumbbells. Rest 15 seconds.
Set 2: 10 repetitions, 3-pound dumbbells. Rest 15 seconds.
Set 3: 10 repetitions, 3-pound dumbbells. Rest 15 seconds.

START

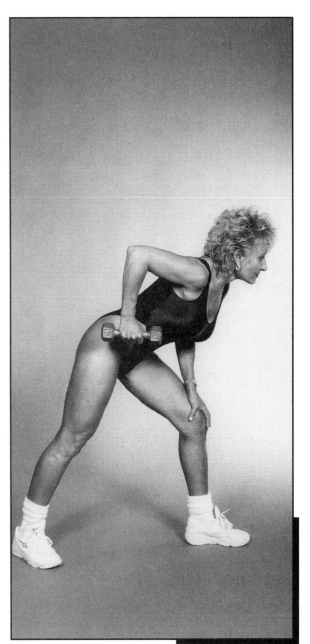

FINISH

DOUBLE-ARM REVERSE ROW

This exercise develops, shapes, strengthens, and defines the latissimus dorsi, the trapezius, the rear deltoid, and the forearm.

POSITION

Stand with your feet about six inches wider than shoulder width apart, with a dumbbell held in each hand, palms away from your body. Bend over until your torso is parallel to the floor. Extend your arms straight down and let them touch the upper-thigh-knee area.

MOVEMENT

Flexing your back muscles as you go, raise the dumbbells up and to the side of your body (about six inches out at the highest point—waist height). Willfully flex your back muscles and return to start position. Feel the stretch in your back muscles and repeat the movement until you have completed your set.

Rest 15 seconds and perform your second set. Rest another 15 seconds and perform your third set. Rest 15 seconds and move to the next exercise—the seated back lateral.

BEWARE

Maintain the near-parallel-to-floor position of your torso. Don't gradually rise up. Don't hold your breath. Breathe naturally.

MACHINES, ETC.

You may use a 20-pound barbell for this exercise. You may substitute this exercise for the lat pulldown to the back as seen on p. 44. Set the weight at 20 pounds.

SETS, REPETITIONS, WEIGHTS

Set 1: 10 repetitions, 3-pound dumbbells. Rest 15 seconds.
Set 2: 10 repetitions, 3-pound dumbbells. Rest 15 seconds.
Set 3: 10 repetitions, 3-pound dumbbells. Rest 15 seconds.

START

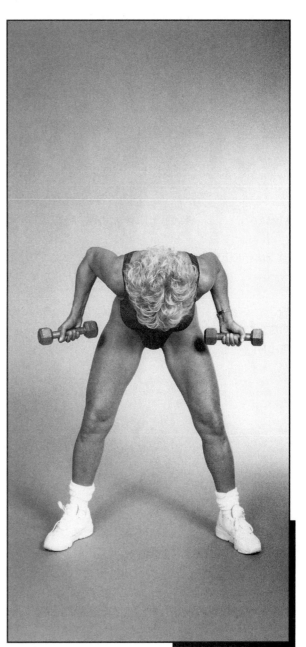

FINISH

SEATED BACK LATERAL

This exercise develops, shapes, strengthens, and defines the upper back and trapezius muscles.

POSITION
Holding a dumbbell in each hand, sit at the edge of a flat exercise bench or chair and lean forward until your upper body is nearly parallel to the floor. Palms facing to the rear, hold the dumbbells behind your ankles, letting the ends of the dumbbells touch.

MOVEMENT
Flexing your upper back muscles as you go, and keeping the dumbbells close to your body, raise the dumbbells up and back, rotating the dumbbells 180 degrees as you go, so that when you reach hip level, the dumbbells are angled to the front, and your palms are facing front. Willfully flex your upper back muscles by making believe you're trying to squeeze a pencil in the middle of your back. Return to start position and feel the stretch in your upper back. Repeat the movement until you have completed your set. (You may want to look at my *Bottoms Up: Upper Body* video to get a better picture of how this is done.)

Rest 15 seconds and perform your second set. Rest another 15 seconds and perform your third set. Congratulations. You have completed your day one workout.

BEWARE
Keep your arms close to your sides throughout the exercise.

MACHINES, ETC.
You may substitute a T-bar rowing machine for this exercise. Use a 5-pound plate, or set the weight at 10 pounds.

SETS, REPETITIONS, WEIGHTS
Set 1: 10 repetitions, 3-pound dumbbells. Rest 15 seconds.
Set 2: 10 repetitions, 3-pound dumbbells. Rest 15 seconds.
Set 3: 10 repetitions, 3-pound dumbbells. Rest 15 seconds.

START

FINISH

DAY 2

LOWER BODY WORKOUT

1 | SQUAT

This exercise develops, shapes, strengthens, and defines the front thigh (quadriceps) muscle, and helps to tighten and tone the buttocks (gluteus maximus). Note: If you can't do squats, double up on side leg lifts, the next exercise.

POSITION

With a dumbbell held in each hand, stand with your feet about shoulder width apart and your toes pointed slightly outward. Let your arms hang down at your sides, holding the dumbbells with your palms facing your body. Keep your back straight and your eyes straight ahead.

MOVEMENT

Feeling the stretch in your front thigh muscles as you go, descend to an approximate 45 degree bend in your knees. Flexing your quadriceps as you go, return to start position. Willfully flex your quadriceps and repeat the movement until you have completed your set.

Rest 15 seconds and perform your second set. Rest another 15 seconds and perform your third set. Rest 15 seconds and move to the next exercise—the side leg lift.

BEWARE

You may not be able to descend the full distance. Go only as far as possible. You may find that you rise on your toes as you descend. If so, you may place a board under your heels. If you have problem knees, use the leg extension machine. Set the weight at 20 pounds (see p. 46 for photo) or double up on the next exercise, the side leg lift (see p. 129 for photo).

MACHINES, ETC.

You may do this exercise with a 20-pound barbell, or on any squat machine set at 20 to 30 pounds (see p. 55 for photo). You may use any leg press machine in place of this exercise. Set the weight at 40 pounds.

SETS, REPETITIONS, WEIGHTS

Set 1: 10 repetitions, 3-pound dumbbells. Rest 15 seconds.
Set 2: 10 repetitions, 3-pound dumbbells. Rest 15 seconds.
Set 3: 10 repetitions, 3-pound dumbbells. Rest 15 seconds.

START

FINISH

127

SIDE LEG LIFT

This exercise tightens, tones, strengthens, and defines the inner thigh muscle, and helps to tighten and tone the entire quadriceps (thigh muscle).

POSITION

Lie on the floor on your side, supporting yourself with your elbow. Bend your nonworking leg at the knee and place the sole of that foot on the ground. Extend your working leg, and place a dumbbell in the middle of your working thigh area.

MOVEMENT

Keeping your working leg extended, and holding the weight on your thigh, flexing your working thigh, lift your working leg off the ground until you cannot go any higher. Keeping the pressure on your working inner thigh muscle, return to start position and repeat the movement until you have completed your set. Repeat the set for the other side of your body.

Rest 15 seconds and perform your second set. Rest another 15 seconds and perform your third set. Rest 15 seconds and move to the next exercise—the leg curl.

BEWARE

Flex your working inner thigh muscle as you raise and lower your leg.

MACHINES, ETC.

You may perform this exercise on any inner thigh machine. Set the weight at 20 pounds.

SETS,
REPETITIONS,
WEIGHTS

Set 1: 10 repetitions, 3-pound dumbbells. Rest 15 seconds.
Set 2: 10 repetitions, 3-pound dumbbells. Rest 15 seconds.
Set 3: 10 repetitions, 3-pound dumbbells. Rest 15 seconds.

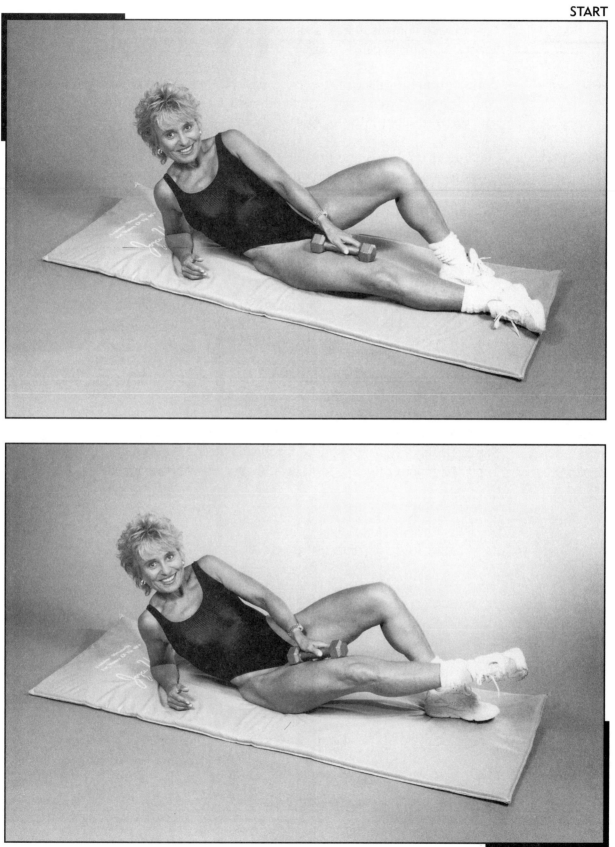

LEG CURL

This exercise tightens, tones, shapes, and defines the back thigh muscles (biceps femoris, or hamstrings).

POSITION
With a dumbbell placed between your feet, lie in a prone position on the floor or a flat exercise bench. Extend your legs straight out behind you and lean on your elbows for support.

MOVEMENT
Bending at the knees and flexing your hamstrings as you go, raise your lower legs until they are perpendicular to the floor. Keeping the pressure on your hamstrings, return to start position and repeat the movement until you have completed your set.

Rest 15 seconds and perform your second set. Rest another 15 seconds and perform your third set. Rest 15 seconds and move to the next exercise—the lunge.

BEWARE
Don't swing the dumbbell up and down. If you squeeze your ankles together, you will better be able to keep the pressure on your back thigh muscles.

MACHINES, ETC.
You may perform this exercise on any leg curl machine, as seen on p. 47. Set the weight at 20 pounds.

SETS, REPETITIONS, WEIGHTS
Set 1: 10 repetitions, 3-pound dumbbells. Rest 15 seconds.
Set 2: 10 repetitions, 3-pound dumbbells. Rest 15 seconds.
Set 3: 10 repetitions, 3-pound dumbbells. Rest 15 seconds.

LUNGE

This exercise tightens, tones, and defines the front thigh muscle (quadriceps) and helps to tighten the buttocks. (Note: If you can't do lunges, double up on leg curls, the exercise before this.)

POSITION

Stand with your feet together or a natural width apart. Keep your back straight. Hold a dumbbell in each hand, palms facing your body, and arms straight down at your sides. Look at a point directly in front of you.

MOVEMENT

Keeping one foot in place, lunge forward about two and a half feet, bending at the knee as you lunge, and keeping your knee in line with your toes. (Do not lunge forward so much that your knee covers the view of your toes.) Feel the stretch in your front thigh muscles in the finish position. Without resting, return to start position, and flex your quadriceps muscle. Without resting, complete the set for the other leg.

Rest 15 seconds and perform your second set. Rest another 15 seconds and perform your third set. Rest 15 seconds and move to the next exercise—and body part—the standing butt squeeze for the hips/buttocks.

BEWARE

Don't quickly drop to the lunge position or jerk up to start. Maintain a fluid movement. You will feel awkward at first, and this will seem impossible. (You should have seen me—I looked drunk, and in fact doing lunges nearly drove me to drink, but in time it became easy.) It will become second nature to you in a few months. In the meantime your awkward attempts are still working to shape your muscle.

MACHINES, ETC.

You may perform this exercise with a 20-pound barbell placed on your shoulders. You may use any leg press machine in place of this exercise (see p. 59). Set the weight at 40 pounds. You may also substitute this exercise for the leg extension (see p. 46). Set the weight at 20 pounds.

**SETS,
REPETITIONS,
WEIGHTS**

Set 1: 10 repetitions, 3-pound dumbbells. Rest 15 seconds.
Set 2: 10 repetitions, 3-pound dumbbells. Rest 15 seconds.
Set 3: 10 repetitions, 3-pound dumbbells. Rest 15 seconds.

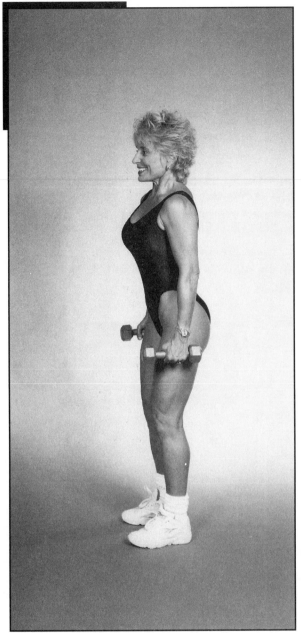

START

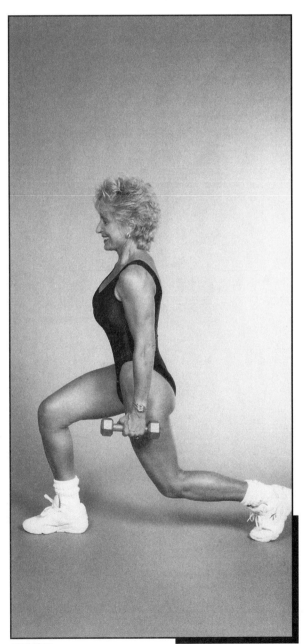

FINISH

133

1

STANDING BUTT SQUEEZE

This exercise tightens, tones, shapes, and defines the entire hips/buttocks area.

POSITION Stand with your feet a natural width apart and with your back erect. Hold a dumbbell in each hand, palms facing your body. Lower your body about four inches by bending at the knee.

MOVEMENT Flexing your entire hips/buttocks area as you go, rise until your knees are locked, thrusting your hips slightly forward as you rise. Willfully flex your buttocks. Keeping the pressure on your buttocks, return to start and repeat the movement until you have completed your set.

Rest 15 seconds and perform your second set. Rest another 15 seconds and perform your third set. Rest 15 seconds and move to your next exercise—the standing back-leg extension.

BEWARE The awkwardness of this exercise will quickly disappear once you get into the swing of it. (See video, Volume II of *The Fat-Burning Workout* for a demonstration of this exercise.)

MACHINES, ETC. You may substitute this exercise for any exercise done on a hips/buttocks machine. Set the weight at 20 pounds.

SETS,
REPETITIONS,
WEIGHTS
Set 1: 10 repetitions, 3-pound dumbbells. Rest 15 seconds.
Set 2: 10 repetitions, 3-pound dumbbells. Rest 15 seconds.
Set 3: 10 repetitions, 3-pound dumbbells. Rest 15 seconds.

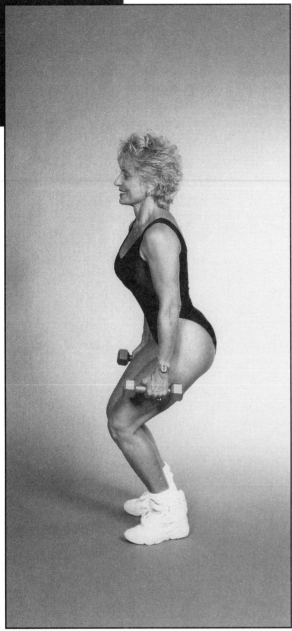

START

FINISH

STANDING BACK-LEG EXTENSION

This exercise tightens and tones the entire hips/buttocks area and helps remove saddlebags.

POSITION Lean against something such as a chair for support on your nonworking leg side. Raise your working leg, bending at the knee so that the ankle of your working leg is just about touching the inner knee area of your non-working leg (hey, just look at the photo, okay!). Your nonworking leg should be relatively straight—serving as a pole to hold you up. Place your free hand on your soon to be working buttocks so you will feel them tightening as you flex.

MOVEMENT Lower your working leg and extend it behind you until your knee is nearly completely unbent—all the while flexing your working buttocks muscle as hard as possible. When you reach finish position, give your buttocks an extra flex and without further ado return to start and repeat the movement until you have completed your set. Repeat the movement for the other side of your body.

Rest 15 seconds and perform your second set. Rest another 15 seconds and perform your third set. Rest 15 seconds and move to the next exercise—the straight-leg kick-up.

BEWARE Don't start twisting your body from side to side. Keep your body still and let your buttocks do the work.

MACHINES, ETC. You may substitute this exercise for any exercise done on a hips/buttocks machine. Set the weight at 20 pounds.

SETS, REPETITIONS Set 1: 10 repetitions. Rest 15 seconds.
Set 2: 10 repetitions. Rest 15 seconds.
Set 3: 10 repetitions. Rest 15 seconds.

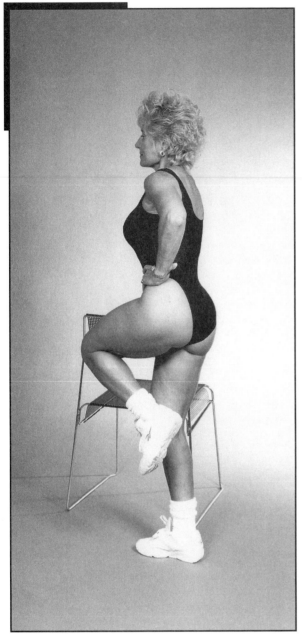

START

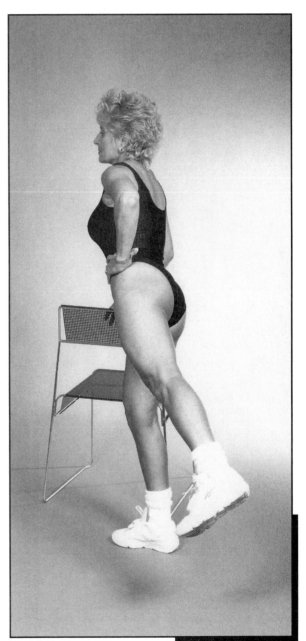

FINISH

STRAIGHT-LEG KICK-UP

This exercise tightens, tones, and lifts the entire hips/buttocks area, especially the upper back–thigh area.

POSITION   Get into an all-fours position on the floor. Flex your toes forward and extend your working leg straight out behind you. (Your nonworking knee will be bent.)

MOVEMENT   Flexing your working butt-thigh area, lift your working heel toward the ceiling, but don't go any higher than parallel to your body. (Look at the photograph.) Give your working butt-back-thigh area an extra-hard flex and quickly return to start and without a second's hesitation repeat the movement until you have completed your set. Complete the set for the other side of your body.

Rest 15 seconds and perform your second set. Rest another 15 seconds and perform your third set. Rest 15 seconds and move to the next exercise—the bent-knee kick-up.

BEWARE   This is a fun exercise, but don't take it for granted. It really reshapes your back thigh and butt—but only if you squeeze (flex) like the madwoman that you are!

MACHINES, ETC.   You may substitute this exercise for any exercise done on a hips/buttocks machine. Set the weight at 20 pounds.

SETS, REPETITIONS
Set 1: 10 repetitions. Rest 15 seconds.
Set 2: 10 repetitions. Rest 15 seconds.
Set 3: 10 repetitions. Rest 15 seconds.

FINISH

BENT-KNEE KICK-UP

This exercise tightens and tones the entire hips/buttocks area, and helps to remove saddlebags.

POSITION

Place yourself in an all-fours position on the floor. Raise your working thigh up and bend at the knee so that your leg takes the shape of an L.

MOVEMENT

Leading with your heel, and flexing your working buttocks muscle, extend your working leg behind you until your leg is slightly higher than parallel to your body. Give your working buttocks an extra-hard flex and return to start position. Repeat the movement until you have completed your set. Repeat the set for the other side of your body.

Rest 15 seconds and perform your second set. Rest another 15 seconds and perform your third set. Rest 15 seconds and move to the next exercise—and body part—the concentrated butt lift for the abdominals.

BEWARE

At first you'll have to think about it (getting your leg back to the L position each time after extending back)—but don't worry, after a while it will become natural to you. This is a powerful exercise and it's worth going through the awkward stage.

MACHINES, ETC.

You may substitute this exercise for any exercise done on a hips/buttocks machine. Set the weight at 20 pounds.

SETS, REPETITIONS

Set 1: 10 repetitions. Rest 15 seconds.
Set 2: 10 repetitions. Rest 15 seconds.
Set 3: 10 repetitions. Rest 15 seconds.

FINISH

CONCENTRATED BUTT LIFT

This exercise tightens, tones, and defines the entire lower abdominal area, and helps to strengthen the lower back.

POSITION
Lie on a mat and place your hands, fingers interlocked, behind your head. Raise your legs off the floor—bending at the knee and crossing them at the ankles. Push your back into the floor so that there is no curve or space in your back.

MOVEMENT
Making believe that your belly button is sewn to the ground, lift your buttocks off the floor about 2 to 3 inches, while at the same time flexing your lower abdominal muscles as hard as possible. (Remember, you can't go much higher even if you tried—your belly button is sewn to the ground.) Repeat this movement until you have completed your set.

Rest 15 seconds and perform your second set. Rest another 15 seconds and perform your third set. Rest 15 seconds and move to the next exercise—the crunch.

MACHINES, ETC.
You may substitute this exercise for the standard knee-in as demonstrated in my book *Bottoms Up!*

SETS, REPETITIONS
Set 1: 10 repetitions. Rest 15 seconds.
Set 2: 10 repetitions. Rest 15 seconds.
Set 3: 10 repetitions. Rest 15 seconds.

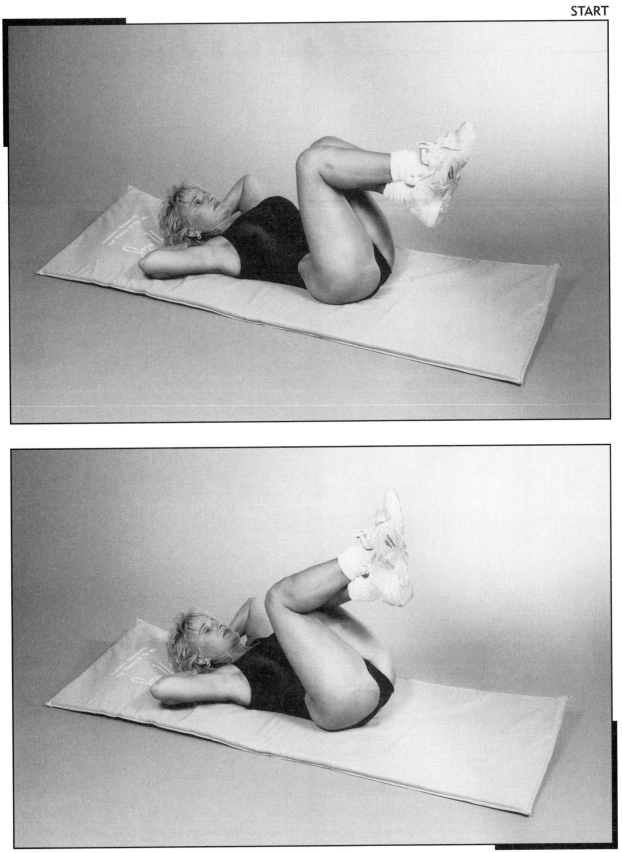

FINISH

CRUNCH

This exercise develops, shapes, and defines the entire upper abdominal area, and helps strengthen the upper abdominal area.

POSITION

Lie flat on your back on the floor, and bend at the knees. Place your feet flat on the floor and your hands behind your neck, fingers crossed.

MOVEMENT

Flexing your entire abdominal area as you go, raise your shoulders off the floor in a curling movement until your shoulders are completely off the floor, all the time flexing your upper abdominal muscles. Keeping the pressure on your abdominal area, return to start, and repeat the movement until you have completed your set.

Rest 15 seconds and perform your second set. Rest another 15 seconds and perform your third set. Rest 15 seconds and move to the next exercise—the ceiling lift.

BEWARE

Don't use your hands behind your neck to jerk yourself up. If you do, you'll know the true meaning of the expression "It's a pain in the neck."

MACHINES, ETC.

You may perform this exercise on any crunch machine. Set the weight at 20 pounds.

SETS, REPETITIONS

Set 1: 10 repetitions. Rest 15 seconds.
Set 2: 10 repetitions. Rest 15 seconds.
Set 3: 10 repetitions. Rest 15 seconds.

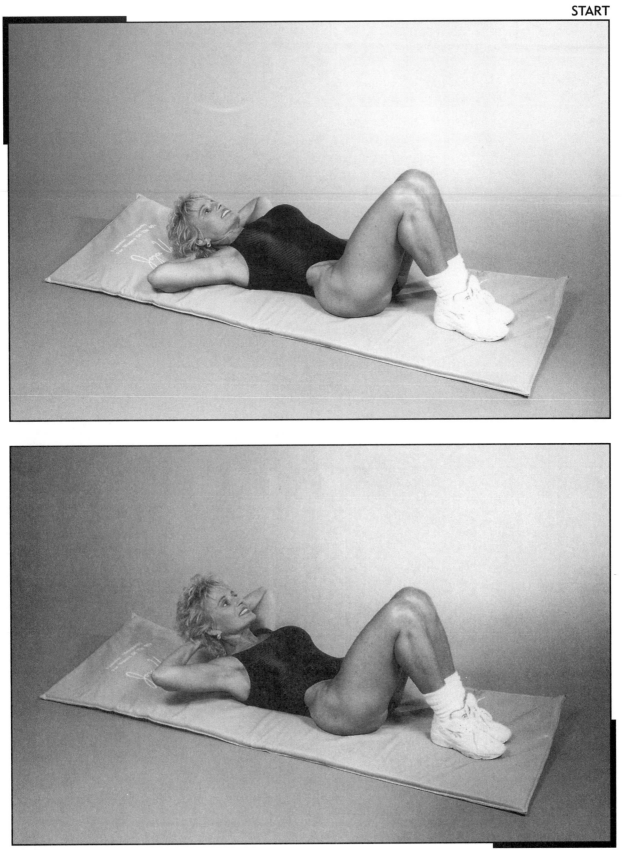

CEILING LIFT

This exercise tightens, tones, and defines the entire lower abdominal area, and helps strengthen the lower back.

POSITION   Lie on a mat and place your hands, fingers interlocked, behind your head. Raise your legs off the floor—extending your legs fully upward, and crossing your legs at the ankles. Push your back into the floor so that there is no curve or space in your back.

MOVEMENT   Making believe that your belly button is sewn to the ground, lift your buttocks off the floor about 2 to 3 inches, while at the same time flexing your lower abdominal muscles as hard as possible. (Remember, you can't go much higher even if you tried—your belly button is sewn to the ground.) Repeat this movement until you have completed your set.

Rest 15 seconds and perform your second set. Rest another 15 seconds and perform your third set. Rest 15 seconds and move to the next exercise— the knee-raised crunch.

MACHINES, ETC.   You may substitute this exercise for the leg raise as demonstrated in my book *Bottoms Up!*

SETS,
REPETITIONS   Set 1: 10 repetitions. Rest 15 seconds.
Set 2: 10 repetitions. Rest 15 seconds.
Set 3: 10 repetitions. Rest 15 seconds.

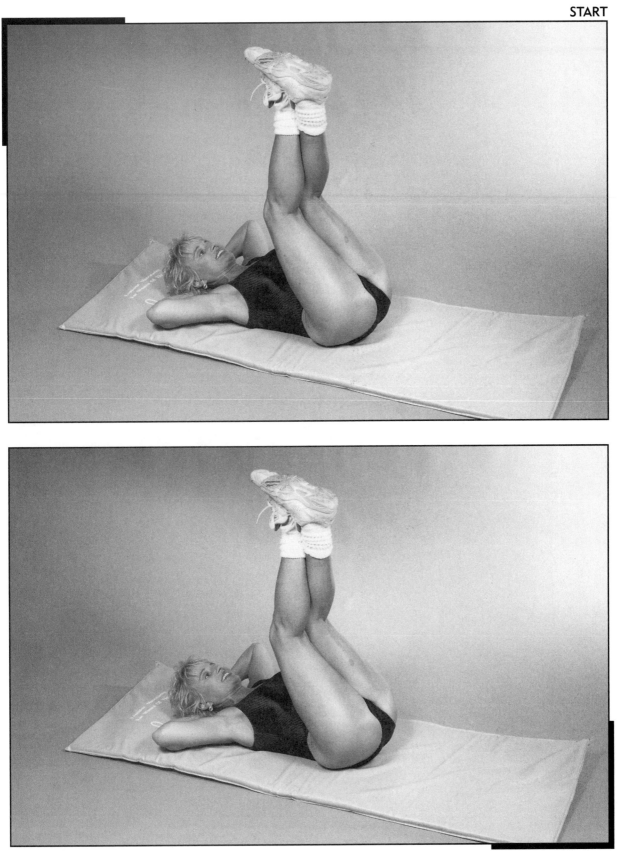

FINISH

KNEE-RAISED CRUNCH

This exercise develops, shapes, strengthens, and defines the entire upper abdominal area, and helps strengthen the lower abdominal area.

POSITION

Lie flat on your back on the floor, and pull your knees up until your legs form an L. You may cross your feet at the ankles. Place your hands behind your head.

MOVEMENT

Flexing your entire abdominal area as you go, raise your shoulders off the floor in a curling movement until your shoulders are completely off the floor, all the while keeping your knees raised so that your legs are still in an approximate L shape. Keeping the pressure on your abdominal muscles, return to start and repeat the movement until you have completed your set.

Rest 15 seconds and perform your second set. Rest another 15 seconds and perform your third set. Rest 15 second and move to the next exercise—and body part—the seated straight-toe raise for the calves.

BEWARE

Don't allow yourself to use your hands behind your neck to jerk your neck. Let your upper abdominals do the work.

MACHINES, ETC.

You may substitute this exercise for the standard sit-up as demonstrated in my book *Gut Busters*.

SETS, REPETITIONS

Set 1: 10 repetitions. Rest 15 seconds.
Set 2: 10 repetitions. Rest 15 seconds.
Set 3: 10 repetitions. Rest 15 seconds.

SEATED STRAIGHT-TOE RAISE

This exercise develops, shapes, strengthens, and defines the entire calf muscle (gastrocnemius).

POSITION   Sit at the edge or corner of a flat exercise bench with a set of dumbbells held on top of your knees. Plant your heels on the ground. Point your toes straight ahead.

MOVEMENT   Keeping your toes pointed straight ahead and flexing your calf muscles as you go, raise your heels until you cannot go any further. Willfully flex your calf muscles and return to start position. Feel the stretch in your calf muscles and repeat the movement until you have completed your set.

    Rest 15 seconds and perform your second set. Rest another 15 seconds and perform your third set. Rest 15 seconds and move to the next exercise—the seated angled-out-toe raise.

BEWARE   You have the option of using a thick book if you feel that you are not getting a full range of motion. In this case, place your toes on the edge of the book and let your heels descend to floor level.

MACHINES, ETC.   You may perform this exercise on any seated calf machine, as seen on p. 48. Set the weight at 20 pounds.

SETS,
REPETITIONS,
WEIGHTS
Set 1: 10 repetitions, 3-pound dumbbells. Rest 15 seconds.
Set 2: 10 repetitions, 3-pound dumbbells. Rest 15 seconds.
Set 3: 10 repetitions, 3-pound dumbbells. Rest 15 seconds.

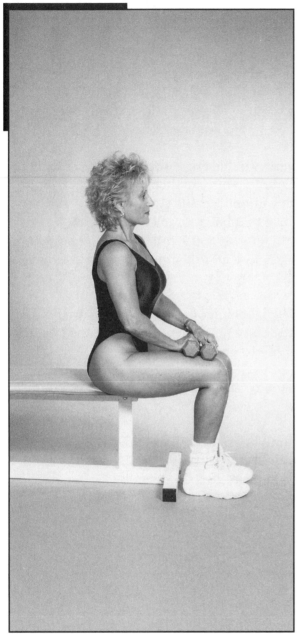

START

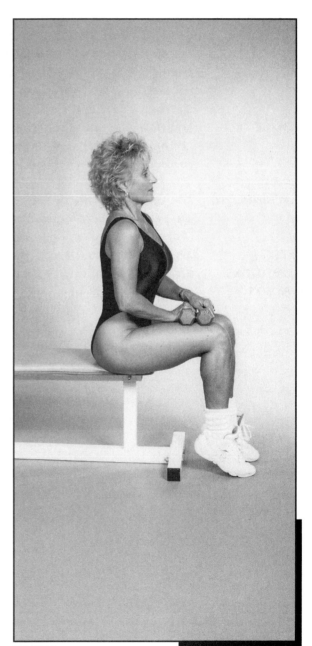

FINISH

SEATED ANGLED-OUT-TOE RAISE

This exercise develops, shapes, strengthens, and defines the entire calf muscle (gastrocnemius) muscle, especially the inner area.

POSITION
Sit at the edge or corner of a flat exercise bench with a set of dumbbells held on top of your knees. Plant your heels on the ground. Point your toes outward as far as possible. Close your eyes and think, "Wow, I'm almost finished."

MOVEMENT
Keeping your toes pointed outward, and flexing your calf muscles as you go, raise your heels until you cannot go any further. Willfully flex your calf muscles and return to start position. Feel the stretch in your calf muscles and repeat the movement until you have completed your set.

Rest 15 seconds and perform your second set. Rest another 15 seconds and perform your third set. Rest 15 seconds and move to the next exercise—the standing straight-toe raise.

BEWARE
You have the option of using a thick book if you feel that you are not getting a full range of motion. In this case, place your toes at the edge of the book, and let your heels descend to floor level.

MACHINES, ETC.
You may perform this exercise on any seated calf machine, as seen on p. 48. Set the weight at 20 pounds.

SETS, REPETITIONS, WEIGHTS
Set 1: 10 repetitions, 3-pound dumbbells. Rest 15 seconds.
Set 2: 10 repetitions, 3-pound dumbbells. Rest 15 seconds.
Set 3: 10 repetitions, 3-pound dumbbells. Rest 15 seconds.

START

FINISH

3 STANDING STRAIGHT-TOE RAISE

This exercise develops, shapes, strengthens, and defines the entire gastrocnemius (calf) muscle.

POSITION   Stand with your feet a natural width apart, and your toes flat on the floor, pointed straight ahead.

MOVEMENT   Flexing your calf muscles as you go, raise yourself as high as possible. When you reach the highest point, willfully flex your calf muscles and return to start position. Feel the stretch in your calf muscles and repeat the movement until you have completed your set.

Rest 15 seconds and perform your second set. Rest another 15 seconds and perform your third set. Rest 15 seconds and move to the next exercise—the standing angled-in-toe raise.

BEWARE   You have the option of using a thick book if you feel that you are not getting a full range of motion. In this case you will probably have to hold on to something in order to keep your balance. You will place your toes at the edge of the book, and let your heels descend to floor level.

MACHINES, ETC.   You may perform this exercise on any standing calf machine. Set the weight at 20 pounds.

SETS, REPETITIONS, WEIGHTS
Set 1: 10 repetitions, 3-pound dumbbells. Rest 15 seconds.
Set 2: 10 repetitions, 3-pound dumbbells. Rest 15 seconds.
Set 3: 10 repetitions, 3-pound dumbbells. Rest 15 seconds.

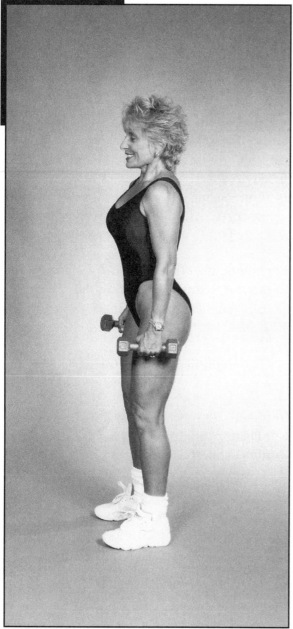

START

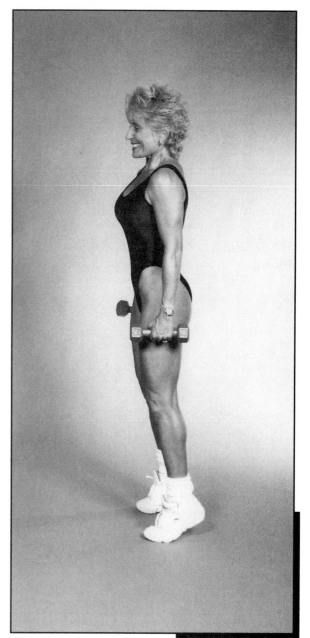

FINISH

STANDING ANGLED-IN-TOE RAISE

This exercise develops, shapes, strengthens, and defines the entire gastrocnemius (calf) muscle, especially the outer area.

POSITION

Stand with your feet a natural width apart, and your toes flat on the floor, pointed straight in as far as possible.

MOVEMENT

Flexing your calf muscles as you go, raise yourself as high as possible. When you reach the highest point, willfully flex your calf muscles and return to start position. Feel the stretch in your calf muscles and repeat the movement until you have completed your set.

Rest 15 seconds and perform your second set. Rest another 15 seconds and perform your third set. Congratulations. Wow. You have completed your day two workout—and the entire body workout, as a matter of fact.

BEWARE

You have the option of using a thick book if you feel that you are not getting a full range of motion. In this case you will probably have to hold on to something in order to keep your balance. You will place your toes at the edge of the book, and let your heels descend to floor level.

MACHINES, ETC.

You may perform this exercise on any standing calf machine. Set the weight at 20 pounds.

SETS, REPETITIONS, WEIGHTS

Set 1: 10 repetitions, 3-pound dumbbells. Rest 15 seconds.
Set 2: 10 repetitions, 3-pound dumbbells. Rest 15 seconds.
Set 3: 10 repetitions, 3-pound dumbbells. Rest 15 seconds.

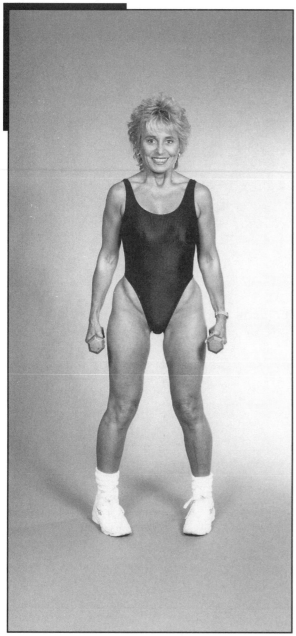

START

FINISH

5

ESTABLISHING A MUSCLE BASE
WORKOUT LEVEL 2

Now that you've learned the moves, it's time to get serious! This chapter is perhaps the most important workout in the book. It teaches you how to build a muscle base that will later allow you to advance to workout levels 3 and 4, where you can add more definition and shape.

The Purpose of This Workout: To Build a Firm Muscle Base— But Why Do You Need Muscle?

If your body were a building, this workout would provide its foundation—a muscle foundation. But why do you need muscle? We've already talked about this on pp. 12–13, but let's take a closer look at the issue now.

The body is made of skin, bone, internal organs, fat, and muscle. But which of the four elements determines the shape and form of the body? While bone size does play a part, it is mainly *fat and muscle!* Most people have too much fat and not enough muscle. Fat is mushy and amorphous. It isn't pleasant to touch and it isn't pretty to look at. Muscle, on the other hand, is firm and shapely—and it is a delight to feel and see. I'm not talking about huge, hulking muscles. I'm talking about sexy, taut muscles that delineate your body and make it a joy to the senses.

This workout, along with the low-fat eating plan found in Chapter 8 (or my diet book *Eat to Trim*, see Bibliography), will rearrange your body composition so that you'll have more muscle and less fat. You can't build and reshape your muscles by dieting—and you can't do it by aerobics. You must use weights— and use them in a specific way. That way is clearly spelled out in this chapter.

If you are a woman, don't worry that you will look like Arnold the minute you pick up a weight. If you are a man, lay aside your fear that soon you will have to replace all your clothing. Yes. Muscles will be popping everywhere, but they will be of moderate size, and will replace fat! Men who do this workout will probably wear the same size clothing—but may go down a few sizes in the waist—and maybe up one size in the chest. Women will go down a few dress or pants sizes. Both men and women will find that the body has "redistributed" itself. It will have an appealing shape and form.

The Advantage of This Workout Over the Other Workouts

This workout will yield you more muscle than any other workout in this book. Why? You will be using heavier weights and will be resting more between each set than with the other workouts. But what is the advantage of getting more muscle—other than the advantages listed above? The more muscle you have on your body, the more you can eat without gaining weight. How so?

Muscle raises your metabolism, so you burn more fat twenty-four hours a day—all things being equal. Let me explain.

After you put on muscle, even a moderate amount of muscle, you burn about 20 percent more fat doing the same thing you used to do. For example, say you used to burn sixty calories when you were sleeping. (We do burn calories when we sleep—it takes energy even to breathe.) Now you'll burn at least seventy-two calories an hour.

One more thought. Did you ever notice that men seem to be able to eat more than women without putting on weight? How can they do this? You guessed it. Men naturally have more muscle (due to a greater amount of the muscle-building hormone testosterone, naturally produced by their bodies).

But we don't have to be victims of our gender. We can work to put on muscle—so that we too can eat more without getting fat. And again, don't worry. You won't look like a bodybuilder. You would have to ingest steroids, work out four hours a day, and lift hundreds of pounds per set. Those women who look like men, and those men who look like the Incredible Hulk—you know, the ones you see in some of those bodybuilding contests—do just that.

Skipping Workout Level 1 and Beginning Here

Okay. If this workout is so great, why not skip workout level 1 and start right here. Fine. You can do it. But if you've never worked out with weights before, you may have some difficulty learning the moves and at the same time learning to do the pyramid system explained later in this chapter (the differing number of repetitions and the graduated weights).

If you are a complete newcomer, it's much better if you start with workout level 1 and stay there for the prescribed three months—or at least for three to six weeks so you can get used to the exercises, the order of the exercises, and what is done on each workout day.

If you do skip workout level 1, keep in mind that the photos here are in reduced size. Also, note that the detailed instructions on how to perform the exercises are found in workout level 1 (Chapter 4) and are not repeated here. However, if you wish to refer back to the detailed instructions it will be easy because the exercises are in the same order here as they are in Chapter 4, only here, as I will later explain, your weights and repetitions will be different.

How Much Time Is Involved?

Your time investment is thirty minutes a day, but it may take a little more or a little less, depending upon how fast or slow you move the dumbbells, and whether you take your full thirty-second rest between sets. If you move the dumbbells quickly (after you get used to the routine, of course) and you opt for the shorter rests (see below: "Getting More Out of the Workout by Increasing the Intensity"), you will in fact find that you can finish the workout in twenty minutes or less. I do—but this is after some experience.

Keep in mind that in the beginning, while you're getting used to the pyramid system and handling the heavier weights, the workout may take as long as forty-five minutes but probably not that long if you've already gotten used to the exercises by doing workout level 1.

You will work out four to six days a week. Details will be discussed below.

Workout Days and Exercises Used in This Workout

You will use the same exercises as demonstrated in workout level 1, only in a different manner. You will be using the pyramid system as explained in the following paragraphs, and as defined in the A–Z Quick-Start Dictionary. Your exercises, as in workout level 1, are divided into two workout days— and again, as in workout level 1, you will exercise the upper body on workout day one and the lower body on workout day two. They are exactly the same as workout level 1, but here is a review. (Remember, you will be doing something different with the exercises in workout level 2.)

▶ Workout Day 1

UPPER BODY
Chest
Shoulders
Biceps
Triceps
Back

▶ Workout Day 2

LOWER BODY
Thighs
Hips/Buttocks
Abdominals
Calves

Here are the specific exercises you will do on each workout day:

DAY 1 WORKOUT

CHEST
- flat press
- incline press
- incline flye
- cross-bench pullover

SHOULDERS
- side lateral raise
- front lateral raise
- alternate shoulder press
- bent lateral raise

BICEPS
- alternate curl
- simultaneous curl
- alternate hammer curl
- concentration curl

TRICEPS
- overhead press
- kickback
- one-arm overhead extension
- cross-face extension

BACK
- upright row
- one-arm dumbbell row
- double-arm reverse row
- seated back lateral

DAY 2 WORKOUT

THIGHS
- squat
- side leg lift
- leg curl
- lunge

HIPS/BUTTOCKS
- standing butt squeeze
- standing back-leg extension
- straight-leg kick-up
- bent-knee kick-up

ABDOMINALS
- concentrated butt lift
- crunch
- ceiling lift
- knee-raised crunch

CALVES
- seated straight-toe raise
- seated angled-out-toe raise
- standing straight-toe raise
- standing angled-in-toe raise

Equipment Needed

You will need three sets of dumbbells: three-, five-, and ten-pounders. As mentioned before, when I give the weight for dumbbells, I mean for each dumbbell.

You will also need a bench or step, preferably one that can be raised to an incline. If you're using a step, make sure that it can be raised eight to ten inches off the floor. See exercise photos for use of a step in place of a bench; pp. 188 for a flat bench.

Adding to Your Knowledge

This workout requires that you remember a little more than you had to remember when doing workout level 1. It is the next step in the workout—and is well worth the effort. In workout level 1, "Learning the Moves," you were introduced to the basics: the moves and the order of the exercises. Now you will learn how to graduate your weights with each set of a specific exercise at the expense of a few repetitions. This method is called the "pyramid system."

The Pyramid System

In workout level 1, all you needed was one set of three-pound dumbbells. Now you will need two additional sets of weights: a set of five-pound dumbbells, and a set of ten-pound dumbbells. In addition, as you get stronger and stronger, you will raise your overall weights so that your muscles continue to grow. (See "progression" in the A–Z Quick-Start Dictionary.)

Technically speaking, we are using the "modified" pyramid system because we are not going down the pyramid—but rather going to the top and stopping there. However, over time, weight-training experts have come to refer to the modified pyramid system as just the plain old pyramid system. What do they call the actual pyramid system? They call it the "true pyramid system." But forget about that now. For your purposes, when you see the words "pyramid system," this is what you'll be doing. For the sake of continuity, I'll compare it to workout level 1.

Instead of doing only ten repetitions for your first set, you take the three-pound dumbbells and you do twelve repetitions. Then you take a rest. Now, for your second set, you pick up a slightly heavier set of dumbbells, five-pounders, and you do your second set, but you do only ten repetitions this time. You take another rest. Now you pick up your last and heaviest set of dumbbells, the ten-pounders, and you do your final set—but this time, you do only eight repetitions. (If the tens are too heavy, repeat with the fives or purchase eight-pounders.)

You do this for every single exercise except for abdominal and the hips/buttocks exercises where no weight is used. In such cases, you simply do fifteen to twenty-five repetitions per set.

Notice that every time I ask you to increase the weight, I give you a break by asking you to do fewer repetitions. The pyramid system encourages you to work hard without getting bored. It's the system used by every champion bodybuilder—male or female, and by nearly every in-the-know body-shaping expert. Let's take a closer look at the pyramid system as it will appear in your workout.

Sets, Repetitions, Weights, and Rests

You will do three sets for each exercise, but you will graduate the weights and reduce the repetitions until you reach your final set. Here's how it looks:

ALL EXERCISES *EXCEPT* ABDOMINAL AND HIPS/BUTTOCKS EXERCISES

SET 1:   12 repetitions, 3-pound dumbbells. Rest 30 seconds.
SET 2:   10 repetitions, 5-pound dumbbells. Rest 30 seconds.
SET 3:   8 repetitions, 10-pound dumbbells. Rest 30 seconds.

ABDOMINAL AND HIPS/BUTTOCKS EXERCISES

SET 1:   15–25 repetitions, no weights. Rest 30 seconds.
SET 2:   15–25 repetitions, no weights. Rest 30 seconds.
SET 3:   15–25 repetitions, no weights. Rest 30 seconds.

Note: You will be holding three-pound dumbbells throughout the standing butt squeeze. They don't count as weights—they're merely used as an anchor.

Notice that you rest longer than you did in workout level 1. This is due to the increase in weights, and also because as you get stronger and stronger, you will increase your weights as well. (Note: when you get used to the routine, you may be able to shorten your rests to 10–15 seconds anyway!)

Changing the Order of the Exercises

The exercises in this workout have been placed in a certain order because they are easiest to do in this order for many people. However, after you have been working out for at least six weeks you can do the following if you wish.

You may change the order of the exercise within the body part. Let me explain, using the shoulders as an example. There are four exercises for the shoulders: the side lateral raise, the front lateral raise, the alternate shoulder press, and the bent lateral raise, in that order. Instead of doing the side lateral raise first, you can do the alternate shoulder press first, or any other one first. In fact, you can completely rearrange the exercises in this group if you wish. But don't start mixing them with the exercises for other body parts. You can only do that in a very special way—and I do it for you in workout level 4.

What about changing the order of the body parts you exercise on a given day? I'll use workout day two as an example. On that day you exercise thighs, hips/buttocks, abdominals, and calves, in that order. Suppose you want to exercise abdominals first, or hips/buttocks or calves? Suppose you want to scramble the body parts and make up your own order. Fine. You can do it.

What about mixing the workout days—taking some from workout day one and some from workout day two—and making up different workout days? Don't do it until you have worked out with weights for at least a year—and have gone through workout levels 1 to 4. By then you will know what you are doing and will be able to make appropriate changes.

Getting More Out of the Workout by Increasing the Intensity

Later, you may want to increase the intensity of this workout, and as a result, get even more out of it. You can do this in three ways: 1) Shorten the rests (you burn more fat). 2) Use heavier weights (you build more muscle). 3) Flex harder and use some dynamic tension on the stretch part of the exercise (you get harder muscles). You can do one, all, or any combination of these.

Stretching

The first set of each exercise provides a natural stretch because you are using relatively light weights—three-pound dumbbells. However, if you wish, you can do a few repetitions of each exercise without weights, just before you start your first set of that exercise.

Breaking In Gently if You've Used Workout Level 1 for at Least Three Weeks

WEEK ONE: First and second sets of each exercise, using three- and five-pound dumbbells.

WEEK TWO: Full workout: first, second, and third sets of each exercise using three-, five-, and ten-pound dumbbells.

Breaking In Gently if You Are Starting Here— And Did Not Do Workout Level 1, or Have Worked with Weights Before

If you are very weak, and never worked with weights before, I suggest that you go to workout level 1 and break in gently. After three weeks, you will have reached the full level of that program, and, if you still want to skip the rest of the three-month break-in, you may go to the above plan.

If you've been working out with weights before, but not with any of my workouts, and you want to skip workout level 1 and start here, break in in the following manner.

WEEK ONE: First set of each exercise using the three-pound dumbbells.

WEEK TWO: First and second sets of each exercise, using the three- and five-pound dumbbells.

WEEK THREE: You are on the full program. First, second, and third sets of each exercise, using three-, five-, and ten-pound dumbbells.

If you've used any of my other workout books for ten weeks or more, you can completely skip the break-in period.

Ready, Set, Go

Okay. You've gathered your three sets of dumbbells and you've set up a place to work out with your bench or step. Now let's get started. Use this reduced-size overview of the entire workout. (Note that you can also use the tear-out wall posters on pp. 263–287.) If need be, reread the exercise instructions found in Chapter 4 (level 1) before you start. For your convenience, the only differences between workout levels 1 and 2 are:

Differences: In workout level 1 you used only one set of weights—you did not pyramid your weights. You did three sets of ten repetitions for each exercise. Now you pyramid your weights. You will do three sets for each exercise, but you will graduate (pyramid) the weights and reduce the repetitions until you reach your final set. By way of review:

SET 1: 12 repetitions, 3-pound dumbbells. Rest 30 seconds.
SET 2: 10 repetitions, 5-pound dumbbells. Rest 30 seconds.
SET 3: 8 repetitions, 10-pound dumbbells. Rest 30 seconds.

WORKOUT LEVEL 2

CHEST ROUTINE

FLAT PRESS

START

FINISH

INCLINE PRESS

START

FINISH

INCLINE FLYE

START

FINISH

CROSS-BENCH PULLOVER

START

FINISH

SHOULDERS ROUTINE

SIDE LATERAL RAISE

FRONT LATERAL RAISE

START   FINISH   START   FINISH

SETS, REPETITIONS, WEIGHTS, AND RESTS
Set 1: 12 repetitions, 3-pound dumbbells. Rest 30 seconds.
Set 2: 10 repetitions, 5-pound dumbbells. Rest 30 seconds.
Set 3: 8 repetitions, 10-pound dumbbells. Rest 30 seconds.

SHOULDERS ROUTINE

ALTERNATE SHOULDER PRESS

START   FINISH

BENT LATERAL RAISE

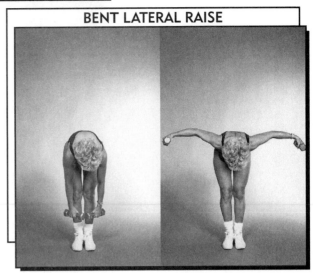

START   FINISH

BICEPS ROUTINE

ALTERNATE CURL

START   FINISH

SIMULTANEOUS CURL

START   FINISH

ALTERNATE HAMMER CURL

START   FINISH

CONCENTRATION CURL

START   FINISH

SETS, REPETITIONS, WEIGHTS, AND RESTS
Set 1: 12 repetitions, 3-pound dumbbells. Rest 30 seconds.
Set 2: 10 repetitions, 5-pound dumbbells. Rest 30 seconds.
Set 3: 8 repetitions, 10-pound dumbbells. Rest 30 seconds.

TRICEPS ROUTINE

OVERHEAD PRESS

START   FINISH

KICKBACK

START   FINISH

ONE-ARM OVERHEAD EXTENSION

START   FINISH

CROSS-FACE EXTENSION

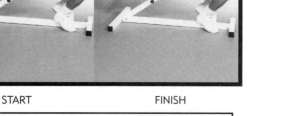

START

FINISH

BACK ROUTINE

UPRIGHT ROW

START   FINISH

ONE-ARM DUMBBELL ROW

START   FINISH

SETS, REPETITIONS, WEIGHTS, AND RESTS
Set 1: 12 repetitions, 3-pound dumbbells. Rest 30 seconds.
Set 2: 10 repetitions, 5-pound dumbbells. Rest 30 seconds.
Set 3: 8 repetitions, 10-pound dumbbells. Rest 30 seconds.

BACK ROUTINE

DOUBLE-ARM REVERSE ROW

START   FINISH

SEATED BACK LATERAL

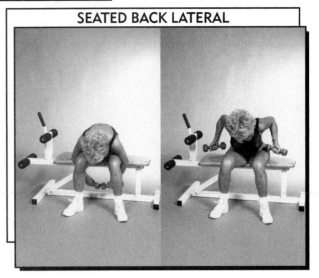

START   FINISH

THIGH ROUTINE

SQUAT

START   FINISH

SIDE LEG LIFT

START

FINISH

LEG CURL

START

FINISH

LUNGE

START   FINISH

SETS, REPETITIONS, WEIGHTS, AND RESTS
Set 1: 12 repetitions, 3-pound dumbbells. Rest 30 seconds.
Set 2: 10 repetitions, 5-pound dumbbells. Rest 30 seconds.
Set 3: 8 repetitions, 10-pound dumbbells. Rest 30 seconds.

STANDING BUTT SQUEEZE

START   FINISH

STANDING BACK-LEG EXTENSION

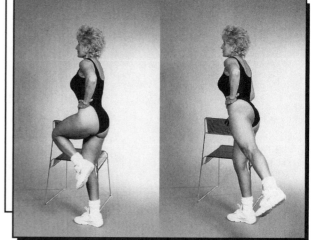

START   FINISH

STRAIGHT LEG KICK-UP

START

FINISH

BENT-KNEE KICK-UP

START

FINISH

ABDOMINALS

CONCENTRATED BUTT LIFT

START

FINISH

CRUNCH

START

FINISH

SETS, REPETITIONS, AND RESTS
Set 1: 15–25 repetitions, no weights. Rest 30 seconds.
Set 2: 15–25 repetitions, no weights. Rest 30 seconds.
Set 3: 15–25 repetitions, no weights. Rest 30 seconds.

ABDOMINALS (CONT)

CEILING LIFT

START

FINISH

KNEE-RAISED CRUNCH

START

FINISH

CALVES ROUTINE

SEATED STRAIGHT-TOE RAISE

START   FINISH

SEATED ANGLED-OUT-TOE RAISE

START   FINISH

STANDING STRAIGHT-TOE RAISE

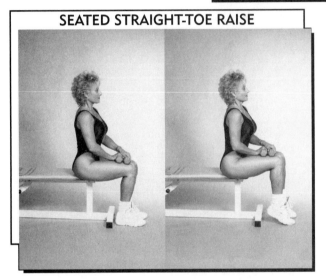

START   FINISH

STANDING ANGLED-IN-TOE RAISE

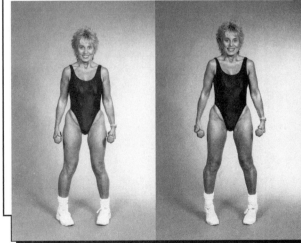

START   FINISH

SETS, REPETITIONS, WEIGHTS, AND RESTS
Set 1: 12 repetitions, 3-pound dumbbells. Rest 30 seconds.
Set 2: 10 repetitions, 5-pound dumbbells. Rest 30 seconds.
Set 3: 8 repetitions, 10-pound dumbbells. Rest 30 seconds.

6

SCULPTING AND DEFINING THE MUSCLES

WORKOUT LEVEL 3

Now that you've learned the moves and have established a muscle base, it's time to sculpt and define your muscles. You'll be using a method called "supersetting within body parts," a technique that enables you to get rid of that last bit of body fat that may be lingering on your body.

The Advantages of This Workout Over the Other Workouts

This workout will yield you more definition than any other workout in this book. When you have definition, you can see the clear delineation and separation of your muscles. You'll also burn more fat as you work out than you did in workout levels 1 or 2 because you'll be taking fewer rests. In addition, once you get used to the workout, it takes less time than either workout levels 1 or 2 because of the limited rest periods.

Now don't get wild and think, "Then why did I waste my time with workout levels 1 and 2?" Workout level 1 is mandatory for learning the moves, and workout level 2 is invaluable for building a muscle base.

Skipping Workout Levels 1 and 2 and Beginning Here

Can you do this workout without having done workout levels 1 and 2? Yes. As mentioned in Chapter 1, if you are a seasoned exerciser and know what you're doing, and want a new routine, of course you can go directly to this workout. But what will happen to those who are completely new to working with weights if they begin right here?

If you skip workout levels 1 and 2—and go straight to this workout: 1) You may have a little more difficulty learning the workout, because you will have to learn the exercises, how to pyramid the weights, and in addition, a slightly more complicated way of doing them at the same time. 2) You will not have established the muscle base that workout level 2 would have given you—so that now you will form some muscle mass and you will achieve some shaping and definition of those muscles, but perhaps you will not have formed as much of a muscle base as you need. If this is so, you can always go back to workout level 2 later, and build the base.

If you choose to begin here, you may want to refer back to the full-size exercise photographs in Chapter 4 (workout level 1) and the detailed instructions on how to perform the exercises. The exercises in this chapter are in the same order as the exercises in Chapters 4 and 5 so it will be easy to find them. In addition, you will want to review Chapter 5 (workout level 2) to make sure you understand how to pyramid the weights and to use the proper repetitions for abdominals and hips/buttocks exercises that do not use weights. This chapter assumes that you know how to do that.

How Much Time Is Involved?

Because you will be taking fewer and shorter rests, once you become accustomed to the routine, your workout will only take you fifteen minutes a day! You'll be working out four to six days a week. See pp. 61–62 for a review of how to set up your workout schedule. Keep in mind that when you are learning the routine, the workout will take longer.

The Purpose of This Workout:
To Sculpt and Define the Muscles and to Burn More Fat

The job of this workout is to shape and define your muscles into a more perfect form—and to help you burn off the excess fat on your body. In order to do that, you will take fewer rests than you took in workout levels 1 or 2, and in addition, those rests periods will be shorter. In other words, this workout is almost aerobic, while at the same time muscle-sculpting.

How can this be? An aerobic activity requires that you keep your heart rate up to between 60 and 80 percent of its capacity for twenty minutes or more. This workout does exactly that. However, you are allowed a fifteen-second rest after doing two sets of exercise—so technically speaking it's not officially aerobic. However, after you get used to the exercise, you can opt to forgo most of your rests, taking one only when you feel it is absolutely necessary. If you do this, your workout will be completely aerobic. Yet you will only be exercising fifteen minutes—not the minimum twenty minutes required by the official aerobic definition.

These days, many experts agree that even if you exercise only twelve minutes or more, and keep your heart rate up to 60 to 80 percent of its capacity, the workout can be considered aerobic.

But let's not split hairs about aerobics. No matter what you officially call this workout, you will burn more fat with this routine than with the other workouts presented thus far, and your heart rate, if monitored at any time during the workout, even after a fifteen-second rest, would most likely be at at least 60 percent of its capacity.

Adding to Your Knowledge of Working Out

This workout requires that you remember a little more than you had to remember when doing workout levels 1 or 2. In workout level 1, "Learning the Moves," you were introduced to the basics—the moves and the order of the exercises. In workout level 2, "Establishing a Muscle Base," you learned to use the pyramid system. In workout level 3, "Sculpting and Defining the Muscles," you will continue to use everything you learned in workout levels 1 and 2—only now you will add to what you have learned. You will learn to use the superset within body parts.

The Superset Within Body Parts

In this workout, you'll be using the technique called the "superset within body parts." You'll be using the same exercises you used in both workout levels 1 and 2, only you'll be doing something different with those exercises. For example, the first body part you will exercise is the chest. You'll be doing the following exercises for the chest: flat press, incline press, incline flye, and cross-bench pullover.

In workout levels 1 and 2 you did one set of repetitions for your first exercise, the flat press. Then you rested a certain amount of time and did another set for that same exercise. You rested again, and did your third and final set for that exercise. You then moved on to the next chest exercise, the incline press. You then went along the same way, doing a set, resting, doing another set, resting, doing your third set, resting, and moving to the third and then the fourth exercises for that body part—and continuing in the same manner until you finished exercising the body parts for that day, in this case, workout day one, the upper body, which includes chest, shoulders, biceps, triceps, and back. You did the same thing for workout day two, the lower body, which includes thighs, hips/buttocks, abdominals, and calves.

Now you will do something different. You will combine your first and second, and then your third and fourth exercises. In other words, instead of doing regular sets, where you get to rest after doing a set for one exercise for a given body part, you'll be doing supersets where you don't get to rest until you've done a set for two exercises of that body part. It's easy. Let's take a look using the chest as an example. The chest routine is:

1. flat press	Superset 1 with 2
2. incline press	
3. incline flye	Superset 3 with 4
4. cross-bench pullover	

Supersets, Repetitions, Weights, and Rests

You will do your first set of the flat press, then, without resting, do your first set of the incline press. (I realize it will take a few seconds to put the bench up to an incline. Don't worry—but move it.) Now you take your first fifteen-second rest. Then, you pick up your next heavy weight and do your second set of the flat press and the incline press—and then take another fifteen-second rest. Finally, you pick up your heaviest weight and do your last set of the flat press and the incline press without resting between the two exercises. Now you take a fifteen-second rest and begin your next superset combination within body parts (in this case you are supersetting within the body part chest), the incline flye and the cross-bench pullover.

You do your first set of the incline flye, and without resting, you do your first set of the cross-bench pullover. Now you rest fifteen seconds. Then you do your second set of the incline flye and the cross-bench pullover—and take another fifteen-second rest. Finally, you do your third and last set of the incline flye and the cross-bench pullover without resting between the two exercises, and then take a fifteen-second rest before starting to superset the first two exercises of the next body part, the shoulders (the side lateral raise and the front lateral raise).

You'll proceed in that manner for all five body parts for the day, combining your first two and your second two exercises for chest, shoulders, biceps, triceps, and back, until you have finished your workout for the day (in this case, workout day one: upper body). Then, on workout day two (lower body) you will do the same thing. You'll combine your first two exercises for your thighs—the squat and the side leg lift—and your second two exercises for that body part, the leg curl and the lunge. You'll do the same for your other three body parts for workout day two: hips/buttocks, abdominals, and calves.

What is the end result? Once you get the hang of it, you'll be breezing through your workout in record time—in about fifteen minutes! But in the beginning, it will take longer—thirty minutes or more—because you'll be getting familiar with the new system.

Note: To make your workout faster, you can switch the cross-bench pullover with the incline press. Then you won't have to keep moving the bench up and down!

All This and, of Course, the Pyramid System Too

You already know what the pyramid system is. (Technically the modified pyramid system, but we'll call it the pyramid system. See pp. 163–164 for an explanation as to why.)

Now let's see exactly how your workout will look when you use the pyramid system. You already used this system if you did workout level 2. (If not, see "pyramid system" in the A–Z Quick-Start Dictionary.)

EXERCISES 1 AND 2 OF THE CHEST ROUTINE:
FLAT PRESS AND INCLINE PRESS

SET 1: 12 repetitions, 3-pound dumbbells: no rest between flat press and incline press. Then rest 15 seconds.

SET 2: 10 repetitions, 5-pound dumbbells: no rest between flat press and incline press. Then rest 15 seconds.

SET 3: 8 repetitions, 10-pound dumbbells: no rest between flat press and incline press. Then rest 15 seconds.

Note: Don't worry that you will be wasting a few seconds to raise and lower the bench from flat to incline, and back to flat. In time, you'll do this very quickly, but as mentioned on pp. 178, you can switch exercises if this annoys you.

EXERCISES 3 AND 4 OF THE CHEST ROUTINE:
INCLINE FLYE AND CROSS-BENCH PULLOVER

SET 1: 12 repetitions, 3-pound dumbbells: no rest between incline flye and cross-bench pullover. Then rest 15 seconds.

SET 2: 10 repetitions, 5-pound dumbbells: no rest between incline flye and cross-bench pullover. Then rest 15 seconds.

SET 3: 8 repetitions, 10-pound dumbbells: no rest between incline flye and cross-bench pullover. Then rest 15 seconds.

Now move through the next body part—the shoulders—then through the next body part, the biceps, and then the triceps, and finally the back, supersetting the first and second and the third and fourth exercises of each body part until your workout day one is completed. You will do exactly the same thing for workout day two—supersetting your first and second, then third and fourth exercises for each body part: thighs, hips/buttocks, abdominals, and calves. When exercising hips/buttocks and abdominals, since weights are not used, you will do fifteen to twenty-five repetitions per set. For the standing butt squeeze, you will simply hold a three-pound dumbbell and do fifteen to twenty-five repetitions for all three sets.

Workout Days and Exercises Used in This Workout

Although what you work out on each day, and the exercises you will do on these days, are the same as in workout levels 1 and 2, it is important to review them here with the new method—supersetting—in mind. Here they are:

▶ **Workout Day 1**

UPPER BODY
Chest
Shoulders
Biceps
Triceps
Back

▶ **Workout Day 2**

LOWER BODY
Thighs
Hips/Buttocks
Abdominals
Calves

Here are the specific exercises you will do on each workout day:

DAY 1 WORKOUT

CHEST
1. flat press
   Superset 1 with 2
2. incline press
3. incline flye
   Superset 3 with 4
4. cross-bench pullover

SHOULDERS
1. side lateral raise
   Superset 1 with 2
2. front lateral raise
3. alternate shoulder press
   Superset 3 with 4
4. bent lateral raise

BICEPS
1. alternate curl
   Superset 1 with 2
2. simultaneous curl
3. alternate hammer curl
   Superset 3 with 4
4. concentration curl

TRICEPS
1. overhead press
   Superset 1 with 2
2. kickback
3. one-arm overhead
   extension
   Superset 3 with 4
4. cross-face extension

BACK
1. upright row
   Superset 1 with 2
2. one-arm dumbbell row
3. double-arm reverse row
   Superset 3 with 4
4. seated back lateral

DAY 2 WORKOUT

THIGHS
1. squat
   Superset 1 with 2
2. side leg lift
3. leg curl
   Superset 3 with 4
4. lunge

HIPS/BUTTOCKS
1. standing butt squeeze
   Superset 1 with 2
2. standing back-leg
   extension
3. straight-leg kick-up
   Superset 3 with 4
4. bent-knee kick-up

ABDOMINALS
1. concentrated butt lift
   Superset 1 with 2
2. crunch
3. ceiling lift
   Superset 3 with 4
4. knee-raised crunch

CALVES
1. seated straight-toe raise
   Superset 1 with 2
2. seated angled-out-
   toe raise
3. standing straight-
   toe raise
   Superset 3 with 4
4. standing angled-in-
   toe raise

Note: You may want to switch the incline press with the cross-bench pullover so you don't have to keep moving the bench.

Changing the Order of the Exercises to Create Different Supersets Within a Given Body Part: Very Important!

After a few weeks, when you have become familiar with the routine, you may decide that you'd like to change the order of the particular supersets within a body part. For example, you may decide that you don't like moving the bench up and down for the flat press and the incline press, and would rather do the incline press and the incline flye as a superset, and the flat press and the cross-bench pullover as a superset. Fine. You may do this.

Why didn't I make it more convenient for you and write the workout that way in the first place? There is a method to my madness. In the beginning, I wanted you to "waste" a few seconds changing the bench—so that you would get to steal a little extra rest and not become discouraged with the workout.

Equipment Needed

You will need three sets of dumbbells: three-, five-, and ten-pounders. As mentioned before, when I give the weight for dumbbells, I mean for each dumbbell.

You will also need a bench or step, preferably one that can be raised to an incline. If you're using a step, make sure that it can be raised eight to ten inches off the floor. See exercise photos in *Definition* for use of a step in place of a bench. If you can't or won't get an incline bench or step, you'll have to repeat the flat exercise—the press, and do the flye flat instead of on an incline. You'll still get a great deal out of the workout.

Getting More out of the Workout by Increasing the Intensity

Later, as you go along, you may want to increase the intensity of the workout, and as a result burn more fat and get finer muscle quality. You can do this in three ways: 1) Shorten or eliminate most of the rests (you burn more fat and get more definition). 2) Use heavier weights as you get stronger—but be sure you can still do your supersets without resting (you add to your muscle base). 3) Flex harder and use some dynamic tension on the stretch part of the muscle (you get harder, more dense muscles). This workout is already somewhat intense because you've eliminated half of the rests by supersetting.

Stretching

The first set of each exercise provides a natural stretch because you are using relatively light weights, three-pound dumbbells. However, you may choose to do your own set of stretches before working out, or, you can simply do a few repetitions of each exercise without weights before you start your workout.

Breaking In Gently if You've Used Workout Levels 1 and 2 for at Least Six Weeks Total

WEEK ONE: First and second sets of each exercise, using three- and five-pound dumbbells.

WEEK TWO: Full workout: first, second, and third sets of each exercise.

If you've used any of my previous exercise books for ten weeks or more, you can try to skip the break-in period.

Breaking In Gently if You Are Starting Here and Did Not Do Workout Levels 1 or 2, or Have Worked with Weights Before

First let me say, if you are very weak and are also not in aerobic shape (you've never done any aerobics), you should go back to workout level 1 and do that for three weeks before you start this break-in gently plan. If you are in aerobic shape, however, even though you've never lifted a weight before, you can test yourself and see if you can cope with this break-in plan. You may surprise yourself and see that in fact you can do it.

WEEK ONE: First set of each exercise using three-pound dumbbells.

WEEK TWO: First and second sets of each exercise using three- and five-pound dumbbells.

WEEK THREE: You are on the full program. First, second, and third sets of each exercise, using three-, five-, and ten-pound dumbbells.

Ready, Set, Go

You've read Chapters 1 through 3. You've carefully read the A–Z Quick-Start Dictionary. You've reviewed Chapter 4 if need be to view the exercise photographs in full size, and to go over the detailed exercise instructions. You've reviewed Chapter 5 if need be (workout level 2) for the pyramid system, and you've gathered your three sets of dumbbells and set up a place to work out with your bench or step.

This workout is the same as workout level 2 in that you continue to pyramid your weights. It is different in that:

Difference: In workout levels 1 and 2 you did not combine exercises. You did what is called "regular" sets. Now you will combine exercises. This is called the "superset." You will superset your first and second, and third and fourth exercises. By way of review, here is what you will do for your entire workout.

Supersets, Repetitions, Weights, and Rests

SET 1: 12 repetitions first exercise and 12 repetitions second exercise, 3-pound dumbbells. Rest 15 seconds.

SET 2: 10 repetitions first exercise and 10 repetitions second exercise, 5-pound dumbbells. Rest 15 seconds.

SET 3: 8 repetitions first exercise and 8 repetitions second exercise, 10-pound dumbbells. Rest 15 seconds.

Now move to your third and fourth exercises for that body part.

SET 1: 12 repetitions third exercise and 12 repetitions fourth exercise, 3-pound dumbbells. Rest 15 seconds.

SET 2: 10 repetitions third exercise and 10 repetitions fourth exercise, 5-pound dumbbells. Rest 15 seconds.

SET 3: 8 repetitions third exercise and 8 repetitions fourth exercise, 10-pound dumbbells. Rest 15 seconds.

Do this for your entire workout, except hips/buttocks exercises.

Supersets, Repetitions, Weights, and Rests for Abdominals and Hips/Buttocks Exercises

SET 1:   15–25 repetitions first exercise, and 15–25 repetitions second exercise, no weights. Rest 15 seconds.

SET 2:   15–25 repetitions first exercise, and 15–25 repetitions second exercise, no weights. Rest 15 seconds.

SET 3:   15–25 repetitions first exercise, and 15–25 repetitions second exercise, no weights. Rest 15 seconds.

Now move to your third and fourth exercises for that body part.

SET 1:   15–25 repetitions third exercise, and 15–25 repetitions fourth exercise, no weights. Rest 15 seconds.

SET 2:   15–25 repetitions third exercise, and 15–25 repetitions fourth exercise, no weights. Rest 15 seconds.

SET 3:   15–25 repetitions third exercise, and 15–25 repetitions fourth exercise, no weights. Rest 15 seconds.

Remember: The photographs in this chapter have been reduced in size. If you want the full-size photos (and the detailed exercise instructions) refer back to Chapter 4. Also realize that this entire workout is found on pp. 263–287—in the form of a tear-out wall poster.

WORKOUT LEVEL 3
CHEST SUPERSETS

FLAT PRESS   AND

START

FINISH

INCLINE PRESS

START

FINISH

INCLINE FLYE   AND

START

FINISH

CROSS-BENCH PULLOVER

START

FINISH

SHOULDERS SUPERSETS

SIDE LATERAL RAISE   AND

START   FINISH

FRONT LATERAL RAISE

START   FINISH

SUPERSETS, REPETITIONS, WEIGHTS, AND RESTS
Set 1: 12 repetitions first exercise and 12 repetitions second exercise, 3-pound dumbbells. Rest 15 seconds.
Set 2: 10 repetitions first exercise and 10 repetitions second exercise, 5-pound dumbbells. Rest 15 seconds.
Set 3: 8 repetitions first exercise and 8 repetitions second exercise, 10-pound dumbbells. Rest 15 seconds.
Now move to your third and fourth exercises for that body part.
Set 1: 12 repetitions third exercise and 12 repetitions fourth exercise, 3-pound dumbbells. Rest 15 seconds.
Set 2: 10 repetitions third exercise and 10 repetitions fourth exercise, 5-pound dumbbells. Rest 15 seconds.
Set 3: 8 repetitions third exercise and 8 repetitions fourth exercise, 10-pound dumbbells. Rest 15 seconds.

SHOULDERS SUPERSETS

ALTERNATE SHOULDER PRESS
AND
BENT LATERAL RAISE

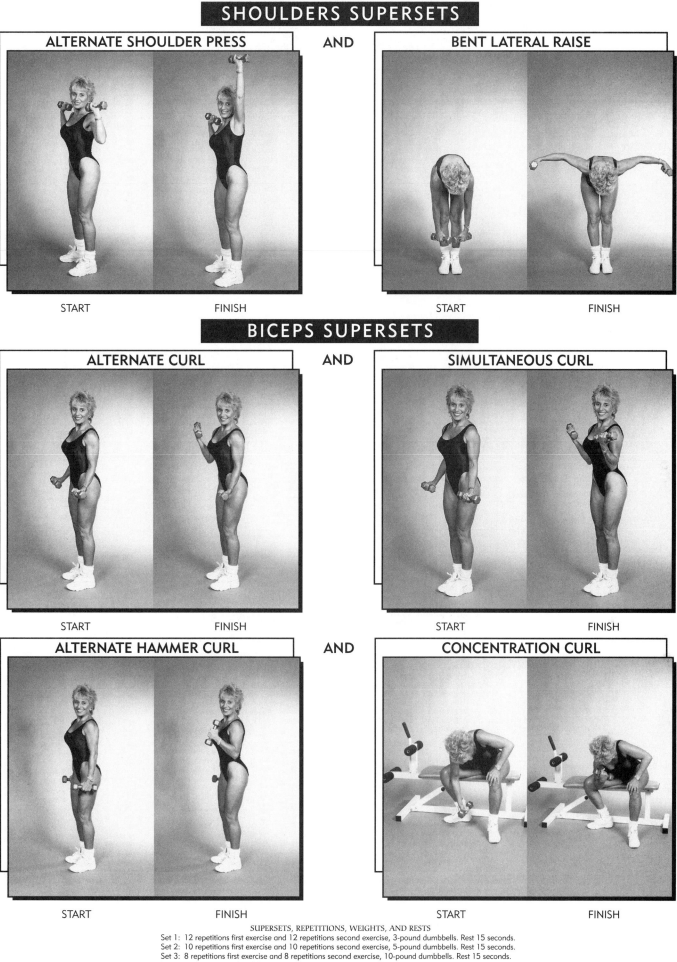

START   FINISH   START   FINISH

BICEPS SUPERSETS

ALTERNATE CURL
AND
SIMULTANEOUS CURL

START   FINISH   START   FINISH

ALTERNATE HAMMER CURL
AND
CONCENTRATION CURL

START   FINISH   START   FINISH

SUPERSETS, REPETITIONS, WEIGHTS, AND RESTS
Set 1: 12 repetitions first exercise and 12 repetitions second svercise, 3-pound dumbbells. Rest 15 seconds.
Set 2: 10 repetitions first exercise and 10 repetitions second exercise, 5-pound dumbbells. Rest 15 seconds.
Set 3: 8 repetitions first exercise and 8 repetitions second exercise, 10-pound dumbbells. Rest 15 seconds.
Now move to your third and fourth exercises for that body part.
Set 1: 12 repetitions third exercise and 12 repetitions fourth exercise, 3-pound dumbbells. Rest 15 seconds.
Set 2: 10 repetitions third exercise and 10 repetitions fourth exercise, 5-pound dumbbells. Rest 15 seconds.
Set 3: 8 repetitions third exercise and 8 repetitions fourth exercise, 10-pound dumbbells. Rest 15 seconds.

TRICEPS SUPERSETS

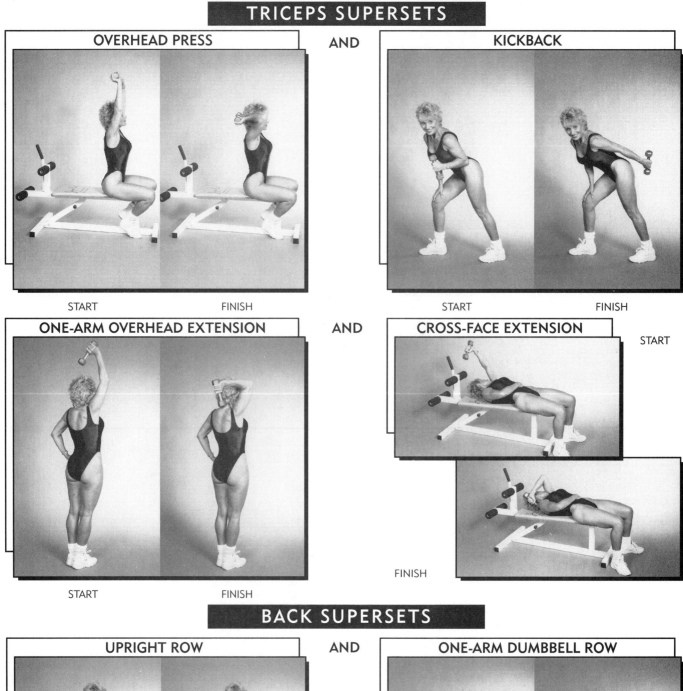

OVERHEAD PRESS   AND   KICKBACK

START   FINISH   START   FINISH

ONE-ARM OVERHEAD EXTENSION   AND   CROSS-FACE EXTENSION

START

START   FINISH

FINISH

BACK SUPERSETS

UPRIGHT ROW   AND   ONE-ARM DUMBBELL ROW

START   FINISH   START   FINISH

SUPERSETS, REPETITIONS, WEIGHTS, AND RESTS
Set 1: 12 repetitions first exercise and 12 repetitions second exercise, 3-pound dumbbells. Rest 15 seconds.
Set 2: 10 repetitions first exercise and 10 repetitions second exercise, 5-pound dumbbells. Rest 15 seconds.
Set 3: 8 repetitions first exercise and 8 repetitions second exercise, 10-pound dumbbells. Rest 15 seconds.
Now move to your third and fourth exercises for that body part.
Set 1: 12 repetitions third exercise and 12 repetitions fourth exercise, 3-pound dumbbells. Rest 15 seconds.
Set 2: 10 repetitions third exercise and 10 repetitions fourth exercise, 5-pound dumbbells. Rest 15 seconds.
Set 3: 8 repetitions third exercise and 8 repetitions fourth exercise, 10-pound dumbbells. Rest 15 seconds.

BACK SUPERSETS

DOUBLE-ARM REVERSE ROW

START FINISH

AND

SEATED BACK LATERAL

START FINISH

THIGHS SUPERSET

SQUAT

START FINISH

AND

SIDE LEG LIFT

START

FINISH

LEG CURL

START AND

FINISH

LUNGE

START FINISH

SUPERSETS, REPETITIONS, WEIGHTS, AND RESTS
Set 1: 12 repetitions first exercise and 12 repetitions second exercise, 3-pound dumbbells. Rest 15 seconds.
Set 2: 10 repetitions first exercise and 10 repetitions second exercise, 5-pound dumbbells. Rest 15 seconds.
Set 3: 8 repetitions first exercise and 8 repetitions second exercise, 10-pound dumbbells. Rest 15 seconds.
Now move to your third and fourth exercises for that body part.
Set 1: 12 repetitions third exercise and 12 repetitions fourth exercise, 3-pound dumbbells. Rest 15 seconds.
Set 2: 10 repetitions third exercise and 10 repetitions fourth exercise, 5-pound dumbbells. Rest 15 seconds.
Set 3: 8 repetitions third exercise and 8 repetitions fourth exercise, 10-pound dumbbells. Rest 15 seconds.

HIP/BUTTOCKS SUPERSETS

STANDING BUTT SQUEEZE
AND
STANDING BACK-LEG EXTENSION

START   FINISH   START   FINISH

STRAIGHT LEG KICK-UP
START
AND
BENT-KNEE KICK-UP
START

FINISH   FINISH

ABDOMINALS SUPERSETS

CONCENTRATED BUTT LIFT
START
AND
CRUNCH
START

FINISH   FINISH

SUPERSETS, REPETITIONS, AND RESTS
Set 1: 15–25 repetitions first exercise and 15–25 repetitions second exercise, no weights. Rest 15 seconds.
Set 2: 15–25 repetitions first exercise and 15–25 repetitions second exercise, no weights. Rest 15 seconds.
Set 3: 15–25 repetitions first exercise and 15–25 repetitions second exercise, no weights. Rest 15 seconds.
Now move to your third and fourth exercises for that body part.
Set 1: 15–25 repetitions third exercise and 15–25 repetitions fourth exercise, no weights. Rest 15 seconds.
Set 2: 15–25 repetitions third exercise and 15–25 repetitions fourth exercise, no weights. Rest 15 seconds.
Set 3: 15–25 repetitions third exercise and 15–25 repetitions fourth exercise, no weights. Rest 15 seconds.

ABDOMINALS SUPERSETS (CONT)

CEILING LIFT

AND

START

FINISH

KNEE-RAISED CRUNCH

START

FINISH

CALVES SUPERSETS

SEATED STRAIGHT-TOE RAISE

AND

SEATED ANGLED-OUT-TOE RAISE

START FINISH

START FINISH

STANDING STRAIGHT-TOE RAISE

AND

STANDING ANGLED-IN-TOE RAISE

START FINISH

START FINISH

SUPERSETS, REPETITIONS, AND RESTS
Set 1: 12 repetitions first exercise and 12 repetitions second exercise, 3-pound dumbbells. Rest 15 seconds.
Set 2: 10 repetitions first exercise and 10 repetitions second exercise, 5-pound dumbbells. Rest 15 seconds.
Set 3: 8 repetitions first exercise and 8 repetitions second exercise, 10-pound dumbbells. Rest 15 seconds.
Now move to your third and fourth exercises for that body part.
Set 1: 12 repetitions third exercise and 12 repetitions fourth exercise, 3-pound dumbbells. Rest 15 seconds.
Set 2: 10 repetitions third exercise and 10 repetitions fourth exercise, 5-pound dumbbells. Rest 15 seconds.
Set 3: 8 repetitions third exercise and 8 repetitions fourth exercise, 10-pound dumbbells. Rest 15 seconds.

7

THE FINISHING TOUCH
WORKOUT LEVEL 4

Y*ou've* learned the moves, you've established a muscle base, and you've sculpted and defined your muscles. What more can you do? Plenty! Now you can add the finishing touches. This workout allows you to do two things at once: to create and solidify muscle mass—and at the same time, burn maximum fat and gain added definition.

The Advantages of This Workout Over the Other Workouts

The wonderful thing about this system is, it kills two birds with one stone: 1) It allows you to build valuable muscle mass—not quite as much as is possible with workout level 2, but more than with workout levels 1 or 3, and at the same time, 2) causes you to burn as much fat—or more than you can burn by doing any other workout in this book. Here's why.

In this system, you are supersetting *between* body parts. The details of this method will be explained later in this chapter. For now, suffice it to say that you never have to take rests, because while one body part is working, the other body part is resting—and so forth. Once you get to know the routine, you rarely, if ever, have to actually stop moving. By continually switching back and forth between two complementary body parts, you burn maximum fat—but you don't exhaust your muscles. Because you don't overtire your working muscle, you can use heavier weights than you can use in workout level 3, and in turn, as mentioned above, you can build more muscle mass.

The reason you can't build quite as much muscle mass as in workout level 2 is due to the fact that you will not be resting more than fifteen seconds between sets—and may not even rest at all. In order to be able to build considerable muscle mass, you would have to eventually handle heavier weights than this workout would allow, and you would have to rest at least thirty seconds between sets.

Skipping Levels 1, 2, and 3 and Beginning Here

"Then why can't I simply skip workout levels 1 to 3 and start here?" you might ask. Well, actually you could, but this is the most complicated of all the workouts—well, not complicated, but involved. You have to know more and do more than you did in any of the previous workouts in this book: 1) You must know the moves introduced in workout level 1. 2) You must understand how to pyramid the weights, as introduced in workout level 2. 3) You must know how to superset the weights—as introduced in workout level 3, only now you learn to superset in a different way.

True—you could learn it all at once, right here. And in fact, a similar workout is found in my book *Bottoms Up!*, and many women who never worked out with weights before started with that workout. But many women wrote to me asking me to write a book that would take them to that workout in simple steps. This is that book. If you take advantage of it, and follow it chapter by chapter, going from workout level 1 to 2 and then to 3, and finally to 4—you really "get it." You build a solid understanding step by step, and it stays in your mind forever.

However, if you are game to learn it all at once, try it and see if you can. If you've had *no previous weight-training experience* and/or are *not in aerobic shape*, you may say to yourself, "What was I thinking? Thank God I have this easy route all charted out for me. I'm going to start at level 1 and work my way up."

For those of you who have used any of my previous workout books, and believe that you are up to it, feel free to start here. However, you may want to refer back to workout level 1 (Chapter 4) for the full-size exercise photographs and the detailed instructions. Keep in mind, however, that the exercises are in a different order here. You will have to thumb through the chapter to find them.

How Much Time Is Involved?

Because you will be taking fewer and shorter rests, once you become accustomed to the routine, your workout will only take you fifteen minutes a day—even less on upper body day. You'll be working out four to six days a week. See pp. 61–62 for a review of how to set up your workout schedule.

The Purpose of This Workout: To Build Muscle Density, Sculpt and Define the Muscle, and Burn Maximum Fat

This workout allows you to build a muscle base, and at the same time burn maximum fat. It is more aerobic than any other workout found in this book—even workout level 3. Why?

Because you will be supersetting between different body parts, your working muscle will not become so exhausted that it will need a mandatory rest. The only time you'll have to take a rest will be when *you* are tired! Your muscles usually won't force you to rest. If you did workout level 3, you will remember that you supersetted two exercises for the same body part. Your muscle needed a rest more often than with this workout, because it was being bombarded straight on with two sets (one each of two different exercises) for the *same* body part.

For example, in workout level 3 you did one set of your first chest exercise, the flat press, and without resting, one set of the next chest exercise, the incline press. In this workout, you'll do one set of your first chest exercise, the flat press, and instead of doing another chest exercise, you'll do one set of your first triceps exercise, the overhead press. You give your chest muscles a rest while you work your triceps, so you are able to go right back and work your chest without resting. You won't feel as desperate for that fifteen-second rest as you may have felt when supersetting within the body part as in workout level 3.

As you perform the exercises in this routine, your heart rate will go up to between 60 and 70 percent of its capacity—and remain there for the entire workout. This makes the workout qualify as aerobic, but what's more, it enables you to burn maximum fat. (See the A–Z Quick-Start Dictionary for the definition of aerobic.)

Adding to Your Knowledge of Working Out

This workout requires that you learn a little more than you had to learn in order to do workout levels 1 to 3. In workout level 1, "Learning the Moves," you were introduced to the basics: the moves and the order of the exercises. In workout level 2, "Establishing a Muscle Base," you learned to use the pyramid system and to graduate your weights. In workout level 3, "Sculpting and Defining the Muscles" you learned how to superset within the same body part. Now you will add to that knowledge. You will take the principle of the superset and expand it to switching back and forth from one body part to a different, complementary body part. This method is called "supersetting between body parts," or doing a "twin set." (Another word for twin set is "interset.")

The Twin Set: Supersetting Between Body Parts

In this workout, you'll be using a technique called the "twin set," better known among bodybuilders as "supersetting between body parts." I've invented the name "twin set" because I wanted to create a different term for those who may get a headache when thinking about supersetting and having to say "superset within, superset between, superset among, superset without, I'm so confused." So I invented the term "twin set" to distinguish it from superset.

When you are doing a twin set you are doing exercises for two different body parts at the same time without taking a rest. When you are doing a superset, you are doing two exercises for the same body part without taking a rest. In this chapter, from now on I'll refer to your supersets between body parts as twin sets.

In this workout, lucky for you, you won't have to stretch your brain and have to learn new exercises. You'll be using the same exercises used in all the workouts that came before this—levels 1 to 3, only now you'll be combining those exercises in a different way. Let's get into the details.

In workout levels 1 to 3, you exercised the chest first. You did four exercises for that body part, and then moved to the next body part, the shoulders. You did four exercises for that body part and moved to the next body part, the biceps. You finished the biceps and then you did the triceps. Finally, you did your last body part for workout day one, the back. The next time you worked out (workout day two), you did the lower body, which included the thighs, hips/buttocks, abdominals, and calves.

The thing that is the same about this workout, well, almost the same, is you will exercise the same body parts that you worked in all the other workouts in this book on each workout day—except you will do the back on workout day two instead of workout day one. The thing that is different is, you will be exercising in unlike combinations. You will work everything in twin sets, complementary body part combinations.

Your first twin set is the chest and triceps. You will do your first set of your first chest exercise, the flat press, and then without resting, you will do your first set of your first triceps exercise, the overhead press. Then you will take an optional fifteen-second rest and perform your second set of that combination. Again, you will take an optional fifteen-second rest and move to your next twin set combination for these two body parts—the incline press and the kickback.

You will continue to work in twin sets combining the other two exercises for those body parts: the incline flye for the chest with the one-arm overhead extension for the triceps, and the cross-bench pullover for the chest with the cross-face extension for the triceps.

Let's take a look at this in chart form.

CHEST	AND	TRICEPS	TWIN SET
1. flat press		overhead press	(Twin set 1)
2. incline press		kickback	(Twin set 2)
3. incline flye		one-arm overhead extension	(Twin set 3)
4. cross-bench pullover		cross-face extension	(Twin set 4)

You will be pairing the following body parts:

▶ **Workout Day 1**

UPPER BODY
Chest-Triceps
Shoulders-Biceps

▶ **Workout Day 2**

LOWER BODY
Abdominals-Hips/Buttocks
Thighs-Back
Calves (superset as in level 3)

The beauty of this system is, your workout seems to go so quickly. It feels as if you only worked one body part—but in the meantime you've worked two. For example, on workout day one, after you do your chest-triceps routine, it will feel as if you only did four exercises. But you actually did eight. The same will hold true when you do your shoulders-biceps routine. It will seem as if you've only done four exercises, when in fact you will have done eight, and will have conquered two more body parts. You won't believe that you've actually finished your entire upper body workout. You'll think, "It can't be true." But it will be. That's the beauty of this workout.

Sets, Repetitions, Weights, and Rests

Let's use the first twin set combination, the chest and triceps, as an example. As in all other routines, there are four exercises for each body part.

1. FLAT PRESS (CHEST) AND OVERHEAD PRESS (TRICEPS)

You will do your first set of twelve repetitions of your chest exercise, the flat press, and without resting, your first set of twelve repetitions of your triceps exercise, the overhead press. Now you will take an optional fifteen-second rest.

Then you will pick up your next heavy weight and do your second set of ten repetitions of the flat press and ten repetitions of the overhead press. Now you will take an optional fifteen-second rest.

Then you will pick up your final weight and do your third set of eight repetitions of the flat press and eight repetitions of the overhead press. Now you will take an optional fifteen-second rest.

2. INCLINE PRESS (CHEST) AND KICKBACK (TRICEPS)

Then you will do your first set of the next twin set for the chest and triceps: the incline press and the kickback. You will do your first set of twelve repetitions of the incline press, and without resting, your first set of twelve repetitions of the kickback. Now you will take an optional fifteen-second rest.

Then you will pick up your next heavy weight and do your second set of ten repetitions for the incline press and the kickback. Now you will take an optional fifteen-second rest.

Then you will pick up your final weight and do your third set of eight repetitions of the incline press and eight repetitions of the kickback. Now you will take an optional fifteen-second rest.

3. INCLINE FLYE (CHEST) AND ONE-ARM OVERHEAD EXTENSION (TRICEPS)

Then you will do your first set of the next twin set for the chest and triceps: the incline flye and the one-arm overhead extension. You will do your first set of twelve repetitions of the incline flye, and without resting, your first set of twelve repetitions of the one-arm overhead extension. Now you will take an optional fifteen-second rest.

Then you will pick up your next heavy weight and do your second set of ten repetitions for the incline flye and the one-arm overhead extension. Now you will take an optional fifteen-second rest.

Then you will pick up your final weight and do your third set of eight repetitions of the incline flye and the one-arm overhead extension. Now you will take an optional fifteen-second rest.

4. CROSS-BENCH PULLOVER (CHEST) AND CROSS-FACE EXTENSION (TRICEPS)

Then you will do your first set of the last twin set for the chest and triceps: the cross-bench pullover and the cross-face extension. You will do your first set of twelve repetitions of the cross-bench pullover, and without resting, your first set of twelve repetitions of the cross-face extension. Now you will take an optional fifteen-second rest.

Then you will pick up your next heavy weight and do your second set of ten repetitions for the cross-bench pullover and the cross-face extension. Now you will take an optional fifteen-second rest.

Then you will pick up your final weight and do your third set of eight repetitions of the cross-bench pullover and the cross-face extension.

THE BEAT GOES ON!

Now you will take an optional 15-second rest and move to the first twin set of your next combination, the shoulders and biceps: the side lateral raise and the alternate curl—and so on. You'll proceed in this manner until you have completed all four exercises for shoulders and biceps. Then you will have completed your workout day one upper body workout. (As mentioned above, the back has now been moved to workout day two.)

For workout day two, as you can see in the chart above, you will exercise abdominals and hips/buttocks in twin sets, and then thighs and back in twin sets. But there is an "odd man out," the calves. You will do them at the end of your workout in supersets, exactly the same way you supersetted them in workout level 3.

The photographs will be arranged in the correct order.

All of This and, of Course, the Pyramid System

You already know how to pyramid your weights. If you've used workout levels 2 and/or 3, you've already used that system. If you need more information on the pyramid system, review the A–Z Quick-Start Dictionary and/or workout level 2, pp. 163–164. Here is an exact picture of how your workout will look as you twin-set and pyramid the weights.

EXERCISE 1 OF THE CHEST-TRICEPS ROUTINE:
FLAT PRESS AND OVERHEAD PRESS

SET 1: 12 repetitions, 3-pound dumbbells. No rest between flat press and overhead press. Then optional rest 15 seconds.

SET 2: 10 repetitions, 5-pound dumbbells. No rest between flat press and overhead press. Then optional rest 15 seconds.

SET 3: 8 repetitions, 10-pound dumbbells. No rest between flat press and overhead press. Then optional rest 15 seconds.

EXERCISE 2 OF THE CHEST-TRICEPS ROUTINE:
INCLINE PRESS AND KICKBACK

SET 1: 12 repetitions, 3-pound dumbbells. No rest between incline press and kickback. Then optional rest 15 seconds.

SET 2: 10 repetitions, 5-pound dumbbells. No rest between incline press and kickback. Then optional rest 15 seconds.

SET 3: 8 repetitions, 10-pound dumbbells. No rest between incline press and kickback. Then optional rest 15 seconds.

EXERCISE 3 OF THE CHEST-TRICEPS ROUTINE:
INCLINE FLYE AND ONE-ARM OVERHEAD EXTENSION

SET 1: 12 repetitions, 3-pound dumbbells. No rest between incline flye and one-arm overhead extension. Then optional rest 15 seconds.

SET 2: 10 repetitions, 5-pound dumbbells. No rest between incline flye and one-arm overhead extension. Then optional rest 15 seconds.

SET 3: 8 repetitions, 10-pound dumbbells. No rest between incline flye and one-arm overhead extension. Then optional rest 15 seconds.

EXERCISE 4 OF THE CHEST-TRICEPS ROUTINE:
CROSS-BENCH PULLOVER AND CROSS-FACE EXTENSION

SET 1: 12 repetitions, 3-pound dumbbells. No rest between cross-bench pullover and cross-face extension. Then optional rest 15 seconds.

SET 2: 10 repetitions, 5-pound dumbbells. No rest between cross-bench pullover and cross-face extension. Then optional rest 15 seconds.

SET 3: 8 repetitions, 10-pound dumbbells. No rest between cross-bench pullover and cross-face extension. Then optional rest 15 seconds.

Then move to the next twin set combination: shoulders and biceps, twin-setting the first shoulder exercise with the first biceps exercise, the second shoulder exercise with the second biceps exercise, and so on, until you have completed the shoulders-biceps routine. You will then have completed your day one upper body workout

You will do exactly the same thing for workout day two—twin-setting your abdominals and hips/buttocks and your thighs and back. Then, as mentioned above, you will superset your calves. At this point you will have completed your day two lower body workout routine. (Note: As you will recall, for abdominals and hips/buttocks you are not using weights, so there is no pyramiding to be done. You simply do fifteen to twenty-five repetitions per set.

Of course, as time goes by and you can handle more weight, you will increase your weight—5, 8, and 12; 8, 12, and 15; and so on.

Workout Days and Exercises Used in This Workout

The exercises are the same as those you used in workout levels 1 to 3, but the order is quite different. Here is the new order of exercises.

▶ Workout Day 1

UPPER BODY
Chest-Triceps
Shoulders-Biceps

▶ Workout Day 2

LOWER BODY
Abdominals-Hips/Buttocks
Thighs-Back
Calves (Superset)

DAY 1 WORKOUT

TWIN SETS FOR CHEST AND / **TRICEPS**

1. flat press	overhead press
2. incline press	kickback
3. incline flye	one-arm overhead extension
4. cross-bench pullover	cross-face extension

TWIN SETS FOR SHOULDERS AND / **BICEPS**

1. side lateral raise	alternate curl
2. front lateral raise	simultaneous curl
3. alternate shoulder press	alternate hammer curl
4. bent lateral	concentration curl

DAY 2 WORKOUT

TWIN SETS FOR ABDOMINALS AND / **HIPS/BUTTOCKS**

1. concentrated butt lift	standing butt squeeze
2. crunch	standing back-leg extension
3. ceiling lift	straight-leg kick-up
4. knee-raised crunch	bent-knee kick-up

TWIN SETS FOR THIGHS AND / **BACK**

1. squat	upright row
2. side leg lift	one-arm dumbbell row
3. leg curl	double-arm reverse row
4. lunge	seated back lateral

SUPERSET FOR CALVES

1. seated straight-toe raise	Superset 1 with 2
2. seated angled-out-toe raise	
3. standing straight-toe raise	Superset 3 with 4
4. standing angled-in-toe raise	

Changing the Order of Exercises to Create Different Complementary Supersets (Twin Sets) Between Body Parts

After a few months, when you have become familiar with the whole idea of twin-setting, you may decide you'd like to try to pair different body parts. For example, you may want to pair chest and shoulders, biceps and triceps, thighs and hips/buttocks, and back and calves, and superset abdominals the way I have paired them in *Bottoms Up!* Or, you may want to pair chest and biceps and shoulders and triceps, and so on, making up your own combinations. Feel free to experiment. Your body will tell you whether or not it is working for you. As mentioned above, I have carefully chosen these specific combinations to make your work the least taxing on your muscles—so that you will have to take the least amount of rests.

Equipment Needed

You will need three sets of dumbbells: three-, five-, and ten-pounders. As mentioned before, when I give the weight for dumbbells, I mean for each dumbbell.

You will also need a bench or step, preferably one that can be raised to an incline. If you're using a step, make sure it can be raised eight to ten inches off the floor. See exercise photos in *Definition* for demonstrations.

Getting More out of the Workout by Increasing the Intensity

Later, you may want to further increase the intensity of this workout, and as a result burn more fat and get finer muscle quality. You can do this in three ways: 1) Shorten or eliminate most of the rests (you burn more fat and get more definition). 2) Use heavier weights as you get stronger—but be sure you can still do your twin sets without resting between the two exercises. 3) Flex harder and use some dynamic tension on the stretch part of the muscles (you get harder muscles). This workout is already intensified to some extent because half of the rests are eliminated through the twin set. Later, as mentioned before, you can eliminate nearly all rests.

Stretching

The first set of each exercise provides a natural stretch because you are using relatively light weights, three-pound dumbbells. However, you may choose to do your own set of stretches before working out, or you can simply do a few repetitions of each exercise without weights before you start the workout.

Breaking In Gently if You Are Not in Aerobic Shape and Have Never Used Weights Before

This is difficult. Try to use the three-week break-in program below. If you find that it is simply too taxing and/or confusing, go back to workout level 1—break in gently with that program, do it a few weeks, and move through levels 2 and 3. Then come here and do this workout. If you give workouts 1 to 3 three weeks each you should have no problem with this workout.

Breaking In Gently if You're Starting Here and Did Not Do Workout Levels 1, 2, or 3, but Have Worked Out with Weights Before and Are in Aerobic Shape

WEEK 1: First set of each exercise for the body parts for that day, using three-pound dumbbells

WEEK 2: Second set of each exercise for the body parts for that day, using three- and five-pound dumbbells.

WEEK 3: You are on the full program. First, second, and third sets of each exercise for the body parts for that day, using three-, five-, and ten-pound dumbbells.

Breaking In Gently if You Have Done Workout Levels 1, 2, and 3 for a Total of at Least Nine Weeks, or Have Done Any of the Workouts Found in Any of My Books for Ten Weeks

You may do the entire workout immediately—or, if you choose, just to get used to the new arrangement of exercise, you may opt for the three-week break-in program above.

Ready, Set, Go

Okay. You've read Chapters 1 through 3. You've carefully read the A–Z Quick-Start Dictionary. If necessary, you've reviewed Chapters 4 through 6 (workout levels 1 to 3). You've gathered your dumbbells and have placed them near a bench or step.

As you do this workout, you will quickly notice that the exercise photographs are in a different order than they were in all the other workouts. This is due to the fact that you will be supersetting between body parts (twin-setting) as described above. If you wish to review the exercise instructions for any particular exercise, or if you need to see the full-size photographs, since they are not in the same order as in Chapter 4, it may be easier to look up that exercise by its name in the index rather than flip through Chapter 4 to find them.

This workout is the same as workout levels 2 and 3 in that you still pyramid your weights. It is the same as workout level 3 in that you still superset. Note that this workout is also duplicated in the tear-out wall poster on pp. 255–281.

Difference: In this workout, you superset between body parts—twin-setting—instead of supersetting the exercises within the same body part. As a review, here are your sets, repetitions, and weights for all exercises:

Since there is no partner for calves, they are supersetted as in workout level 3. You do seated straight-toe and seated angled-out-toe together, and standing straight-toe and standing angled-in-toe together. If you need a review, reread this chapter, specifically p. 199, where supersetted calves are discussed.

WORKOUT LEVEL 4

CHEST AND TRICEPS TWIN SETS

A   B

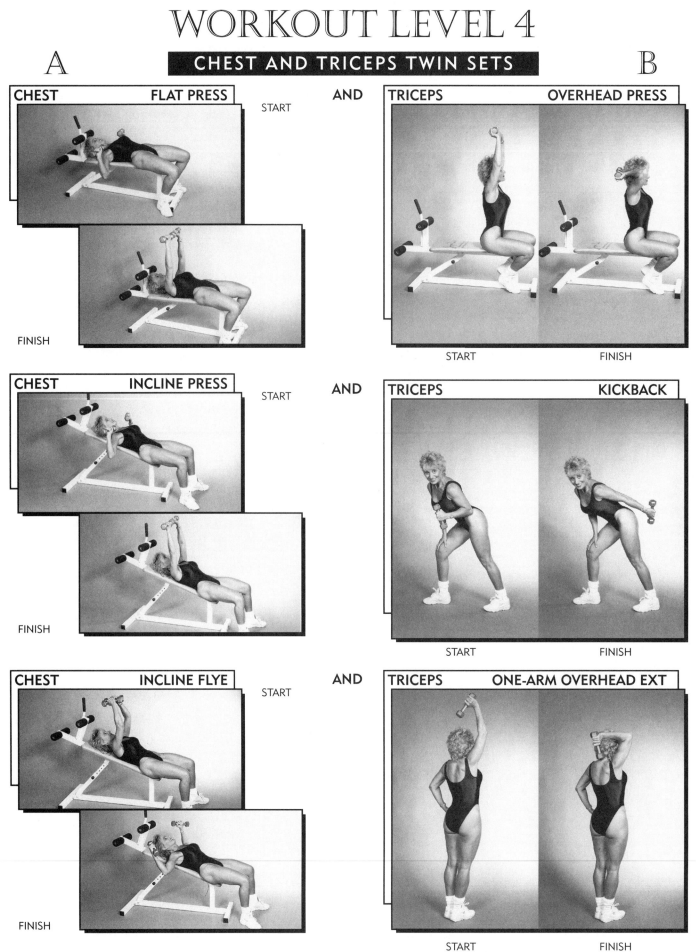

CHEST   **FLAT PRESS**   START

AND

TRICEPS   **OVERHEAD PRESS**

FINISH

START   FINISH

CHEST   **INCLINE PRESS**   START

AND

TRICEPS   **KICKBACK**

FINISH

START   FINISH

CHEST   **INCLINE FLYE**   START

AND

TRICEPS   **ONE-ARM OVERHEAD EXT**

FINISH

START   FINISH

TWIN SETS, REPETITIONS, WEIGHTS, AND RESTS
Set 1: 12 repetitions Body Part A and 12 repetitions Body Part B, 3-pound dumbbells. Rest 15 seconds.
Set 2: 10 repetitions Body Part A and 10 repetitions Body Part B, 3-pound dumbbells. Rest 15 seconds.
Set 3: 8 repetitions Body Part A and 8 repetitions Body Part B, 3-pound dumbbells. Rest 15 seconds.
Repeat for all four twin sets.

A CHEST AND TRICEPS TWIN SETS B

CHEST   CROSS-BENCH PULLOVER   AND   TRICEPS   CROSS-FACE EXT

START

START

FINISH

FINISH

SHOULDERS AND BICEPS TWIN SETS

SHOULDERS   SIDE LATERAL RAISE   AND   BICEPS   ALTERNATE CURL

START   FINISH

START   FINISH

SHOULDERS   FRONT LATERAL RAISE   AND   BICEPS   SIMULTANEOUS CURL

START   FINISH

START   FINISH

TWIN SETS, REPETITIONS, WEIGHTS, AND RESTS
Set 1: 12 repetitions Body Part A and 12 repetitions Body Part B, 3-pound dumbbells. Rest 15 seconds.
Set 2: 10 repetitions Body Part A and 10 repetitions Body Part B, 3-pound dumbbells. Rest 15 seconds.
Set 3: 8 repetitions Body Part A and 8 repetitions Body Part B, 3-pound dumbbells. Rest 15 seconds.
Repeat for all four twin sets.

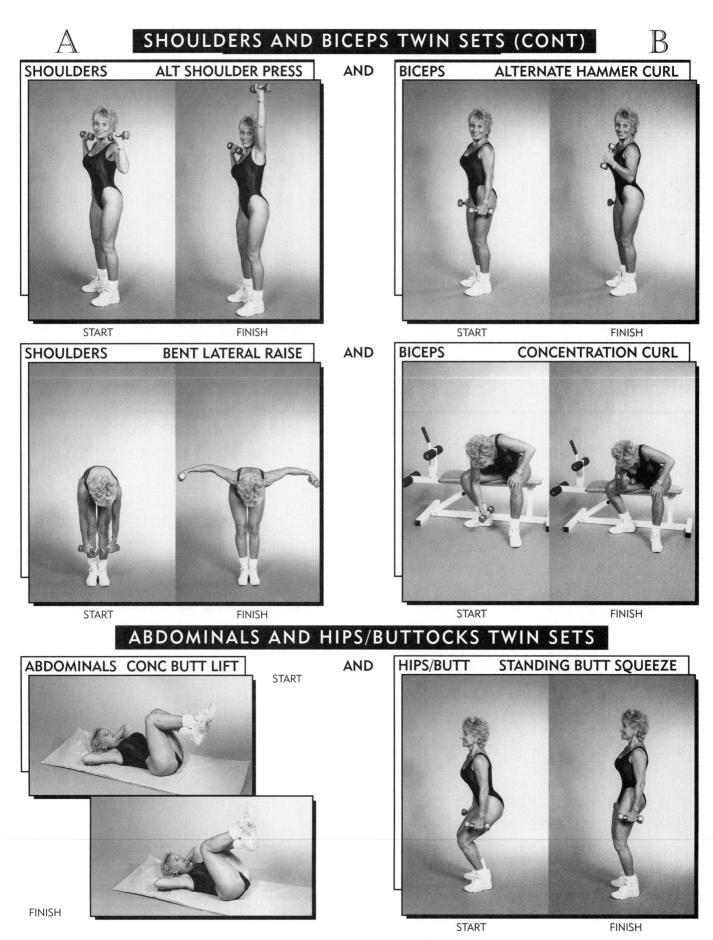

A SHOULDERS AND BICEPS TWIN SETS (CONT) B

SHOULDERS	ALT SHOULDER PRESS	AND	BICEPS	ALTERNATE HAMMER CURL

START · FINISH · START · FINISH

SHOULDERS	BENT LATERAL RAISE	AND	BICEPS	CONCENTRATION CURL

START · FINISH · START · FINISH

ABDOMINALS AND HIPS/BUTTOCKS TWIN SETS

ABDOMINALS CONC BUTT LIFT	START	AND	HIPS/BUTT	STANDING BUTT SQUEEZE

FINISH · START · FINISH

TWIN SETS, REPETITIONS, AND RESTS FOR ABDOMINALS AND HIPS/BUTTOCKS EXERCISES
Set 1: 15–25 repetitions Body Part A and 15–25 repetitions Body Part B. Optional rest 15 seconds.
Set 2: 15–25 repetitions Body Part A and 15–25 repetitions Body Part B. Optional rest 15 seconds.
Set 3: 15–25 repetitions Body Part A and 15–25 repetitions Body Part B. Optional rest 15 seconds.
Repeat for all four twin sets.

A   B

ABDOMINALS AND HIPS/BUTTOCKS TWIN SETS

ABDOMINALS   CRUNCH

START

FINISH

AND

HIPS/BUTTOCKS   STANDING BACK-LEG

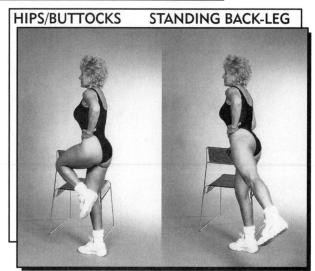

START   FINISH

ABDOMINALS   CEILING LIFT

START

FINISH

AND

HIPS/BUTT   STRAIGHT LEG KICK-UP

START

FINISH

ABDOMINALS   KNEE-RAISED CRUNCH

START

FINISH

AND

HIPS/BUTT   BENT-KNEE KICK-UP

START

FINISH

TWIN SETS, REPETITIONS, AND RESTS FOR ABDOMINALS AND HIPS/BUTTOCKS EXERCISES
Set 1: 15–25 repetitions Body Part A and 15–25 repetitions Body Part B. Optional rest 15 seconds.
Set 2: 15–25 repetitions Body Part A and 15–25 repetitions Body Part B. Optional rest 15 seconds.
Set 3: 15–25 repetitions Body Part A and 15–25 repetitions Body Part B. Optional rest 15 seconds.
Repeat for all four twin sets.

THIGHS   SQUAT

START   FINISH

AND

BACK   UPRIGHT ROW

START   FINISH

THIGHS   SIDE LEG LIFT

START

FINISH

AND

BACK   ONE-ARM DUMBBELL ROW

START   FINISH

THIGHS   LEG CURL

START

FINISH

AND

BACK   DOUBLE-ARM REVERSE ROW

START   FINISH

TWIN SETS, REPETITIONS, WEIGHTS, AND RESTS
Set 1: 12 repetitions Body Part A and 12 repetitions Body Part B, 3-pound dumbbells. Rest 15 seconds.
Set 2: 10 repetitions Body Part A and 10 repetitions Body Part B, 3-pound dumbbells. Rest 15 seconds.
Set 3: 8 repetitions Body Part A and 8 repetitions Body Part B, 3-pound dumbbells. Rest 15 seconds.
Repeat for all four twin sets.

THIGHS   **LUNGE**   AND   **BACK**   **SEATED BACK LATERAL**

START   FINISH   START   FINISH

SUPERSETS FOR CALVES

SEATED STRAIGHT-TOE RAISE   AND   **SEATED ANGLED-OUT-TOE RAISE**

START   FINISH   START   FINISH

STANDING STRAIGHT-TOE RAISE   AND   **STANDING ANGLED-IN-TOE RAISE**

START   FINISH   START   FINISH

TWIN SETS, REPETITIONS, WEIGHTS, AND RESTS
Set 1: 12 repetitions Body Part A and 12 repetitions Body Part B, 3-pound dumbbells. Rest 15 seconds.
Set 2: 10 repetitions Body Part A and 10 repetitions Body Part B, 3-pound dumbbells. Rest 15 seconds.
Set 3: 8 repetitions Body Part A and 8 repetitions Body Part B, 3-pound dumbbells. Rest 15 seconds.
Repeat for all four twin sets.

8

EATING MADE SIMPLE

Why didn't I title this chapter *dieting* made simple? The word "diet" has gotten such a bad reputation that I hesitate to use it. But what you eat *is* your diet! In fact, the dictionary definition of diet is "food and drink regularly consumed." Some people "regularly consume" high-fat foods, others low-fat foods. Both are on a specific diet. With this in mind, I hope you will rethink the word "diet," and forgive me for using it from time to time in this chapter.

In this chapter, you'll find out how to make sure that your diet includes nutritious, low-fat foods that will ultimately result in the loss of any excess fat that may be lingering on your body. If you follow the simple food formula presented here, in time you'll be able to stand in front of the mirror in the nude and say, "I like what I see." At that point, you will be given a plan to maintain that beautiful body—a system so simple that at first you'll think it can't be true. But first the facts.

Why We Get Fat

All food contains potential energy—calories. When we eat food, either we burn the food up as energy, or it gets stored on our body as fat. If we keep eating more than we burn, we get fat—in fact we can build up quite a store-house of fat.

Perhaps *you* have a grand storehouse of fat. Even a hundred pounds of fat. How do you get rid of it? Slowly, calmly, you follow a plan that will day by day force your body to use up the stored fat. In time, the entire store-house will be depleted, and the tight, toned muscles you have been developing with this workout will be displayed. You'll love your body.

But how can you make this happen? You've already taken the first fat-burning step without even having begun a low-fat diet. How so? As mentioned before, you've begun the workout, which will ultimately put small, shapely muscles all over your body, muscles that raise your metabolism and cause you to burn more fat twenty-four hours a day. Now for the next step. But before I give you the food plan, you should know some basic facts about nutrition.

Food Facts

Food is traditionally divided into three groups: fats, proteins, and carbohydrates. In order to lose excess body fat and still maintain healthful eating, your daily food intake should consist of approximately 15 percent fat, 15 percent protein, and 70 percent carbohydrates. But why that division?

FAT

In simple terms, eating fat is what makes you fat. Why? It has more than twice the number of calories per gram as do carbohydrates and proteins. In addition, when fat is digested, little energy is expended, whereas proteins and carbohydrates burn about 20 percent of their calories in the digestive process.

Where is fat found? Everywhere! It's even found in the most healthful foods—in modest amounts. Even an apple has a gram of fat. You will consume most of your fat allotment in your protein requirement. The rest will be spread out—a gram here, a gram there—until you reach your full allowance.

PROTEIN

Protein is necessary for a balanced diet. Only small amounts can be productively used by the human body. Overindulgence in protein is stored on the body as fat. Therefore, only 15 percent of your total intake will be protein. Protein is found in all meat, poultry, and fish—and in eggs, beans, and dairy products. As you can see, since most protein comes in foods that are high in fat, you have to be careful where you get your protein. You'll be given the best sources of protein later in this chapter.

CARBOHYDRATES

Carbohydrates provide you with energy for both your body and mind. If you deplete your body of carbohydrates, not only do you feel weak and enervated, you can't even think straight. For this reason, 70 percent of your food allotment comes from carbohydrates.

Carbohydrates fall into two categories: simple and complex. Simple carbohydrates include *good* simple carbohydrates and *bad* simple carbohydrates. Good simple carbohydrates are fruits. Bad simple carbohydrates are processed carbohydrates—all sugars!

You must keep your bad simple carbohydrate intake (sugar) low because it can hinder fat-burning. Why? When you consume a substantial amount of sugar, a heavy dose of glucose is released to your bloodstream—causing your body to produce high levels of insulin—which in turn inhibits hormone-sensitive lipase—the enzyme that is responsible for draining fat from the cells. So the bottom line is, keep the sugar to a bare minimum—and if in doubt, leave it out.

Complex carbohydrates include all vegetables, breads, cereals, rice, pasta, and grains. When you are on a regular exercise program, such as the plan found in this book, your body will actually crave carbohydrates. (On the other hand, as you might have noticed, if you do no exercise, your body craves fat.)

It is always better to eat whole grain bread, pasta, or rice as opposed to "white." Why? The white varieties are processed, and behave as sugars—which, as mentioned above, can hinder your body's ability to burn fat. I like regular white pasta and white rice, but I discipline myself and try more and more to opt for the whole grain variety.

Note: If you cook your white pasta "al dente" (slightly firm), it does not behave as sugar.

How Much of Each Group Should You Eat?

In the beginning of this chapter I talked in terms of percentages. But now I'm going to tell you that you can throw away your calculator because I'm not going to ask you to figure out the percentage of anything. I've done it for you. If you follow the food plan given below, you will automatically be consuming about 15 percent fat, 15 percent protein, and 70 percent carbohydrates.

Fat Grams Are Limited!

The only math you'll have to do is addition—and that will be for fat grams. If you are a woman, you must keep your daily fat grams between 20 and 25, and if you're a man, to between 30 and 40. Naturally, the lower end is better for faster fat loss. If you want to keep your daily fat intake even lower, that's okay, only don't go lower than 10 percent of your daily caloric intake, or you'll feel hungry and won't know why you keep wanting to eat. Also, most nutritionists agree that this is the minimum amount for good health. By way of example, this would mean you would have a minimum of 15 grams of fat for a 1500 calorie diet.

A Balanced Diet

What is a balanced diet? The U.S. Department of Agriculture studied the matter and came out with what is called the food pyramid. Health and nutrition experts agree that a daily balanced diet should contain the following:

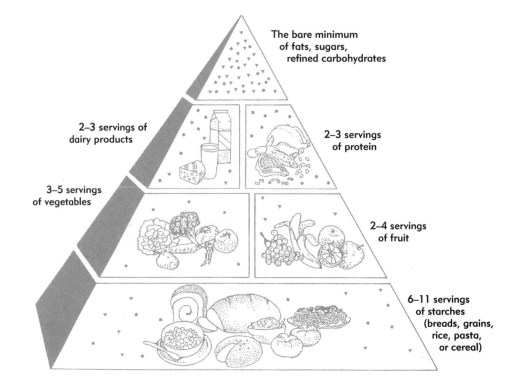

The bare minimum
of fats, sugars,
refined carbohydrates

2–3 servings of
dairy products

2–3 servings
of protein

3–5 servings
of vegetables

2–4 servings
of fruit

6–11 servings
of starches
(breads, grains,
rice, pasta,
or cereal)

I have taken that guideline and modified it to fit in with a low-fat weight loss plan. I've adjusted the pyramid so that you can lose the maximum weight and at the same time ensure optimum health. You will be eating a lot more vegetables—for a minimum, and an unlimited amount of vegetables for your maximum.

In the following paragraphs you will be told which foods are acceptable for the low-fat eating plan, and how much of each of these foods constitutes a serving. In the end, it will be a simple matter for you to make up your own daily meal plan. All you will have to do is pick out servings from each group. You need never be bored. You can have something different every day of the week—or even every day of the month.

What Is a Serving?

Now let's take a closer look at each specific food group to determine what constitutes a serving of each particular food in the five distinctive food groups.

YOU WILL EAT 6–11 SERVINGS OF STARCHES: LIMITED COMPLEX CARBOHYDRATES

Note: Men will eat the amount closer to the higher end of the scale, women will eat closer to the lower end of the scale. However, women who are more than twenty pounds overweight may opt to eat the higher amount.

This group of complex carbohydrates provides high energy. It includes bread, cereal, rice, pasta, and all grains, plus two high-starch vegetables.

One Serving Equals:

2 slices whole wheat bread
$1/2$ bagel
1 English muffin
3 cups popcorn (made without fat)
$1/2$ cup hot cooked cereal
$3/4$ cup dry cold cereal
$2/3$ cup cooked pasta or rice
$1/2$ cup barley
1 ounce pretzels or 1 "serving" size
8 low-fat medium crackers or 4 rice cakes
1 medium potato, or 1 small-sized yam or sweet potato
1 cup beets or peas
1 cup corn or 1 large corn on the cob
$3/4$ cup Jerusalem artichoke
1 cup acorn squash

Let's go through the day and see how much food you really get to eat—looking at the maximum allowance first—for those of you who are more than twenty pounds overweight and men.

You can have a whole bagel for breakfast (two servings) $1\,1/3$ cups of rice with your lunch (two servings), a generous amount of pretzels for a snack (two ounces—two servings), 2 cups of pasta for dinner (three servings), and two rice cakes for a snack—and still be within the fat-loss range. In addition, of course you get to eat all the other foods.

What? Too much food? You can go to the minimum (about half the amount) or somewhere in between, and still be within the range of healthful eating.

YOU WILL EAT 6 OR MORE (PREFERABLY MORE) SERVINGS OF VEGETABLES: UNLIMITED COMPLEX CARBOHYDRATES

One Serving Equals:

Any vegetable, except for corn, potatoes, beets, Jerusalem artichokes, and acorn squash (they have been included above), is fair game.

(1/2 cup cooked or 1 cup raw equals a serving)

Asparagus	Leeks
Broccoli	Lettuce
Brussels sprouts	Mushrooms
Cabbage, chinese cabbage	Okra
Carrots	Onions
Cauliflower	Parsnips
Celery	Peppers, green or red
Chicory	Radishes
Collard greens	Rutabagas
Cucumber	Shallots
Eggplant	Spinach
Endive	Sprouts
Escarole	Squash (summer or zucchini)
Frozen mixed vegetables	Tomatoes
Green or yellow beans	Turnips
Kale	

Note: One tomato, cucumber, or pepper counts as a serving. Let's think about this. Suppose you ate the maximum amount allowed: twelve or more servings. That's six or more whole cups of vegetables. Wow. Could you really do that and not feel stuffed? Of course you would feel stuffed. That's the whole idea. You can eat as much of and as many of the above vegetables as you please, and still lose weight. How so? They are very low in calories and at the same time filling. The human stomach is incapable of holding more than two pounds of food at a time. You really can't overdo vegetables.

But frankly, I've never heard of anyone overdoing vegetables. What I do hear from my readers is, "Do I *have* to eat vegetables? I hate them."

In order to be healthy you must consume at least one and a half cups of vegetables a day. Why? They are filled with fiber, vitamins, minerals, and other nutrients that not only keep you feeling healthy and looking good, but ward off all kinds of diseases. In addition, they fill up your stomach and thus help keep you from eating fatty foods.

So you must, I repeat, must eat vegetables. No ifs, ands, or buts about it. You will learn to love them and indeed thank God for them. How so? If you limit your food intake to the guidelines in this chapter, you'll be hungry, plain and simple. In time you'll be glad to have anything legitimate to put in your mouth. And what now seems unthinkable, will be your delight: "Thank God for this large bag of frozen broccoli and cauliflower," you'll say. And you'll cook up the whole bag and eat all of it in one sitting! No guilt. In fact, self-praise.

Don't eat the same old vegetables every day. Experiment. Go to the supermarket and buy all kinds of frozen vegetables in family-size bags. Check the label to make sure no fat is added. Go to the produce counter and purchase a variety of fresh vegetables. Soon you'll find yourself looking forward to vegetables instead of dreading them. (For a great variety of easy to fix vegetables, and other recipes, see my diet/meal plan book *Eat to Trim* in the Bibliography.)

YOU WILL EAT 2–4 SIMPLE CARBOHYDRATES (FRUIT) PER DAY

One Serving Equals:

One medium to large piece of any fruit: apple, orange, pear, etc.

1 cup berries of any kind or papaya	15 cherries
1 1/2 cups strawberries, watermelon	20 grapes
1/2 cantaloupe, grapefruit, large plantain	3 persimmons, kumquats
1/4 honeydew or pineapple	2 plums, prunes, or tangerines
1 small banana	

Think of it. if you're going for the maximum, you can actually eat four cups of blackberries and still lose weight—or, grab this, six cups of strawberries, or any combination. What? Too much fruit? Go for the minimum or somewhere in between. Note: *Eat to Trim* gives substitutes such as raisins, candy, nonfat ice cream, etc.

YOU WILL EAT 2–3 SERVINGS OF PROTEIN

One Serving Equals:

4–6 ounces white meat chicken or turkey, or fish, or see "Other Sources of Protein" below and specific serving size.

Low-Fat Sources of Protein

All poultry is without skin and cooked without fat! I'm listing the fat grams for your convenience.

Poultry (4 ounces cooked)	Grams of Fat	Grams of Protein
Turkey breast	1	34
Turkey drumstick	4.5	33
Turkey thigh	5	31
Chicken breast	4.5	35
Chicken drumstick	6.8	37
Chicken thigh	5	31

Fish (4 ounces)	Grams of Fat	Grams of Protein
Mahi-mahi (dolphin fish)	0.8	20.8
Haddock	1	23
Cod	1	26
Abalone	1	16
Sole	1	19
Pike	1	25
Scallops	1	26
Tuna in water	1	34
Squid	1.8	20
Flounder	2.3	34
Red snapper	2.3	26
Sea bass	3.4	25
Halibut	4	31
Trout	4	30

Other (Vegetarian) Sources of Protein

Food Product	Grams of Fat	Grams of Protein
3 egg whites	1	9
1/2 cup beans	1	9
1/2 cup soft tofu	6	10
1/2 cup firm tofu	11	19

But what about your fat allotment? How will you get your 15 percent or 20–25 grams of fat (for men, 30–40 grams) per day? You will have already consumed it in the foods you've eaten. Get yourself a fat-gram counter and count up your daily fat grams. Note that I have given an approximate amount.

YOU WILL EAT 2–3 DAIRY FOODS PER DAY

One Serving Equals:

Food Product	Grams of Fat	Grams of Protein
4 ounces low-fat yogurt	2	6
4 ounces no-fat yogurt	0	7
8 ounces 1 percent fat milk	3	8

Food Product	Grams of Fat	Grams of Protein
8 ounces skim milk	1	8
4 ounces (1/2 cup) 1 percent fat cottage cheese	1	14
2 tablespoons no-fat cream cheese	0	2
1 1/2 slices no-fat cheese	0	9
1/2 cup no-fat ice cream	0	2

I get my daily requirement by putting 1 percent milk in my coffee and cold cereal, and by eating no- or low-fat cottage cheese or yogurt. I usually can't eat the no-fat cheese because one slice seems like nothing. I want to eat the whole pack! The same goes for no-fat ice cream. I buy a pint or a quart, and unless I'm very vigilant, by the end of the evening, it's gone. So, as a general rule, I simply don't buy it! Know yourself.

How Much Should You Eat a Day?

By way of review, how much should you really eat—the minimum or the maximum? Men should eat close to the maximum. Women should eat closer to the minimum (unless more than twenty pounds overweight—then they have an option). Those who want to speed up the fat-loss process should try to stick to the minimum in either case. But not the vegetables. Everyone should eat loads of vegetables.

Do You Have to Count Calories?

Yes and no. If you follow the above guidelines, you will rarely go above 1,800 calories. Your daily caloric intake will be about 1,500—but remember, those 1,500 calories will be equivalent to about 1,200 calories because they will consist mainly of carbohydrates and protein—food elements that burn about 20 percent of themselves up in the digestion process.

No, No, Absolutely Not!

To make your life simple, here are some rules to keep in mind. First the bad news, then the good.

1. No fat of any kind. No butter, margarine, lard, oil, mayonnaise, peanut butter, sour cream, fried foods, cream cheese, cheese, bacon, beef, lamb, veal, nuts, olives, avocados, poultry skin, chocolate, doughnuts, cake,

cookies, chips, or fast foods in general. Except under one condition: to fulfill your minimum daily requirement (see Rule 4 and my new diet book, *Eat to Trim*—check the Bibliography).

2. No excess of sugar. Although sugar is much less damaging to your weight-loss program than fat, in excess it can slow down your body's fat-burning mechanism. Have an occasional tablespoon of jam or jelly, hard candy, or no-fat ice cream, cake, or cookies. Maximum: three servings per week.

3. No more than three alcoholic drinks per week (a drink is a light beer or one ounce [a shot] of any hard liquor with no-calorie soda or juice).

4. No more than 22–25 fat grams a day (30–40 for men)—but don't go under 10 percent of your daily caloric intake. For example, fifteen grams on a 1500 calorie diet.

Yes, Yes, Yes, Absolutely Yes

And now for the yeses.

1. Eat your minimum for the day:
   6–unlimited servings of vegetables
   6–11 servings of limited complex carbohydrates
   2–4 fruits
   2–3 servings of protein
   2–3 servings of dairy products

2. Eat often—five times a day or more. Never go more than four hours without eating.

3. Drink lots of water. Drink six to eight glasses of water a day. It's a good idea to drink a glass first thing in the morning, one before each meal, and one during or after exercising.

4. Rather than break your diet, if you like salty foods, with your doctor's permission, indulge. Sometimes low-fat, high-sodium foods such as pickles or pretzels can satisfy an urge and help prevent you from resorting to fatty foods. (See p. 226 for more information on sodium.)

Make Your Own Meal Plans

Using the above guide, here is a sample meal plan:

(Note: The code for each nutritional requirement is in parentheses: "v" = vegetables; "lcc" = limited complex carbohydrates; "f" = fruit; "p" = protein; and "d" = dairy.)

Breakfast	Fat Grams
1 cup cold cereal (lcc #1)	
with 1 cup 1 percent fat milk (d #1)	(2 milk, 1 cereal)
1 banana (f #1)	(1 banana)
no-calorie drink	

Snack	Fat Grams
1 8-ounce no-fat yogurt (d #2)	(0 no-fat yogurt)

Lunch	Fat Grams
6 ounces tuna in water (p #1) mixed with	
1 chopped cucumber (v #1) and vinegar	(0 cucumber, 5 tuna)
on two slices of whole wheat toast	
(lcc #2 and 3)	(2 whole wheat toast)
large tossed lettuce and	
tomato salad (v #2–4)	(0 salad)

Snack	Fat Grams
1 ounce pretzels (lcc #4)	(1 pretzels)
1 pear (f #2)	(0 pear)

Dinner	Fat Grams
6 ounces broiled flounder (p #2)	(3 flounder)
1 cup mixed vegetables (v #5 and 6)	
1 cup pasta with 1 cup	
tomato sauce (lcc #5 and 6)	(2 pasta, 6 tomato sauce)

Snack	Fat Grams
2 cups broccoli and cauliflower (v #7–10)	(0 fat grams)

223

Now let's count it up and see if we have filled the bill for a nutritionally healthy meal—and at the same time a low-fat meal.

3–12 or more servings of vegetables (v)
6–10 servings limited complex carbohydrates (lcc)
2–4 fruits (f)
2–3 protein (p)
2–3 dairy (d)

We have ten servings of vegetables—well over the bare minimum! Great. Vegetables are the thing to overdo—because you *can't* overdo them. Only six servings of limited complex carbohydrates. Great. The minimum. Only two fruits—again, the minimum. Two proteins—again the minimum. And two dairy—the minimum. Now think about it, would you starve if you got to eat all of the above each day—changing the particular foods? No, you wouldn't. And note, only twenty-four grams of fat.

But what if you did eat all of the above and were still hungry? You could eat more free vegetables, and the rest of your limited complex carbohydrate allowance, fruit allowance, protein allowance, and dairy allowance.

Note: For a whole month's worth of meal plans (quick recipes included)—three meals plus two snacks a day, never repeat a meal—get a copy of my book *Eat to Trim* (see Bibliography).

Don't Overdo It!

Be kind to yourself. Listen to your body. If it is screaming at you for more food, and you've been sticking to the minimum plan hoping to lose weight fast, don't push it. Go closer to the middle allowance, and if you must, go up to the maximum. Slowly, as your body becomes accustomed to the new way of eating, you can gently coax yourself down to the minimum. But you never have to go down to the minimum when it comes to vegetables. Thank God for that. You never have to go hungry.

Another thing. If you are kind to yourself and allow your body to go at its own pace rather than punish it and rush it, you will be that much more likely to maintain your fat-free body.

Maintaining Your Fat-Free Body for Life

Good news. It can be done without constant attention. All you have to do is continue to eat exactly as above—forever! Wait. Don't throw this book across the room. I've left out the best part. You eat exactly as above forever, *but*, you can eat anything you want—and I do mean anything—one day a week.

What? Am I crazy? No. It works. You see, if you didn't take one day off, but kept strictly to the eating plan above forever, in time you would lose too much weight. True, when you got closer to your ideal weight, you would lose very slowly—maybe a half a pound or even an eighth of a pound a month. But you would continue to lose over time. Since our goal is not a gaunt, anorectic look, but rather a healthy, shapely look, you must take advantage of your free eating day once you reach your goal.

There's another reason for the free eating day once you reach your goal. In time, your mind and body will rebel against the boredom of the same day-to-day range of food. You will begin to dream about doughnuts, hamburgers, and macaroni and cheese—whatever your favorite fat food is. By allowing yourself to eat whatever you want once a week you not only solve the boredom issue, but you erase the forbidden fruit element. There's no reason to rebel because nothing is permanently prohibited.

"But that could never work for me, I would eat from morning until night." Fine. Try it. If you go overboard and indulge from dawn until midnight, stuffing your face with every junk food imaginable, the next day your body will feel sluggish and sick, and will stop you from going as crazy the next time. Eventually you'll find yourself being more realistic on your free eating days. In addition, once you realize that a week goes by quickly, and that this will not be the last free eating day of your life, you'll be more willing to wait for the next week to enjoy some other delights that you may not have been able to schedule in to your feast day this week. In time your free eating day will be no big deal. You'll see. (For a Plan B, where, once you reach your goal, you can have a previously forbidden food once a day, see *Eat to Trim*.)

But What About . . . ?

You know the basic nutritional facts for eating a healthful, low-fat diet, but what about things I didn't mention: details about caffeine, sodium, and so on. Here are some answers to questions you may have.

WHAT ABOUT CAFFEINE?

The caffeine story is constantly being rewritten by medical experts. Check with your doctor as to your specific situation. I drink two to three cups of full-caffeine coffee per day—but lately I've taken to the "lite coffee" that has half the amount. Why? I found myself getting hyper, and was able to trace it to the coffee.

You will have to be honest with yourself. Go by the way your body reacts to caffeine. If you feel off balance, cut your caffeine and see if you feel better.

WHAT ABOUT SODIUM?

The minimum daily requirement for sodium is between 1,500 and 2,400 milligrams. But most of us go way over that. We consume canned foods that contain as much as 1,000 grams per serving. If most of your meals come from cans, that can amount to double the daily requirement—or more.

So what if that happens? You will not get fat. You can't get fat from too much sodium. What you can do is temporarily retain water—which will make your scale weight go up from one to even ten pounds, depending upon how much water you are retaining. In addition, you'll appear swollen in the mirror and you'll feel bloated.

But what about health? It depends upon your particular situation. Of course it's always best to keep within the recommended daily limit—but if you don't have a problem with blood pressure, and your doctor says it's okay, you can do what I do. From time to time I eat many pickles (very high in sodium) and indulge in canned foods. I feel like a bloated pig. But guess what? I didn't break my low-fat eating plan and after five days of keeping my sodium within the daily limit, I lose the bloat. For me, no harm done.

WHAT ABOUT VITAMINS, MINERALS, AND FIBER?

Vitamins, minerals, and fiber are needed in various amounts to keep your body in the best of health. If you follow the above guideline for eating, and if you vary the foods, getting a wide assortment over the week, you will have all the vitamins, minerals, and fiber needed for optimum nutrition. For more detailed information on vitamins, minerals, and fiber, see *Eat to Trim*.

WHAT ABOUT EMERGENCIES?

Suppose you're out all day and haven't eaten in four hours. Your stomach is growling. You have the self-control to wait another three hours, but you know that it isn't a good idea to go more than four hours without eating.

You can usually find at least one of these three items: a soft pretzel (sold in most malls and in various stores and by street vendors), a bagel, or a bag of pretzels. The soft pretzel, the bagel, or two ounces of pretzels (a good amount) will cost only two of your ten limited complex carbohydrate allowances.

What's so great about these quick snacks is, they will provide the gradually released energy that complex carbohydrates give—and will prevent you from going home and bingeing because of weakness and the feeling of deprivation.

WHAT ABOUT CHOLESTEROL—GOOD FAT AND BAD FAT?

If you follow the food guidelines above, you will not be consuming too much cholesterol. But what about good and bad fat? You've heard much about polyunsaturated fat (the kind that does not clog arteries) and saturated fat—the kind that does. Forget it for now. For your purposes, all fat is bad. All fat makes you fat. So for now, no fat—and this includes "a little olive oil." Forget it! For more detailed information on this subject, see my book *Eat to Trim*, where I add tiny amounts of olive or canola oil to certain recipes to make sure you fulfill your daily minimum fat intake. But I don't want *you* to use oils yourself! Right. I don't trust you—not when you're trying to lose fat. I'd rather you use my preset meal plans until you are at your goal and in control.

9

IT'S NOT A GOOD IDEA— AND YOU HEARD WRONG

So many times, I get letters from readers telling me, "I'm using your workout, but I had an idea. I decided to change . . ." And then they'll describe something in the workout they've altered that will guarantee they don't get the promised results. Other times I'll get letters saying, "I heard . . ." And they'll relate some outlandish myth about fitness that someone they know swears is gospel.

The goal of this chapter is to set some things straight—in the hope that I can prevent you from making mistakes and/or worrying over nothing. First I'll talk about the most common not-so-bright "bright ideas" that people have regarding changing the workout to fit their needs. Then I'll dispel some ridiculous myths.

1. **"I want to burn more fat so I decided to increase my repetitions. Now I do thirty repetitions for everything. Is that a good idea?"**

Bad idea. The repetitions required for the specific exercises found in the workouts in this and my other books are carefully calculated to enable you to build just the right amount of muscle and burn maximum fat. If you increase your repetitions for the upper body beyond the maximum twelve allowed for the upper body, for example, you will wear away the muscle as you are creating it.

The only area that you can go up to thirty or even fifty repetitions is the abdominal area—and frankly, more than fifteen to twenty-five reps per set is not a good idea except upon occasion, just to test your strength!

You can do fifteen to twenty-five repetitions for all hips/buttocks work without weights—and some people do up to fifteen repetitions for all thigh work. This is perfectly fine. But other than that, please, don't change the repetitions. You won't burn more fat. You'll just wear away muscle!

2. **"I decided to do only one or two exercises per body part instead of the required four. Is that okay?"**

No. Although something is always better than nothing, I can't guarantee satisfactory results unless you do the required amount. Cutting out exercises is the first step to breaking down the workout. If you can't perform a certain exercise, then double up on any other exercise for that body part, but don't just leave it out.

3. **"I can't afford weights. Is it okay to work out with cans of food?"**

You can, but it's not the best idea. Food cans are clumsy to hold. Also, it's difficult to find the right weights—especially when you're pyramiding the weights. It's much better to invest in the dumbbells—which can be purchased for about fifty cents to two dollars a pound—and they never wear out! You'll have them for life. And unlike fitness club memberships, you never have to renew them. Call around after looking up "Exercise Equipment" in the Yellow Pages.

4. **"I'm going on a liquid diet—just to give me a head start. What do you think?"**

No no no. A thousand times no. Liquid diets work to help you lose a lot of weight quickly, but what happens after that is the problem. The moment you go off a liquid diet, the "starvation response" is triggered. You start eating solid food and you just can't stop—and this holds true even if your liquid diet allowed you one regular meal a day. You'll feel an uncontrollable urge to put food in your mouth until your stomach is so full you can hardly move. You will do this until you've gained every ounce you lost—with a hefty addition. Then and only then will your body's survival instinct let up.

A much better idea is to lose weight the right way in the first place. Learn that food is not an enemy and that you can eat lots of delicious, nutritious solid food and still lose weight. Remember, once you reach your goal you can have your free eating day once a week, and can even enjoy those forbidden foods you've been craving.

5. **"I'm weighing myself every day—to keep myself in check. What do you think?"**

I think you'll drive yourself crazy! The scale goes up and down depending upon water retention, which can vary on an average by two to ten pounds a day (if you are consuming high sodium or taking water pills the variation will be on the higher side of the variation range).

Another point. Muscle weighs more than fat, but it takes up less space. You may have lost three pounds of fat but gained two pounds of muscle. You get on the scale, and you say, "I'm depressed. It's been three weeks, and all I lost is one pound. Yet I do look better in clothing and in the nude. But why didn't I lose more weight?"

Forget the scale. The new scale is your mirror. Once you've been working out for about two years, you can begin to weigh yourself again if you wish, because by then your body will have recomposed itself. You will have more muscle—but it will stay about the same at that point—so your scale weight will be a truer reflection of your actual weight. Let me explain using myself as an example.

Before I ever picked up a weight, I used to have to weigh 105 pounds to look great. Now to look the way I used to look I can be 115 pounds! How is that? Muscle weighs more than fat. I now have ten pounds of muscle on my body—that muscle takes up less space, gives me a better shape, and makes me feel tight and toned.

Why does muscle weigh more than fat? It is composed of condensed material—whereas fat is composed of fluffy material. Think of it as gold to feathers. A pillow weighs less than a brick of gold. The gold is the muscle—it weighs more (and indeed is more valuable) but it takes up less space. Also the gold is solid but the feathers are soft. Do you want to be solid or soft? Do you want gold or feathers?

6. "I'm not a very good dieter. Can I just do the workout and eat what I want and still get into some kind of shape?"

Most people would rather not have to think about what they eat. They would like to be free to eat whatever, whenever. So don't think you're alone when you say, "I'm not a good dieter." We become good dieters with practice.

Sure. If you're a skinny-fat, and don't need to lose weight, you can follow your own eating plan and just do the workout. Your entire body will become shapely, tight, and toned. But if you are overweight, of course you can't keep eating the way you've been eating. Otherwise the fat will cover your developing muscles.

Be comforted also by one thing. In time your body will become unaddicted to poisonous foods and will thrive on the healthful diet in Chapter 8—and will actually crave these foods. It takes six months to a year for this to happen. Give it time.

7. "I hate to look at books. Can't I forget the book and just follow one of your videos?"

You can get one of my videos to do the workout in that video, but it's a good idea to also get the book that accompanies the specific video for all the information I give you. In the book I give you many tips about the exercises, nutrition, motivation, and so on that simply cannot fit in the video. Also, the book gives you stills of the exercises, and always contains variations—alternative exercises from the video. I can send you my videos if you wish. See p. 245.

8. **"I'm using fat-reduction cream as a backup to your program. Is that a good idea?"**

Terrible idea. Fat-reduction creams work only to temporarily reduce the size of the body part to which you apply the cream (by removing the water from that area). The moment you stop applying the cream, the body part returns to its original size. In addition, these creams do nothing to give firmness to the body. How could they? They don't grow muscle you know!

In addition, I believe that in time these creams will prove dangerous to your health. Please, I beg you. Don't take the chance. Do the right thing and work out to develop muscle and follow the low-fat eating plan.

9. **"Can I continue to do the _____ workout (with weights) along with your workout?"**

Why do that? If you're so eager to do more work, go on the maximum workout plan in *Bottoms Up!*, *The Fat-Burning Workout*, or *Definition*. Other weight-training workouts may cause you to overtrain the muscle. There is no reason whatsoever to do another weight-training workout along with this workout.

But you can do other workouts along with this workout if they are strictly aerobic. That is fine. No problem.

10. **"I've been losing the same twenty pounds again and again for the past five years. What's wrong?"**

Once you reach your weight goal, instead of taking only one free eating day a week, you're probably taking three or four, or just eating what you please every day. Reread the diet chapter or get a copy of *Eat to Trim* and realize that you can eat what you want only one day a week once you reach your goal. Also, if you do find yourself regaining (you'll know it by the mirror and your clothing), get on the scale and see if it is more than seven to ten pounds. If it is, start your diet again, until you are satisfied with the way you look, then eat what you want only one day a week.

I deliberately keep losing the same five to seven pounds again because I love to eat and it's worth it to me. But to lose and gain much more than that over and over again can be bad for your health, your budget, and your psychology! (You'll need a set of fat clothes, your doctor won't approve, and you'll feel depressed.)

11. **"I guess I'll have to keep raising my weights forever, in order to make progress. Is that true?"**

No. As explained in the A–Z Quick-Start Dictionary, "plateau," once you reach your goal—you like the way your muscularity looks—you can stay on the same weights forever. For example, I started out with three-, five-, and ten-pound dumbbells, and built up to ten- fifteen-, and twenty-pound dumbbells. I stayed at that weight, and to this day, many years later, that's what I use—and you see my body over the years (the covers of my books).

12. "I was told that if you stop working out, the muscle will turn to fat!"

Sure. And I can turn iron into gold too! And I'll sell you the Brooklyn Bridge. Muscle and fat cells are structurally and functionally different, and never the twain shall metamorphosize!

If you stop working out, what *will* happen is, your muscles will slowly shrink back to their original size. It will take about the same amount of time you were working out for this to happen. For example, if you worked out for a year, it would take a year to lose all the muscle you gained. But.

Here's the good part. Even though it will appear as if you've lost all your muscle, you will never really lose all of your muscles, because muscles have permanent "memory." If you ever start working out again, it will take only one third the time to get your muscles back. Using the above example, if you originally worked out for a year and then stopped for a year, and then started working out again, it would take only four months to get back!

13. "I'm fat—if I work out, won't I get muscles and look bigger than I already am?"

Don't worry. The kind of muscles you'll get with this workout can't make you look bigger than you are. They will be much too small to increase your size. In addition, the muscles will help you burn more fat as you go along.

It's not a good idea to diet first and lose all the weight, and then start working out. If you do this, you'll be depressed to see your flabby skinny-fat body after all your hard dieting work. It's much better to work out as described in this book as you diet. Then when you lose your excess fat, your sexy, defined, toned body will be waiting for you.

14. "I heard that it is impossible to thicken bones after a certain age— the best you can do is to prevent further thinning."

Wrong. You can thicken your bones even at ninety! Medical authorities are in full agreement. Study after study has proven that you can increase bone density at any age by working out with weights. How so?

As you work out with weights, an increased flow of blood carrying nutrients surges through the bone, and an electrical charge stimulates the bone cells. Eventually, the bone thickens. Because of my workout, at fifty-three, my bone density is *double* the density of women my age (see pp. 4–5).

15. "My butt is flat. How can I make it rounded and shapelier without getting fat?"

One thing is for sure. You don't want to try doing it by gaining fat—in which case your butt would just sag. You must build up to heavy squats and lunges. These two exercises, when done with a barbell and plates (see p. 54), help to raise and round the buttocks—even though they are front-thigh exercises. Go back to workout level 2 and use a barbell and plates, or get a copy of *Now or Never* or *Top Shape* to achieve this goal.

16. "I hate my calves—they are so muscular. How can I get rid of them?"

You'll have to stop walking. But since you can't do that, stop running. Running develops muscular calves. Also wearing high heels.

I can't imagine why anyone would hate muscular calves—but I do get such letters. If for some reason you hate your muscular calves, realize that it took a lifetime to develop those muscles, so it will take a long time to get rid of them. Will the calves workout in this book make them even bigger? No. But if you wish, you can skip the calves workout. Okay?

17. "I like to do aerobics. How can I fit them in and still do your workout?"

You can do aerobics six days a week—twenty to forty minutes. You can do them just before you weight-train, or any time of the day. You can do them on the days you work out or on the day you don't or both. Aerobics are a fine complement to any workout in this book. They help you to burn extra fat and to get your heart and lungs into great shape. What do I mean by aerobics? See pp. 11–13 and the A–Z Quick-Start Dictionary.

If it comes down to either/or, choose weight training of course. See pp. 13–16 to review why. If you want the closest thing to a combination weight training and aerobic workout, try my book *Definition*.

18. "Joyce, do you believe in cosmetic surgery—can you do exercises to make your face and neck look young?"

For the face yes. For the body no. You can't get your face in shape with dieting or weight training. Such efforts will only make you look older. Get too thin after forty, and your face looks gaunt and haggard. Do facial exercises and you'll get definition on your face and neck (lines). Forget it.

So as for me, off to the cosmetic surgeon I shall go if I decide that it will help me to grow old more gracefully!

But what about the body? Liposuction is not the way to reshape the body. It permanently removes fat from the specific area, but if you gain weight, the fat will go somewhere else. My luck, I would get it removed from my big butt and it would go on my stomach. So I'll get it removed from my stomach. Well, maybe it will go to my neck! I'll end up looking like a freak. I say when it comes to liposuction, don't fool with Mother Nature.

19. "My five-year-old wants to do your workout with me—is that okay?"

For children of any age, show the workout to your pediatrician. If he or she agrees, let your child work out *without* weights, or with very light weights, say, one-pound dumbbells. As they get older and they're preteen, again with the pediatrician's consent, you can gradually bring them into your full workout, with weights they can easily handle.

20. "I saw you on TV talking about your self-help book *Look In, Look Up, Look Out*. You talked about the eight keys to achieving your goals and motivating yourself. I was also interested to see how much of your strength is inner strength and spiritual. Can you tell me how I can get as strong and as motivated as you?"

Yes. You can do it by developing the eight keys I discuss in that book: *inner voice*; *self-esteem*; learning to let go of the *past*, learning to own up and take *responsibility*; learning to use the power of your *will*; learning to do things *alone*; learning to *motivate yourself*; and finally, learning to call upon the most powerful force in the universe through a simple *prayer* of faith. I spell out these methods in my book and audiotape *Look In, Look Up, Look Out*. (See Bibliography.) I also talk a little bit about my life. I've gotten hundreds of letters from people telling me that this book changed their lives. I asked God to help me to write it—so I'm not surprised.

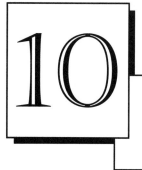

PRESERVING THE NATIONAL TREASURE FOR LIFE!

Okay. You're in shape—or you will be after following the workout plans in this book. But what happens then? Do you have to keep working out until the day you die? If so, what do you have to do?

The Good News and the Bad News

The good news is, it's *much easier to maintain* your in-shape body than it was to get your body in shape. The bad news is (well, I don't think it's bad because by now working out has become a part of my daily routine and it will for you too), you can't just vegetate once you've gotten in shape. Working out must become a habit—a part of your daily routine—like brushing your teeth or getting dressed every morning. You don't argue about it. You just do it! Make up your mind to devote twenty to thirty minutes a day to working out for now and forevermore. The prize is well worth the price. Not only will you feel sexy and appealing, but you'll have more energy and confidence—and you'll live longer.

Using This Workout in a Unique Way—Prevent Workout Burnout

Those of you who worked out with my books before, and those of you who've familiarized yourself with all four levels of this workout—even if you haven't done them for three months each, may want to try something that is fun and very boredom-preventing. You can skip workout level 1 and do the following. Do workout level 2 for two days (upper and lower body), then the next time you work out, do workout level 3 for two days (upper and lower body) and the next time, workout level 4 for two days (upper and lower body). Then you go back to level 2 and keep repeating the cycle.

I discovered this method while writing this book; and in fact that's exactly the way I do this workout. I really look forward to working out because it feels like I'm always doing something new. I never get bored—in fact, on those days when I just don't feel like working out, I remember that I will be doing something completely different, and it gives me that little push. I approach the workout with more energy—and I get more out of it. I almost *never* dread working out anymore. In addition, this plan really ensures a balanced muscle-definition, fat-burning combination. I love it! But every so often, I switch to one of my other books for a few months.

Varying Your Routine to Keep Your Body Improving: Choose Your Workout

Suppose you want to continue using this book, switching back and forth between workout levels 1 and 4 for the rest of your life. You could do it! But it would not be the ideal situation. In order to be challenged in the most beneficial way, muscles need to be asked to do some different exercises and/or different exercise combinations. For this reason, I'm going to present a plan here that will allow you to pick and choose between workouts that will net you even better results than you have gotten. I'll discuss the new workouts as they relate to the workout levels found in this book—explaining their correlations and differences, and what they can do for you.

In all, you'll have seven workouts to choose from—each found in a separate book dealing just with that workout. You'll also be able to take advantage of two special stomach workouts, one in book form, the other in video form.

Will you be able to cope with the workouts presented in the various books and videos I will recommend? Absolutely yes. Because you have gone through workout levels 1 to 4, you are now a veteran body shaper and will have no trouble using any of them.

FOR MUSCLE HARDNESS, LAZY TIME, VACATION TIME

The 12-Minute Total-Body Workout is a continuation of workout level 1—but with a different time frame and many new exercises. Instead of working out only twenty minutes a day, four days a week, you work out twelve minutes every day doing different body parts. This is a great workout if you are looking to take it easy for a while, if you're on vacation and don't want to carry weights, if you are pregnant (in this case, your doctor will probably recommend that you do it without dynamic tension and continual pressure), or if you are pressed for time.

The workout is different from workout level 1 in that it emphasizes the sustained use of dynamic tension and continual pressure—ensuring that your muscles become more and more firm to the touch. It is as simple to perform as workout level 1. You use three-pound dumbbells or no weights, and do three sets of ten repetitions for everything. But many of the exercises are changed, and all the combinations are different—a good idea for maximum benefit to your muscles.

FOR BUILDING MORE OF A MUSCLE BASE—
FOR ALL OR CERTAIN BODY PARTS

Now or Never or *Top Shape* use the same workout system as workout level 2—only with different time frames and many new exercises. *Now or Never* is a forty- to sixty-minute workout, and *Top Shape* is a thirty- to forty-minute workout.

These workouts are ideal if you want to establish yet more of a muscle base than you have gotten with workout level 2, and you don't feel like doing the same old exercises and routines that you did in that workout. Changing the exercises and combinations will encourage your muscles to go one step further toward perfect symmetry. In addition, it will prevent workout boredom.

If you are a woman, switch to *Now or Never* first—and do that for three months to a year, then, if you still want more of a muscle base, switch to *Top Shape* for three months to a year. If you are a man, go in reverse. Switch to *Top Shape* first for three months to a year, and then, if you're still not satisfied, switch to *Now or Never* for three months to a year. Why?

Now or Never is specifically addressed to women, but men can do the workout—only the hips/buttocks workout is optional for men. *Top Shape* is addressed to men, but women can do the workout. However, there is no hips/buttocks workout in *Top Shape*, so if you are a woman and do *Top Shape*, be sure to continue your hips/buttocks workout from one of the workout levels in this book, or from one of my other workout books, perhaps *Bottoms Up!* (this workout will be discussed below).

Another good thing about both of the above workouts is, in addition to the dumbbell workout, they each have a complete machine workout section that provides photographs for doing exercises with various workout equipment.

Both *Now or Never* and *Top Shape* are as simple to perform as workout level 2. Just as in workout level 2, you use three sets of dumbbells in graduated weights, and you use the pyramid system.

If you only want to put more muscle on your front thighs or your triceps, or any other body part for that matter, you can use just the specific body part exercise from either of these books, and do your other body parts from workout levels 1, 3, or 4, or from any other book mentioned in this chapter.

FOR ADDED FAT-BURNING, SUPER-FAT-BURNING, ULTIMATE FAT-BURNING

Workout level 3 introduced you to supersets within a body part—for more fat-burning than you were able to get with workout levels 1 or 2. If you want still further fat-burning, take the next step and move to the giant set workout presented in a very simply written book I wrote with my daughter, *The College Dorm Workout*. You don't have to be a college student to do it.

With the giant set, instead of doing two exercises for a given body part without resting (as you do in workout level 3), you do three exercises for a given body part without resting.

The advantage to *The College Dorm Workout* is, you don't need a bench or step to do it (although you can use one)—all you need is a chair, and you can do the workout in a very small space. In addition, you don't have to pyramid your weights. You can use one set of five-pound dumbbells for every exercise. You can, though, opt to pyramid your weights, for even greater results.

For even more fat-burning, you can use *The Fat-Burning Workout*, where you are required to pyramid your weights, and in addition, where you are offered not only the giant set but the super giant set (four exercises for a body part without resting—the Intensity Workout) and the super-super giant set (five exercises for a body part without resting—the Insanity Workout).

Each of the above workouts has different exercises and varying exercise combinations, so that you will be able to further encourage your muscles to become sculpted and defined.

The *most* fat-burning and definition-yielding of all the workout books I've written is *Definition*. It introduces the true pyramid system, a system not found in any of the workouts in this book, or in any of my other workout books.

The thing that will be familiar to you if you use *Definition* is the superset within body parts that you encountered in workout level 3. *Definition* utilizes this supersetting system—only with the added two sets per exercise for the true pyramid system. Instead of going up the pyramid and stopping there, as in workout level 3, you are asked to descend the pyramid with two additional sets.

In *Definition*, fewer rests are taken, and more fat is burned. The workout takes only fifteen minutes because one-limb-at-a-time exercises are eliminated, fewer exercises are required, you move fast, and you rarely rest.

In addition *Definition* and *Top Shape* are the only workouts that give you the option of exercising your entire body in one workout day. If you choose this option, your workout will take thirty minutes, but you'll only have to work out two or three days a week, and it will be the equivalent of four or six days a week for any other workout.

But isn't this a contradiction against the split routine and the forty-eight-hour recovery principle? No. if you choose the total-body plan, as long as you don't work out with weights the next day, you won't be violating these principles.

But doesn't exercising the whole body in one day contradict what I said before—about being too tired by the end of your workout to do justice to the last few body parts? No. *Definition* has been carefully composed of exercises designed to go quickly (as mentioned above, no time-consuming one-limb-at-a-time exercises), and in addition, you are required to do fewer exercises because, as mentioned above, you are doing two additional sets per exercise. The two additional sets allow you to eliminate other time-consuming exercises.

Who *can* do *Definition*? Anyone who has done workout level 3 will be able to do *Definition* without any trauma! But who *should* do it? This workout is completely aerobic! Anyone who wants to burn maximum fat and get a complete aerobic effect, and at the same time get premier definition should do this workout.

By way of review, thinking of the above workouts in terms of levels, workout level 3 is your base—your beginning level; let's call it A. *The College Dorm Workout* would be your next level, B. *The Fat-Burning Workout* is C, and *Definition* is D—deadly to fat! Try each for three to six months! Note: *The Fat-Burning Workout* is also in video. I can send it to you, or you can order it through my club/newsletter (see p. 246).

BURN FAT AND BUILD MUSCLE AT THE SAME TIME

The workout discussed in this section, *Bottoms Up!* is similar to—you guessed it—workout level 4. It allows you to continue to burn maximum fat (if you shorten or don't take your optional rests) and at the same time to further establish your muscle base.

Just as in workout level 4, you are supersetting between body parts, or, better expressed, you are using the twin set. But *Bottoms Up!* has an additional feature. It combines the exercises into pairs that require a more intense workout. In addition, besides giving a challenging upper body workout, it provides not four, but seven exercise combinations for the hips/buttocks and thigh areas. You can really zone in on cellulite, saddlebags, and inner thigh flab. It also gives six stomach exercises.

Rather than stay with workout level 4 forever, if you want to continue solidifying your muscle base, challenge your muscles with different exercises and combinations and switch to *Bottoms Up!* for three months to a year—and then see how you feel. (The entire *Bottoms Up!* workout is now on video in three volumes. I can send them to you, or you can order them through my club/newsletter [see p. 246]).

FOR EXTRA STOMACH WORK—ANYTIME

I often get letters from readers saying, "I've been doing your workout for X amount of time. I'm thrilled with the results *but* . . ." Then they go on to say something like, "My entire body is tight, toned, and shaped except for one area. My stomach. Is there anything more I can do to get rid of that lower pot and get more definition?"

If you want to perfect your abs, try my bombs-away stomach workout, *Gut Busters.* It has the seven exercises that are done by champion bodybuilders to create the "beer-can abs" you only dream about. The workout accomplishes this by providing the most intense stomach exercises, which hit your abdominal muscles from seven different angles.

If you'd rather work with a video, and/or you have a problem back, try *The Bottoms Up Workout: Middle Body* (see p. 245). It provides ten exercises that zone in on your stomach muscles, but these exercises have been chosen especially for those who can't do sit-ups, knee-ins, or leg raises, or any other abdominal exercise that puts a strain on the back.

Either *Gut Busters* or *The Bottoms Up Workout: Middle Body* would do the trick in putting the finishing touches on your stomach. You can incorporate either of these workouts into your routine by eliminating your present stomach workout and simply replacing it with one of the above. However, you should do it six days a week until you reach your ideal stomach. Then you can do it every other workout day.

Another idea is to continue doing your present abdominal workout on alternate days—one day the easier abdominal workout, the next day either *Gut Busters* or *The Bottoms Up Workout: Middle Body*.

If you follow either *Gut Busters* or *The Bottoms Up Workout: Middle Body* for six months to a year, your abdominal area will be flat, firm, defined, and sexy. Of course, this assumes that you are also following the low-fat eating plan described in any of my workout books or in *Eat to Trim*, my diet book. Otherwise your gorgeous abdominal muscles will be obscured by that last bit of fat that lingers on the stomach area even if you are only a few pounds overweight.

Let's Pull It All Together

You are now able to pick and choose which workout you want to use at any point of your life. If you're lazy, and want to do the bare minimum, keep doing workout level 1 or do *The 12-Minute Total Body Workout* until you're ready for more of a challenge. If you want more of a muscle base, do workout level 2, or *Now or Never*, or *Top Shape* until you're satisfied with your muscularity. If you want to burn more fat and become more defined, continue with workout level 3, or do *The College Dorm Workout*, *The Fat-Burning Workout*, or *Definition* until you are satisfied with the delineation of your muscles. If you want to continue to establish your muscle base and at the same time burn maximum fat and get definition, do *Bottoms Up!* until you accomplish both goals. If you need more work on your stomach, do *Gut Busters* or the video *The Bottoms Up Workout: Middle Body* until your abdominal area meets your standards.

If you don't want to think about it, pick any of the workouts and do them for three months to a year and then switch to any workout you feel in the mood to do. This will work, because over time, your body will have the advantage of all the weight-training principles, and a wide variety of exercises and exercise combinations.

If You Are Happy with Your Body and Don't Know What to Do

If you look in the mirror and say to yourself, "I like my body. I'm content. I don't know what to do," my advice is, do *Bottoms Up!* Do it until you get bored with it. Then do *Definition*. Do it until you are bored with it. Then go to one of the other workouts mentioned here. But no matter what, keep working out. Don't be crazy and stop. Why punish yourself that way?

Do You Ever Get a Break? When to Take a Week Off

Good news. Yes. In fact, you *must* take a week off every so often or you'll become burned out and may be tempted to stop working out for months. You have the option of taking a week off every six months, but you should try to take a week off once a year.

You don't have to stop moving completely during that week. You can do aerobics, sports, walking, dancing, whatever. Just stay away from the weights. By the time that week is up, you'll miss the weights and will be happy to start up again. And don't worry. Your muscles will not disappear in a week. In fact, a week after you start up again, you'll see more progress than usual. It seems that muscles respond to time off by making up for the lost time.

But what about times when you can't work out? Can't work out? There's no such thing except for injury—and even then you can work the body parts that are not injured. In cases of incapacitating sickness, just start up again when you are well after consulting with your doctor. In a matter of weeks your body will more than make up for lost time.

As you already know, vacations, business trips, and so forth are not the issue. You can always work out using workout level 1, *The 12-Minute Total-Body Workout*, or by applying dynamic tension and continual pressure to whatever workout you are doing, and doing the workout with no weights.

The Insurance Policy: Never Get Fat Again If . . .

Now I'm going to give you an insurance policy. If you promise to never stop working out with weights (accept for the allowed weeks off) and you continue to use one of the workouts in this book or in any of the books mentioned in this chapter, even if you eat like a pig for two to three months at a time, you will not go back to where you started—not ever. How can this be?

Even if you ate like a pig for twelve weeks—if you kept working out, your muscles will be intact under the fat. You would probably gain up to ten pounds of fat—and that fat would cover your muscles to some extent, but you would be in shape under the fat.

If you don't stop working out, as you are overeating, week after week, your body will begin to nag you for good food. Your muscles will crave the nutritious diet you had been eating before. But if you stop working out and pig out for twelve weeks, you are in trouble. Why?

In this case, your muscles will begin to atrophy, your metabolism will go down, and you'll feel even more sluggish than you already feel (the fat you have been eating will make you feel lethargic enough). In addition, you'll get out of the workout habit. It will be hard to reestablish it once you decide to get in shape again.

Finally, you'll feel discouraged—even depressed. Your body will feel fat, because of some muscle atrophy, much fatter than it would feel if you were just overeating but still working out. You'll be tempted to tell yourself, "Forget it. It's too late. I'm tired anyway. I'll just be fat."

So if you want to be naughty, I recommend that you don't throw it all to the wind. At least keep working out. Then when you've had enough of it, and you're sick and tired of feeling sluggish, and you want those pretty muscles to show again, all you have to do is return to the eating plan, and week by week the excess fat will melt away, and voilà, your in-shape body will be there waiting for you. Except for the week off once a year, I *never* stop working out. That's my secret!

Do I advise you to eat like a pig for three months? No. I would much rather see you stick to the free eating day only once a week. But we are all human. I'm writing this section because I want to emphasize that no matter what, don't stop working out! That's the secret to a lifetime of fitness. I speak from experience. I come from a family that loves to eat. I love to eat. Sometimes I get sick and tired of eating right. Every so often I eat whatever I please for up to three months. The fat covers my muscles. But I don't panic. I know that gaining and losing fat follows the scientific laws of nature. Eat less (consume less food energy), spend more food energy, and slowly but surely the body must use up its fat reserve!

Think of It as Maintenance

One final word. We give proper respect to our cars—we maintain them, changing the oil and getting tune-ups. We make sure our homes are cleaned, our lawns mowed and maintained. And as mentioned above, we already devote certain nonnegotiable time to our bodies: brushing our teeth and getting dressed. All I'm asking you to do is set aside twenty to thirty minutes a day, four to six days a week, to maintaining your muscles so that your body will look and feel sexy, healthy, and strong—forever. When you consider the prize, it's a real bargain, don't you agree!

BIBLIOGRAPHY

VIDEOS BY JOYCE VEDRAL

Vedral, Joyce. *The Bottoms Up Workout: Upper Body.* New York: Good Times Video, 1995. $15.98. (See below to order.)

Vedral, Joyce. *The Bottoms Up Workout: Middle Body.* New York: Good Times Video, 1995. $15.98. (See below to order.)

Vedral, Joyce. *The Bottoms Up Workout: Lower Body.* New York: Good Times Video, 1995. $15.98. (See below to order.) Note: $39.98 if you buy all three.

Vedral, Joyce. *The Fat-Burning Workout: Volume I.* Regular Workout. (20 minutes a day). New York: Time-Life Video, 1993. $24.98. (See below to order.)

Vedral, Joyce. *The Fat-Burning Workout: Volume II.* Intensity and Insanity Workout. (40 minutes a day). New York: Time-Life Video, 1993. $24.98.

BOOKS BY JOYCE VEDRAL

Vedral, Joyce, Ph.D. *Eat to Trim: Get it Off and Keep it Off.* New York: Warner Books, 1997. $23.98.

Vedral, Joyce, Ph.D. *Look In, Look Up, Look Out: Be the Person You Were Meant to Be.* New York: Warner Books, 1996. (Also in audio.) $17.00.

Vedral, Joyce, Ph.D. *Definition: Shape Without Bulk in Fifteen Minutes a Day.* New York: Warner Books, 1995. $14.98.

Vedral, Joyce, Ph.D. *Top Shape.* New York: Warner Books, 1995. $14.98.

Vedral, Marthe S., and Joyce L. Vedral. *The College Dorm Workout.* New York: Warner Books, 1994. $8.95.

Vedral, Joyce, Ph.D. *Bottoms Up!* New York: Warner Books, 1993. $12.98.

Vedral, Joyce, Ph.D. *Get Rid of Him!* New York: Warner Books, 1993. $8.95.

Vedral, Joyce, Ph.D. *Gut Busters.* New York: Warner Books, 1992. $8.95.

Vedral, Joyce, Ph.D. *The Fat-Burning Workout.* New York: Warner Books, 1991. $12.98.

Vedral, Joyce, Ph.D. *The 12-Minute Total-Body Workout.* New York: Warner Books, 1989. $12.98.

Vedral, Joyce, Ph.D. *Now or Never.* New York: Warner Books, 1986. $12.98.

Joyce Vedral
P.O. Box 7433
Wantagh, NY 11793-0433

A FINAL NOTE

You've read the book, but you may have a question. If you do, I'll be happy to personally answer you *but* you must enclose a stamped, self-addressed envelope. Address your letter to me at the above P.O. Box. And no matter what, keep going. You are in my prayers!

INDEX

ABOUT THE AUTHOR

We'll never forget the day in 1991, when Joyce Vedral appeared on the *Sally Jessy Raphael Show*. It was a quiet July morning and Joyce had been invited on the program to promote her new book, *The Fat-Burning Workout*. With a built-in flair for the dramatic, Joyce decided to appear on camera in a provocative gold bikini that showed off her toned, enviable forty-eight-year-old figure to best effect.

If we told you that all hell broke loose a mere five minutes into the broadcast, it wouldn't begin to describe the pandemonium that followed as viewers all over the country raced out to find copies of Joyce's workout. "If she can do it, I can do it too," they cried to bookstore owners, the Warner switchboard, and to anyone who would listen. In no time, Joyce was a recognized fitness guru, well on her way to the *New York Times* bestseller list.

If anyone ever tells you that lightning does not strike twice, don't believe them. Joyce did it again. She appeared on the *Montel Williams Show* and had an even greater reaction to her book *Bottoms Up!* For the week of January 1, 1994, her book beat all books in print in America, including books by Howard Stern, Rush Limbaugh, and Michael Crichton—making number one on the *USA Today* list for that week. That same book, *Bottoms Up!*, reached number one on the *New York Times* bestseller list.

Today, at a fit and classy fifty-three, Joyce's fitness library combines for an in-print total of well over one million copies. The reason books like *Bottoms Up! Top Shape, Definition, Gutbusters, The 12-Minute Total-Body Workout, Now or Never, Eat to Trim,* and *The College Dorm Workout* have sold so well is simple: They achieve the promised results.

But there's another reason for Joyce's success: Joyce, with her trademark upbeat voice, is a real person who convinces people in lectures and on television shows all over the country that "if I can do it, so can you." She isn't shy about the before picture of herself, fat at twenty-six, nor is she afraid to poke fun at her "bad genetics." "I come from a Russian heritage," she says. "My whole family look like boxes on wheels."

When Joyce gives a lecture, people are mesmerized. She has a way of relating to an audience as if she knows each and every one personally, and a gift for getting right down to the level of each eager listener. In the words of Paul Adamo of The Learning Annex in New York City, "In all the years of my having lecturers I have never seen anything like this in my life. She arrests the audience and keeps each and every one of them in the palm of her hand throughout. People walk away with love in their eyes. No one can have a Joyce Vedral 'experience' without being touched."

Joyce is a frequent guest on *Oprah*, the *Today* show, *Sally Jessy Raphael*, and CNN, and has been written up in the *New York Times*, the *Daily News*, and the *Post*. She is a sought-after speaker in women's groups, fitness centers, and shopping malls across the country.

Perhaps what makes Joyce most interesting is her unusual background. Unlike so many other fitness experts who are one-dimensional, Joyce earned her Ph.D. in English literature from New York University. Her knowledge of fitness came after years of teaching high school and college English, getting "fat and out of shape," and by luck, landing free-lance assignments to *Muscle and Fitness* and *Shape* magazines, where she became acquainted with the techniques that now fill her books and lectures. Joyce says, "My mission is to help others who lead busy lives and are interested in getting healthy and in shape in minutes rather than hours a day."

Always a women's advocate, Joyce is, in addition, the author of the international best-seller, with Warner Books, *Get Rid of Him!*, a book that helps women build their self-esteem, discover their inner strength, and move on when it's time—and to find the right man—and her new self-help book, *Look In, Look Up, Look Out!*

APPENDIX
THE WEIGHT TRAINING MADE EASY
LEVELS 1 TO 3
Tear-Out Wall Chart

Once you have learned the Weight Training Made Easy workout (whether level 1, 2, or 3) you may use the following pages as a convenient tear-out wall chart. If you paste the pages together, you will have an overview of the entire workout in the order in which it is done. You can paste it on oaktag and shove it under a couch until needed, or put it up on the wall.

Note that workout level 4 requires a separate wall chart because the exercises are in a different order.

Note also that even though the chart works for levels 1, 2, and 3, you will be using different methods for each level—it is only the order that is the same for each of these workouts.

WORKOUT LEVELS 1, 2, AND 3
(SEE INDIVIDUAL CHAPTERS FOR METHOD, SETS, REPS, ETC.)

CHEST ROUTINE

FLAT PRESS

START

FINISH

INCLINE PRESS

START

FINISH

INCLINE FLYE

START

FINISH

CROSS-BENCH PULLOVER

START

FINISH

SHOULDERS ROUTINE

SIDE LATERAL RAISE

START   FINISH

FRONT LATERAL RAISE

START   FINISH

SHOULDERS ROUTINE

ALTERNATE SHOULDER PRESS

START   FINISH

BENT LATERAL RAISE

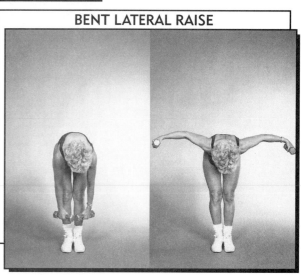

START   FINISH

BICEPS ROUTINE

ALTERNATE CURL

START   FINISH

SIMULTANEOUS CURL

START   FINISH

ALTERNATE HAMMER CURL

START   FINISH

CONCENTRATION CURL

START   FINISH

TRICEPS ROUTINE

OVERHEAD PRESS

START   FINISH

KICKBACK

START   FINISH

ONE-ARM OVERHEAD EXTENSION

START   FINISH

CROSS-FACE EXTENSION

START

FINISH

BACK ROUTINE

UPRIGHT ROW

START   FINISH

ONE-ARM DUMBBELL ROW

START   FINISH

BACK ROUTINE

DOUBLE-ARM REVERSE ROW

START   FINISH

SEATED BACK LATERAL

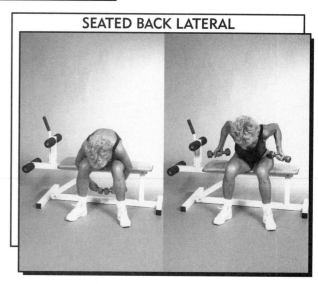

START   FINISH

THIGH ROUTINE

SQUAT

START   FINISH

SIDE LEG LIFT

START

FINISH

LEG CURL

START

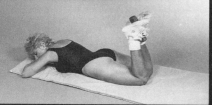

FINISH

LUNGE

START   FINISH

HIPS/BUTTOCKS ROUTINE

STANDING BUTT SQUEEZE

START   FINISH

STANDING BACK-LEG EXTENSION

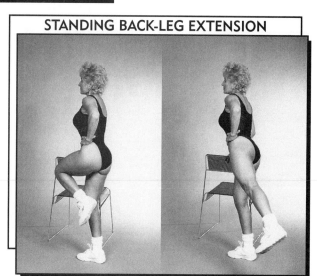

START   FINISH

STRAIGHT LEG KICK-UP

START

FINISH

BENT-KNEE KICK-UP

START

FINISH

ABDOMINALS ROUTINE

CONCENTRATED BUTT LIFT

START

FINISH

CRUNCH

START

FINISH

ABDOMINALS ROUTINE (CONT)

CEILING LIFT

START

FINISH

KNEE-RAISED CRUNCH

START

FINISH

CALVES ROUTINE

SEATED STRAIGHT-TOE RAISE

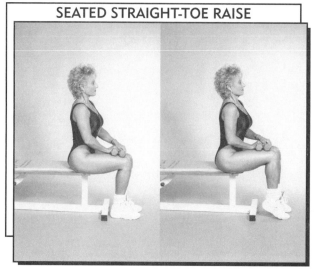

START   FINISH

SEATED ANGLED-OUT-TOE RAISE

START   FINISH

STANDING STRAIGHT-TOE RAISE

START   FINISH

STANDING ANGLED-IN-TOE RAISE

START   FINISH

THE WEIGHT TRAINING MADE EASY

LEVEL 4

Tear-Out Wall Chart

Once you have learned the Weight Training Made Easy workout level 4, you may use the following convenient wall chart. If you paste the pages together, you will have an overview of the entire workout in the order it is done. You can paste it on oaktag and shove it under a couch until needed, or paste it on the wall.

WORKOUT LEVEL 4

CHEST AND TRICEPS TWIN SETS

CHEST — FLAT PRESS
START **AND**

FINISH

TRICEPS — OVERHEAD PRESS

START   FINISH

CHEST — INCLINE PRESS
START **AND**

FINISH

TRICEPS — KICKBACK

START   FINISH

CHEST — INCLINE FLYE
START **AND**

FINISH

TRICEPS — ONE-ARM OVERHEAD EXT

START   FINISH

CHEST AND TRICEPS TWIN SETS

CHEST   CROSS-BENCH PULLOVER   AND   **TRICEPS   CROSS-FACE EXT**

 START

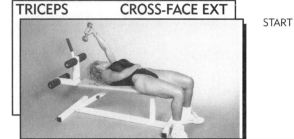 START

FINISH

FINISH

SHOULDERS AND BICEPS TWIN SETS

SHOULDERS   SIDE LATERAL RAISE   AND   **BICEPS   ALTERNATE CURL**

START   FINISH   START   FINISH

SHOULDERS   FRONT LATERAL RAISE   AND   **BICEPS   SIMULTANEOUS CURL**

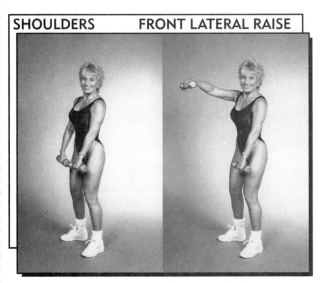

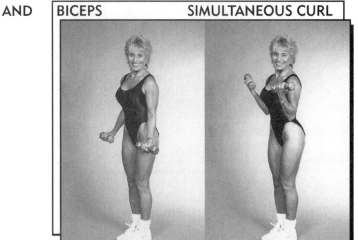

START   FINISH   START   FINISH

SHOULDERS AND BICEPS TWIN SETS

SHOULDERS   ALT SHOULDER PRESS   AND   BICEPS   ALTERNATE HAMMER CURL

START   FINISH   START   FINISH

SHOULDERS   BENT LATERAL RAISE   AND   BICEPS   CONCENTRATION CURL

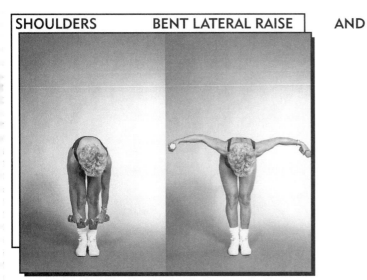

START   FINISH   START   FINISH

ABDOMINALS AND HIPS/BUTTOCKS TWIN SETS

ABDOMINALS   CONC BUTT LIFT   AND   HIPS/BUTT   STANDING BUTT SQUEEZE

START

FINISH

START   FINISH

ABDOMINALS AND HIPS/BUTTOCKS TWIN SETS

ABDOMINALS	CRUNCH	START

FINISH

AND

HIPS/BUTT	STANDING BACK-LEG

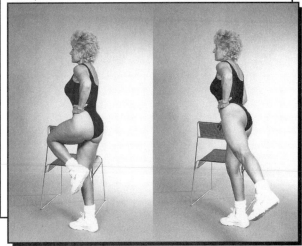

START   FINISH

ABDOMINALS	CEILING LIFT	START

FINISH

AND

HITS/BUTT STRGHT LEG KICK-UP	START

FINISH

ABS	KNEE-RAISED CRUNCH	START

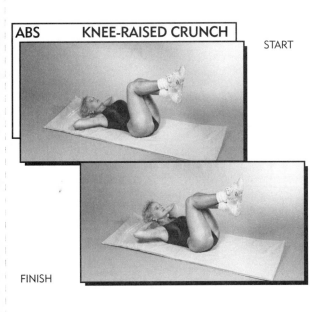

FINISH

AND

HIPS/BUTT	BENT-KNEE KICK-UP	START

FINISH

THIGHS AND BACK TWIN SETS

THIGHS	SQUAT	AND	BACK	UPRIGHT ROW

START   FINISH

START   FINISH

THIGHS	SIDE LEG LIFT	AND	BACK	ONE-ARM DUMBBELL ROW

START

FINISH

START   FINISH

THIGHS	LEG CURL	AND	BACK	DOUBLE-ARM REVERSE ROW

START

FINISH

START   FINISH

THIGHS AND BACK TWIN SETS

THIGHS   LUNGE   AND   BACK   SEATED BACK LATERAL

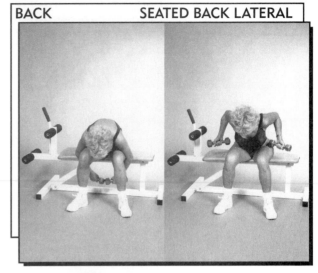

START   FINISH   START   FINISH

SUPERSETS FOR CALVES

SEATED STRAIGHT-TOE RAISE   AND   SEATED ANGLED-OUT-TOE RAISE

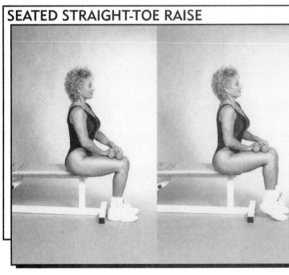

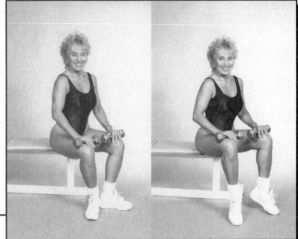

START   FINISH   START   FINISH

STANDING STRAIGHT-TOE RAISE   AND   STANDING ANGLED-IN-TOE RAISE

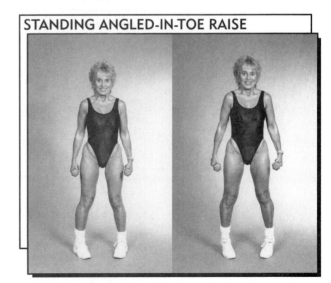

START   FINISH   START   FINISH